05/07

UNIVERSITY OF
WOLVERHAMPTON

ONE WEEK LOAN

− 6 OCT 2010

Telephone Renewals: 01902 321333 or 0845 408 1631
Please RETURN this item on or before the last date shown above.
Fines will be charged if items are returned late.
See tariff of fines displayed at the Counter.   (L2)

Prisoner Resettlement
Policy and practice

Edited by

**Anthea Hucklesby and
Lystra Hagley-Dickinson**

WILLAN
PUBLISHING

Published by

Willan Publishing
Culmcott House
Mill Street, Uffculme
Cullompton, Devon
EX15 3AT, UK
Tel: +44(0)1884 840337
Fax: +44(0)1884 840251
e-mail: info@willanpublishing.co.uk
website: www.willanpublishing.co.uk

Published simultaneously in the USA and Canada by

Willan Publishing
c/o ISBS, 920 NE 58th Ave, Suite 300,
Portland, Oregon 97213-3786, USA
Tel: +001(0)503 287 3093
Fax: +001(0)503 280 8832
e-mail: info@isbs.com
website: www.isbs.com

First published 2007

ISBN   978-1-84392-253-7 paperback
       978-1-84392-254-4 hardback

British Library Cataloguing-in-Publication Data

A catalogue record for this book is available from the British Library.

•

Project managed by Deer Park Productions, Tavistock, Devon
Typeset by GCS, Leighton Buzzard, Bedfordshire
Printed and bound by Ashford Colour Press, Gosport, Hants.

Contents

Preface

This book primarily arose out of a one-day conference organised by the authors, Maureen Cain and Paul Kiff under the auspices of the British Society of Criminology in December 2005. While organising the conference we recognised that there was a substantial amount of knowledge, experience and evidence about prisoner resettlement which was not written down and could easily be lost if there was a shift in government priorities. Furthermore, one of us was acutely aware that some important evidence was not in the public domain. This book is an attempt to record the evidence base about prisoner resettlement which has been amassed at the start of the twenty-first century.

A number of people have been crucial in producing this book. First and foremost, we would like to thank the contributors who readily agreed to participate, produced the chapters we asked for and dealt with our queries swiftly. They also agreed with our suggestion that the fees should go to charity. Our thanks also go to Maureen Cain and Paul Kiff for their assistance with organising the original conference and Brian Willan and his team for sticking with us despite the delays. Anthea would especially like to thank Emma Wincup who has often been the voice of calm and reason during the four years we have been doing resettlement research together.

Finally, we thank our respective partners, John and Peter, 'who end up doing all the things we don't have time to do because we're working'.

Notes on contributors

Susie Atherton is a Research Assistant in the Centre for Criminal Justice Policy and Research at the University of Central England, Birmingham. She is currently undertaking her PhD in policing problematic drug use in two EU member states (Lithuania and England & Wales). Previous research projects include the resettlement of black and minority ex-offenders and two European-wide studies looking at services for problematic drug and alcohol users in juvenile secure settings and police custody.

Andrew Cole is the Programme Manager for PS Plus. Before joining PS Plus in 2002, he worked for the National Probation Service in Merseyside.

Ian Galbraith is the Interventions Programme Manager for PS Plus. Previously, he was a probation officer. He has also worked extensively in the field of housing, employed by the local authority managing funding for supported housing and by Nacro managing their Housing Advice Services.

Loraine Gelsthorpe is Reader in Criminology and Criminal Justice at the Institute of Criminology, University of Cambridge, and a Fellow of Pembroke College. She has extensive publications in relation to gender and justice in particular, but more generally in relation to youth justice and community penalties. Recent books include: *Exercising Discretion: Decision-making in the Criminal Justice System and Beyond* (edited with N. Padfield, 2003), *Sexuality Repositioned:*

Diversity and the Law (edited with B. Brooks-Gordon, M. Johnson and A. Bainham, 2004) and the *Handbook of Probation* (edited with Rod Morgan, 2007). Current research revolves around provision for women offenders in the community. She is also involved in the evaluation of the Home Office's Together Women Programme and an evaluation of community housing initiatives for women. Having had a short career in social work some years ago, she now keeps one foot firmly in the real world through her work as a psycho-therapist.

Lystra Hagley-Dickinson is a Senior Lecturer in Criminology at the University of Northampton. She has a long-standing involvement in working with offenders in some shape or form for the past 15 years. She has pursued careers in government, the European Union and the community and voluntary sectors. Her main research and teaching interests revolve around prisons, dispute resolution and a restorative justice that advocates for victims and community involvement in crime prevention and reducing offending. She has undertaken research and published in relation to ethnicity, the criminal justice system and the effects of imprisonment.

Carol Hedderman is Professor of Criminology at the University of Leicester and a member of the Griffins Society Council. She was formerly Assistant Director of the Home Office Research and Statistics Directorate where she had lead responsibility for statistics and research concerning the management and impact of the Prison and Probation Services. Carol is currently conducting action research with the Together Women projects in the North West, Yorkshire and Humberside. Her other research interests include the effectiveness of sentencing, 'rational' approaches to sentencing, the comparative effectiveness of different approaches to enforcing court penalties, 'what works' in prison and probation, reconviction studies and the development of alternative measures of effectiveness, the treatment of female offenders at different stages of the criminal justice system, domestic violence and rural crime.

Anthea Hucklesby is a Senior Lecturer in Criminal Justice and Deputy Director of the Centre for Criminal Justice Studies at the University of Leeds. She has recently undertaken research on the remand process, electronic monitoring, compliance, pre-trial drugs interventions, drugs in prison and the resettlement of offenders. With Emma Wincup, she has researched three resettlement initiatives, one managed by the statutory sector (Connect) and two voluntary sector projects (the Pyramid Project and the ROTA Project).

Kirsty Hudson is Lecturer in Criminology and Criminal Justice in the School of Social Sciences, Cardiff University. She has undertaken research on the treatment and management of sex offenders and the resettlement of prisoners – the latter from research on the results of the Prisoner Resettlement Pathfinders and her research with South West Integration (SWing), a regional resettlement project designed to bring together a variety of public, private and voluntary service providers to deal with the resettlement needs of short-term prisoners.

Hazel Kemshall is Professor of Community and Criminal Justice at De Montfort University. Her research interests include the assessment and management of high-risk offenders, multi-agency public protection panels and community responses to sexual offenders. She has written extensively on risk, public protection and dangerousness, and has completed research for the Home Office, Scottish Executive and the ESRC. She has evaluated work by multi-agency public protection panels with high-risk offenders and management strategies for violent and sexual offenders. She is the lead author for the recent *Risk of Harm Guidance and Training Resource* CD-ROM produced for NOMS and the Home Office Public Protection Unit.

Philippa Lyon is the Lead Programme Manager for PS Plus. Prior to joining PS Plus in 2002, Phillippa worked in a number of criminal justice related posts including prison-based employment and mentoring work at HMYOI Thorn Cross/HMP Risley and a variety of voluntary sector management roles.

Mike Maguire is Professor of Criminology now working part-time at both Cardiff and Glamorgan Universities. He was formerly a Senior Research Fellow at the Oxford University Centre for Criminological Research. He has published in many areas of crime and justice, including parole and resettlement, burglary, victim issues, complaints systems, risk, violent offending and policing. He is a co-editor of *The Oxford Handbook of Criminology* (4th edition, 2007). He conducted several studies under the Home Office Crime Reduction Programme, including an evaluation of the Probation Resettlement Pathfinders. He was formerly a member of the Parole Board and is currently a member of the Correctional Services Accreditation Panel. He is also senior academic advisor to the Home Office research team based in the Welsh Assembly. He has recently conducted with colleagues a short study of accommodation issues in relation to ex-prisoners in the South West region.

Jane Nolan is a lecturer in Criminology and Criminal Justice at the Centre for Criminology, Glamorgan University. Prior to this she was a part-time Criminology lecturer at Glamorgan University, an Associate Tutor at Cardiff University and a Research Assistant for both institutions. Jane has been involved in various research projects on a variety of topics including street violence, anti-social behaviour, child abuse and homicide, drug use, resettlement and accommodation for ex-prisoners.

Peter Raynor is Professor of Criminology and Criminal Justice at the University of Wales, Swansea. A former probation officer, his research over the last 30 years has included work on victims, drugs, youth justice, pre-sentence reports, throughcare and resettlement of prisoners, risk and need assessment, the effectiveness of probation and programmes, and the impact of probation on minority ethnic offenders. He has published widely on criminal justice issues, including the recent books *Rehabilitation, Crime and Justice* (with Gwen Robinson, 2005) and *Race and Probation* (with Sam Lewis, David Smith and Ali Wardak, 2005). He is a member of the Correctional Services Accreditation Panel.

Heather Ross is a Senior Performance Manager with PS Plus and is responsible for the management and delivery of PS Plus in two areas in the Eastern Region. She joined PS Plus in 2004. Prior to this, she was a prison psychologist latterly at HMP Barlinnie. She has also lectured on the MSc in Forensic Psychology at Glasgow Caledonian University.

Douglas Sharp is Professor of Criminal Justice at the University of Central England. He was formerly a senior police officer, having served for 30 years in the West Midlands Police and with HM Inspectorate of Constabulary. He was a member of the working parties on police interview training and on the Special Constabulary. In addition, he has acted as an advisor to the Polish Police and the Commissioner of Police in Lesotho (Southern Africa) on the reorganisation of policing. His previous research includes the experiences of young people from black and ethnic minorities involved in the criminal justice system and alcohol-related criminality.

Gilly Sharpe is a doctoral research student at the Institute of Criminology, University of Cambridge. She has previously worked with young people in the voluntary sector, as a social worker in a Youth Offending Team, and on a national evaluation of Intensive Supervision and Surveillance Programmes (ISSP) for prolific and serious young offenders. Her doctoral research focuses on girls in the youth justice system.

Julie Vennard is a Senior Research Fellow at the Law School, University of Bristol. She was formerly a senior member of the Home Office Research, Development and Statistics Directorate. She has carried out research and written on a number of aspects of crime and criminal justice. In recent years her main focus has been upon rehabilitative responses to offending, prisoner resettlement and the ongoing restructuring of the Prison and Probation Services. Since moving to Bristol (in 1999) she has completed a national evaluation of Pathfinder resettlement schemes for short-term prisoners (with Mike Maguire and Peter Raynor), evaluated one of the first multi-agency schemes targeted on prolific offenders, and conducted an evaluation of Pathfinder employment schemes for offenders (with Carol Hedderman). Between 2002 and 2004, she also carried out a Department of Constitutional Affairs (DCA)-funded study of racism in the courts from the perspective of ethnic minority magistrates (with Gwynn Davis and John Baldwin), the results of which were published within the DCA Courts and Diversity Research Programme.

Kate Willams is a Research Fellow at the Centre for Criminal Justice Policy and Research, University of Central England in Birmingham. Her research interests focus on voluntary citizen involvement in policing, vigilantism and sex work, using ethnographic methodologies. She is the Secretary of the British Society of Criminology's Advisory Council and also sits on their Executive Committee, chairs the Postgraduate Committee and is a member of their Professional and Ethics Committee. Her publications include '"Caught between a rock and a hard place": police experiences with the legitimacy of street watch partnerships', *Howard Journal* (2005), 44 (5): 527–37.

Emma Wincup is a Senior Lecturer in Criminology and Criminal Justice at the University of Leeds and Deputy Director of the Centre for Criminal Justice Studies. Her research interests relate to social exclusion and crime. She is currently (with Anthea Hucklesby) evaluating two resettlement projects in prisons in the North East.

Previous research related to resettlement has included an evaluation of the Approved Premises Pathfinder (funded by the National Probation Directorate) and a study of the housing needs of female offenders (funded by the National Probation Service, Eastern Region). Emma has published widely on criminological research and a second edition of *Doing Research on Crime and Justice* will be published by Oxford University Press in Autumn 2007.

Jackie Worrall is the Director of Policy and Public Affairs at Nacro, the crime reduction charity. She has worked for Nacro since 1982, initially as the manager of a youth training scheme and more recently as the lead on prisons and resettlement. She has a particular interest in youth crime and her PhD thesis explored the impact of prison education on young men. Before joining Nacro she was a probation officer in the West Midlands and Warwickshire.

Introduction

This book is a product of its time. Prisoners' resettlement is high on current political and policy agendas. While the problems faced by prisoners leaving prison have been acknowledged for many years, a decade ago interest in the issues raised by prisoners returning to society after imprisonment was low. There was an awareness that reconviction rates for prisoners were high but the drive to tackle the crime problem was focused elsewhere. This has changed markedly in the last five years. The rapid rise in the prison population has meant that more prisoners than ever before are released and this together with the pressure this puts on the infrastructure of the prison estate has concentrated attention on attempts to ensure that prisoners do not return to prison once released. Contemporaneously, two influential reports, one by the Social Exclusion Unit (SEU 2002) and one by the Prisons and Probation Inspectorates (HM Inspectorates of Prison and Probation 2001), highlighted the problems faced by prisoners leaving prison and ensured that government attention was directed at this issue. The 'resettlement' of prisoners is now a priority policy area linked directly to government initiatives to reduce reoffending. Consequently, the Government has initiated a resettlement policy, which focuses on seven pathways to resettlement (Home Office 2004) and ensures that each region has an action plan to reduce reoffending by released prisoners. The pathways (accommodation; education, training and employment; mental and physical health; drugs and alcohol; finance, benefits and debt; children and families; and attitudes, thinking and behaviour) ensure that the issues and responsibilities for prisoners' resettlement extend beyond criminal justice agencies to other statutory agencies.

The renewed interest in prisoners' resettlement forms the context to this volume and the current policy framework is discussed extensively in Chapter 1. Indeed this volume aims to bring together current knowledge and understanding about prisoners' resettlement. An important objective is to capture the knowledge gained by the recent upsurge in interest in resettlement and subsequently the number of resettlement initiatives and research projects which have evaluated them. This is of particular importance as many of the recent initiatives have received limited or no statutory funding. Consequently, they are run on time-limited funding and often cease to exist or metamorphose into different projects when funding runs out (see Chapter 8). Additionally, as Wincup and Hucklesby note in Chapter 4, the projects are rarely evaluated adequately nor are the reports disseminated to produce an evidence base to identify effective practice. This volume aims to provide a comprehensive discussion of the issues raised by the resettlement of prisoners at the beginning of the twenty-first century. However, space is limited and difficult decisions were made about what to include. In large part, the content reflects the current state of knowledge about prisoners' resettlement. It brings together current theory, policy, research and practice while acknowledging that gaps exist, especially around provisions for particular groups of prisoners such as lifers and young offenders and the role of families in supporting resettlement, yet these largely reflect a lack of research and evidence in these areas.

Defining what we mean by resettlement is no easy task as Raynor's contribution eloquently argues in Chapter 2. Certainly for many prisoners the process of leaving prison and returning to the community is not 'resettlement'. Often their pre-prison lives were not settled in any sense with homelessness, unemployment and unsettled and disturbed childhood and schooling common (SEU 2002). Indeed many prisoners' lives are blighted not only by unsettled backgrounds but current or past problematic use of drugs and/or alcohol, all of which are exacerbated by the problems which arise as a result of imprisonment (SEU 2002). Consequently, prisoners are often returning to environments which are more conducive to offending than desistance. In common with others (see Raynor, this volume) we use the term resettlement guardedly and with some reluctance, mainly due to the lack of a suitable alternative.

The current resettlement agenda is inextricably linked with reoffending as government policy in this area is almost always expressed in terms of targets to reduce reoffending (Home Office 2004). It follows that resettlement policy should be linked with theories of desistance, i.e. the process by which offenders stop offending (Farrall and Sparks 2006; Maguire and Raynor 2006). However, as Raynor notes in Chapter 2, these linkages are relatively unexplored theoretically and empirically. In the absence of these connections prisoners' resettlement lacks the necessary underpinning to explain how and why some things work while others do not. Without this, an evidence base for resettlement activity will continue to be elusive. While acknowledging that reducing reoffending must be the ultimate aim of resettlement activity, the reality is that desistance is a process, not a single event, which occurs over time and often includes lapses back into offending (Farrall 2002; Maruna 2001). Consequently, more realistic interim measures of success are required to ensure that resettlement initiatives are not labelled as failures because they are unable to tackle entrenched offending behaviour directly. Interim measures such as finding accommodation for prisoners, improving job and life skills, dealing with debt and providing advice and support are often used and are important in a number of respects, not least to ensure that initiatives have some positive outcomes. However, the precise relationship between such factors and resettlement, their relative importance and the relationship between them is largely unexplored and, as Maguire and Nolan note in Chapter 7, are more likely to be necessary rather than sufficient factors in desistance.

Resettlement practice varies and Hucklesby and Wincup explore some of the ways in which activities are organised in Chapter 3. Key elements of resettlement work involve working inside prison and in the community and crucially linking the two, i.e. continuity through the prison gate (Clancy *et al.* 2006; Lewis *et al.* 2003). Part 2 provides some examples of initiatives which are currently operating in England and Wales, namely SWing and PS Plus, and discusses some of their successes and the challenges, which they have faced. The National Offender Management Service (NOMS) was created expressly to improve joint working and communication between the Prison and Probation Services. Of all the areas of its work, this should enhance the resettlement experiences of prisoners most markedly. In theory, offender managers will plan, facilitate and execute prisoners' resettlement from the point at which they enter prison to the end of their sentence. It is too early to judge how effective this move may be but the introduction of NOMS has the potential to change the landscape of resettlement practice. Nevertheless, putting theory into practice is fraught with difficulties, especially when the two services

3

involved have markedly different traditions and cultures. How this may be achieved is discussed in many of the chapters in this volume.

One of the potential issues with the end-to-end management approach brought in under NOMS is that it becomes a one size fits all model. Indeed the National Reoffending Action Plan (Home Office 2004) makes no allowance for the possibility that different groups of offenders have varied pathways out of crime. There are many different groups of prisoners who require resettlement services and one important question for resettlement practice is whether their resettlement needs vary and therefore require different services. Currently, different services are provided for some groups. For example, prisoners serving sentences of 12 months or more and prisoners who are under 21 are subject to statutory supervision whereas short-term prisoners who are 21 or over (serving under 12 months) are not. Consequently, recent initiatives have concentrated on the provision of services for short-term prisoners. Many of these have been provided by the voluntary and community sector and the issues which arise from this are discussed by Hucklesby and Worrall in Chapter 8. Other groups such as women and prisoners from minority ethnic groups have been targeted by individual initiatives (see Chapters 9 and 10). However, as Williams *et al.* note in Chapter 10, it is not always clear whether or indeed how the needs of these groups differ and what resettlement initiatives are required for such groups.

At the time of writing, the context in which resettlement activities are undertaken is changing. Most recently, the Home Office has been split into two, creating a Ministry of Justice which has lead responsibility for the resettlement agenda. It is too early to say what impact this will have but the chapters contained in this volume were completed prior to the split being announced and implemented. Other changes have resulted in a considerable degree of uncertainty about the future direction of policy at the time this volume was being compiled, namely the future of Custody Plus and contestability. The changes proposed have arisen mainly but not exclusively as a consequence of the introduction of NOMS, the Offender Management Model and associated policies (Home Office 2006). It was intended that Custody Plus would deal with the anomaly of prisoners serving under 12 months receiving no statutory supervision upon release despite having one of the highest reconviction rates. Custody Plus introduced in the Criminal Justice Act 2003 is a completely new sentence which involves offenders spending some time in custody followed by a period of supervision in the community. The proposals were well received mainly because they enabled this group of prisoners to be supervised after release from prison although there was some concern about the possibility of net-widening and the impact on the prison population. However, at the time of writing the implementation of the proposals has been postponed indefinitely because of resourcing issues. This obviously has enormous implications for the future direction of resettlement policy and has left many organisations and initiatives in limbo while they await information about whether Custody Plus will ever be implemented.

The second area of uncertainty is contestability. Contestability is a fundamental part of the creation of NOMS. Under proposals to introduce it, key functions in criminal justice will be put out to tender with statutory, voluntary and private sectors being invited to bid to operate services. Officially, the purpose of contestability is to increase the efficiency and effectiveness of services and provide better value for money (NOMS 2006). It is of particular relevance to the provision of resettlement services as many of these are already provided by the voluntary and community sector (see Chapter 8). However, proposals to introduce contestability have taken much longer than anticipated. At the time of writing the Offender Management Bill 2006 is still going through Parliament and it appears that proposals to introduce contestability on a large scale have been watered down. The delay has caused significant problems, not least for some initiatives which have faced funding gaps as they were expecting to be able to bid for statutory funding in late 2006 or early 2007. It is not yet clear when contestability will be introduced nor the extent to which it will apply to services currently provided by the Prison and Probation Services. Indeed, it has been suggested that the threat of contestability is all that is required to raise the game of existing providers and improve value for money (Baumol and Willig 2001). If this is so, the policy of contestability may well continue to be advocated without being put into practice.

Despite these uncertainties, there is a considerable amount of work being undertaken to enhance prisoners' experiences of resettlement. Coupled with its high place on the political and policy agendas this is cause for optimism. For the first time, the impetus appears to exist to tackle the issues faced by prisoners leaving custody and to assist and encourage them to desist from offending. This book attempts to capture the essence of the work being undertaken currently, to enhance our knowledge and understanding of the process of resettlement and desistance and to disseminate knowledge and experiences of doing resettlement work with a variety of prisoners.

The structure of the book

The book has three parts. Part 1 provides a critical review of current policy, theory, practice and research on prisoners' resettlement. Part 2 explores practice issues and includes case studies of two resettlement initiatives and an examination of accommodation provision and voluntary sector involvement in prisoners' resettlement. Part 3 focuses on the particular issues raised by the resettlement of different groups of prisoners including women, minority ethnic groups, prolific and (priority) offenders and high-risk offenders. These chapters draw on the authors' extensive experience as researchers and practitioners in these areas to explore current knowledge about the resettlement needs of these groups and identify issues relating to policy and practice when dealing with particular groups of prisoners. The final chapter explores how resettlement policies and practice may develop and discusses some of the opportunities and threats to its continued development.

References

Baumol, W.J. and Willig, R.D. (2001) 'Contestability: developments since the book', *International Library of Critical Writing in Economics*, 126 (3): 493–520.

Clancy, A., Hudson, K., Maguire, M., Peake, R., Raynor, P., Vanstone, M. and Kynch, J. (2006) *Getting Out and Staying Out: Results of the Prisoner Resettlement Pathfinders*. Bristol: Polity Press.

Farrall, S. (2002) *Rethinking What Works With Offenders*. Cullompton: Willan Publishing.

Farrall, S. and Sparks, R. (2006) 'Introduction', *Criminal Justice*, 6 (1): 7–17.

Her Majesty's Inspectorates of Prisons and Probation (2001) *Through the Prison Gate: A Joint Thematic Review*. London: Home Office.

Home Office (2004) *Reducing Re-offending National Action Plan*. London: Home Office.

Home Office (2006) *Offender Management Model 1.1*. London: Home Office, National Offender Management Service.

Lewis, S., Vennard, J., Maguire, M., Raynor, P., Vanstone, M., Raybould, S. and Rix, A. (2003) *The Resettlement of Short-term Prisoners: An Evaluation of Seven Pathfinders*, RDS Occasional Paper No. 83. London: Home Office.

Maguire, M. and Raynor, P. (2006) 'How resettlement of prisoners promotes desistance from crime: or does it?', *Criminal Justice*, 6 (1): 19–38.

Maruna, S. (2001) *Making Good: How Ex-convicts Reform and Rebuild Their Lives*. Washington, DC: American Psychological Association Books.

National Offender Management Service (NOMS) (2006) *Restructuring Probation to Reduce Reoffending*. London: Home Office.

Social Exclusion Unit (2002) *Reducing Re-offending by Ex-prisoners*. London: Office of the Deputy Prime Minister.

Part 1

Prisoner resettlement: theory, policy and research

Chapter 1

Rediscovering resettlement: narrowing the gap between policy rhetoric and practice reality

Carol Hedderman

Introduction

This chapter sets out to explore the reasons that the concept of resettlement has undergone something of a renaissance in recent penological policymaking and to discuss how that relates to the practical assistance ex-offenders receive in helping them to lead law-abiding lives. While Raynor (see Chapter 2) provides a detailed consideration of the history of resettlement, this chapter summarises some of the key policy developments in order to show how the concept of resettlement has gone in and out of fashion over time. This is followed by a discussion of why resettlement was rediscovered and the factors which have affected current policy. Evidence about the way resettlement work is conducted in practice is then considered. The chapter ends by considering how the policy rhetoric and practice reality might be brought closer together.

The term resettlement appears in ministerial speeches, central government policy statements, regional action plans and academic papers, but whether we are all thinking of the same thing is debatable. In some contexts, resettlement refers to the services which enable ex-prisoners to access benefits or employment, tackle drug problems and secure satisfactory accommodation on, or preferably before, release (see, for example, HM Prison Service 2006). In other contexts, it includes a sense of social reintegration and acceptance (McNeill 2004a). In some circumstances, resettlement only seems to relate to ex-prisoners whereas in others it also includes offenders on community orders (UNHCR 1990). Commentators have also queried how far we really mean resettlement and reintegration or are actually discussing the settlement and integration of individuals who were excluded from society well before they got caught up in the criminal justice system (Social Exclusion Unit 2002). Either as a cause or a consequence of this ambiguity, as Maruna *et al.* (2004) point out, there is no coherent theory of resettlement and recent criminological theorising about desistance seems to have played little part as yet in influencing either policy or practice (see McNeill (2004b) for a full discussion of the implications of this neglect). In the next chapter, Peter Raynor discusses these issues in the detail they deserve. The issue is noted here for two reasons: first, in order to explain that the term is used in this chapter both to refer to the social integration of prisoners on release and to address their practical service needs; second, it is almost too obvious to comment on this, but the very fact that we may not all mean the same thing when we use the term resettlement may, in itself, contribute to the disjuncture between the policy and practice which later parts of this chapter consider.

Inventing and losing sight of resettlement

Histories of probation and prisons in the United Kingdom show that until the mid-1800s, state-run prisons were primarily a holding pen for debtors or for the soon-to-be transported or executed. In the UK, the pressure to work with offenders to ensure their resettlement grew once prison became a place of punishment in its own right and as industrialisation increased the demand for a sober and reliable workforce (Garland 1985). From her examination of the operation of the London Police Courts in the late nineteenth century, Davis (1984) concludes that the courts not only existed to suppress law-breaking but also to provide access to financial assistance and social support. By balancing these two objectives, Davis (1984: 315) argues, the courts served '... not merely to suppress law-breaking but also to win lower-class acceptance of the law and, thus, implicitly, of the social order'. Similarly, Garland (1985) and Vanstone (2004) conclude that the origins of probation-style resettlement work were inspired partly by a mix of humanitarian and (Christian) evangelical concerns for the most socially excluded elements of society and partly by a concern that this substratum posed a threat to the social order which must be managed by being repressed or reformed.

The resettlement of prisoners only became a statutory responsibility in 1862. More than 30 years later the Departmental Committee on

Prisons chaired by Lord Gladstone (1895) expressed its dissatisfaction with the variable quality of the assistance received by discharged prisoners. Although the Probation Service was set up in 1907 to do very similar work with those on non-custodial court orders, it was not until the 1960s that the service became responsible for the resettlement of prisoners. Raynor's more detailed history in the next chapter considers how the concept of resettlement changed during that period. Also in the 1960s, the National Association for the Care and Resettlement of Offenders (now Nacro) was set up both to support the Probation Service in its work and to develop new ways of working with offenders to secure their resettlement (Crow 2006).

The next decade (the mid-1960s to the mid-1970s) has been described as the heyday of the Probation Service because it was respected by sentencers as a source of expert advice and because of widespread confidence that its activities could bring about rehabilitation (Chui and Nellis 2003). However, even during this golden age there was scepticism about whether it was possible to reform as well as punish offenders, leading the New York State Prison Service to commission a review into the rehabilitative impact of interventions in institutional and non-institutional settings. The review, conducted by Robert Martinson (1974), supported the sceptics' perspective in that it concluded that very few interventions had a significant effect on further offending. Although Martinson pointed out that the results were not clear-cut because of the methodological shortcomings of some of the studies, the overall message was taken to be that 'Nothing Works'. Similar overall conclusions were reached in the UK by Brody (1976) and Folkard et al. (1976).

Of course, then as now, research results were not received in a political vacuum. Raynor (2003) has suggested that one reason Martinson's caveats, and the methodological limitations of the UK studies, were ignored was that 'Nothing Works' was what the conservative US and UK governments of the 1980s and early 1990s wished to hear. In other words, Martinson's conclusion meshed with their pre-existing desire to limit public expenditure on prisons to that needed to contain and punish offenders while they were inside. The stark prison conditions which resulted were expected to also have a deterrent effect. This is what one of the British Home Secretaries of the period meant when he (in)famously claimed that 'prison works' (Howard 1993). The concordance between research results and political ideology may explain why the results of a methodologically superior Canadian review by Gendreau and Ross (1979), which found that some interventions were effective, was ignored in the US and the UK during this period.

In the 'Nothing Works' era, public expenditure on supervision could no longer be justified to 'advise, assist and befriend' offenders, but the 1991 Criminal Justice Act recast its purpose as 'punishment in the community'. As Maguire and Raynor (1997: 3) explain: 'This idea, of course, was a key element of the government's attempted solution to the chronic problem of prison overcrowding: to remain credible in a punitive climate, any diversion policy had to appear to involve "tough" alternative penalties.' In Chapter 2 of this volume, Raynor details how this change came about. Not only did punishment in the community ease overcrowding, Home Office figures (1999) also show that it was at least ten times cheaper per month than the £2,070 cost of imprisonment.

In so far as supervision to resettle offenders was discussed at this time, it was portrayed as mainly, if not very successfully, being concerned with the policing of offenders' behaviour during the licence period (i.e. when they might otherwise be in custody). While this demoralised many of those working with offenders to secure their resettlement, there is little evidence that government policy had much practical impact on the *nature* of resettlement work in the community. However, official statistics show that its *extent* was certainly curtailed because of the associated reduction in funding for non-statutory aftercare. In 1991, 26,699 prisoners received some form of voluntary support from the Probation Service pre- or post-release; five years later the number had dropped to 4,653 (Home Office 2001a). While the number of adult offenders on statutory throughcare more than doubled (from 22,628 to 58,396) over the same period, policy documents of the time, including the newly introduced national standards for supervision (Home Office 1992, 1995), emphasised the importance of protecting the public by securing attendance and compliance. In contrast, practitioners saw their efforts in terms of what they might achieve with regard to reintegrating offenders, albeit with the long-term aim of reducing reoffending (Maguire and Raynor 1997). The gap between policy rhetoric and practice reality can be identified most clearly from this time.

The renaissance of resettlement

A natural consequence of the long-term tenure (1979–97) of a Conservative government, which asserted that prison was effective in reducing offending and reoffending, was that the sentenced prison population began to rise. Having been 33,046 in 1993 it went up 15,000 in the next four years (Home Office 2003). Unfortunately, the then government's confidence concerning the benefits of such an increase was not reflected in two-year reconviction rates which rose from 53 per cent to 58 per cent over the same period (Home Office 2003).[1] However, both these trends probably made the incoming Labour government more willing to consider alternative approaches to dealing with offenders. Their arrival also coincided with the publication of two government-sponsored reviews (Vennard et al. 1997; and Underdown 1998) which confirmed the 'what works' conclusions of earlier influential reviews by Hollin (1990) and McGuire (1995) and of Canadian meta-analyses (e.g. Andrews et al. 1990; Lipsey 1992). In essence, the message of this research was that it was possible to identify some combined approaches (usually including, but not restricted to, cognitive behavioural work) which were effective with some groups of offenders who were otherwise at moderately high risk of reoffending (interventions worked less well with the highest and lowest risk groups). The new government quickly committed itself to ensuring that all work with offenders should be evidence-based (e.g. Home Office 1999). In fact, Raynor (2004) has suggested that, even under the previous government, senior policymakers were already a receptive audience to the 'What Works?' approach. This is supported by the fact that, while Vennard et al. (1997) and Underdown (1998) reported after the Labour government came to power, both reviews were commissioned before the general election.

Faced with a further escalation in both the prison population and prison reconviction rates, the newly formed Social Exclusion Unit (SEU) was tasked with providing a clearer picture both of who was in prison and the effects of imprisonment. Its report (Social Exclusion Unit 2002) concluded that characteristics of those in prison showed them to be among the most socially excluded, displaying very low levels of literacy and numeracy and exceptionally high levels of mental illness and drug dependency. Their childhoods were characterised by time in care and as adults they experienced very high rates of unemployment. The report also noted that on release from prison two-thirds of those who had been in employment had lost their jobs, a third had lost their homes, two-fifths lost contact with their families and one-fifth faced increased financial difficulties on release. The report was particularly critical of short prison sentences which were, it concluded, of limited overall value '... as the disruption they cause to support networks and protective factors can outweigh the limited opportunity they present to do positive work' (Social Exclusion Unit 2002: 123). As the Halliday Review (Home Office 2001b) had pointed out in the previous year, this group of prisoners had higher reconviction rates than those serving longer sentences but were not subject to statutory supervision on release. A joint Prison and Probation Inspection also pointed out that even statutory throughcare and aftercare was sometimes little more than a paper exercise (HM Inspectorates of Prisons and Probation 2001) which was, consequently, unlikely to make an appreciable difference to an ex-prisoner's resettlement prospects.

Many of the SEU's recommendations for change, such as measures to improve access to drug treatment and housing and employment services, were a direct response to the evidence in their report. However, as Crow (2006: 37) notes:

> The Social Exclusion Unit's report (2002) and surveys of the prison population contain quite a lot of factual information illustrating the disadvantaged nature of the prison population. To know that there are such relationships is to know something about what needs to be done. But much of this is familiar territory. Research that tells us what works best in terms of resettlement and how best to do it is much scarcer.

His own review of the evidence suggests that there is little strong support to suggest that getting offenders into work and accommodation or off drugs reduces reoffending (Crow 2006). To some degree the evidence is weak because of the methodological failings in the underlying research, but also, as Crow (2006) and others have noted, little of what was being attempted could be expected to be effective. There is evidence that most offenders have numerous criminogenic needs (see Harper and Chitty 2004, for example). Both research reviews (e.g. McGuire 1995) and common sense tell us that if only one of these issues is tackled, even if it is tackled effectively, this is unlikely to have a measurable impact on their risk of reoffending. In other words, getting a job when you are homeless and drug addicted is not going to make the difference. Despite this, most of the interventions which have been attempted in England and Wales over the last decade have focused on single issues usually with disappointing, but predictable, results. Moreover, as Crow (2006) also points out, even holistic approaches are unlikely to be successful unless offenders are assisted to change their attitudes and social relationships along with their material circumstances.

A further difficulty with the approach devised by the Social Exclusion Unit was that, in following the Labour Party's pre-election mantra of being 'tough on crime, tough on the causes of crime', it left a fundamental resettlement policy dilemma unresolved. Should ex-prisoners be supported to help them overcome their many social problems because these seem so closely related to their risk of reoffending? Or should they be dealt with as self-serving, heartless miscreants who must be coerced into improved behaviour? The SEU's compromise was to recommend a carrot and stick approach, which is still the defining characteristic of Government policy on resettlement work today (see, for example, Carter 2003; Home Office 2004; Home Office 2006a). To some degree the SEU's (in)decision is understandable. To argue that someone's background and circumstances may have contributed to their offending is not the same as arguing that offenders should not be held accountable for their actions or punished for them. The dilemma may be irresolvable, but sidestepping the tough questions, or even failing to acknowledge that the dilemma exists, is not a way to form penal policy which ensures that post-release supervision in practice is coherent, defensible or effective.[2] Without clarity about the point at which supervisors should switch from carrot to stick, there is bound to be inconsistency between supervisors, between supervisees and in the treatment a single ex-prisoner receives over time. Not only is disparate treatment undesirable generally in a legal context which espouses notions of justice and equity, it is also at odds with the literature on pro-social modelling and effective therapeutic relationships, which indicates that to be effective supervision must be consistent (see, for example, Trotter 1999).

The mismatch between policy and practice

In theory, current policy requires that offenders who are sentenced to custody should be assessed immediately afterwards (Home Office 2006a). A single case manager (called an 'Offender Manager') will then be appointed who is expected to design and oversee the implementation of sentence plans after consulting other professionals and relevant voluntary sector agencies. Once offenders have signed up to the plan, it will be operationalised while they are in prison and on release. The transition is expected to be seamless as the Probation and Prison Services will be working to a common master in the National Offender Management Service (NOMS) which was created following the Carter Review (2003) largely in order to improve the way the two services work together.

It is too early to say very much about how far this model has been translated into practice, but it is possible to consider whether current policy addresses the real difficulties to be faced in resettling ex-prisoners. A key ingredient of the current approach is that Prison and Probation Services will in future communicate effectively with each other about what has been done with prisoners before release and their resettlement needs on release. This is obviously important. However, bringing both services under one umbrella suggests the main obstacle to effective co-working was primarily structural and cultural. This may be true in part, but there are other reasons which must be addressed if resettlement work is to be effective. The first issue is the cost of effective communication. One tight public spending round after another, combined with increasing caseload sizes, has meant that probation officers find it hard to justify the time involved in visiting offenders serving a long sentence many miles from home. They may not even be able to get the petrol money to do so.[3] There is also evidence that communication *within* each service about resettlement needs and the services available is also sometimes less than ideal (see Webster *et al.* (2001) concerning prison-based employment schemes and Haslewood-Pocsik *et al.* (2004) concerning community-based schemes).

While Lewis *et al.*'s (2003) report on the implementation of seven resettlement 'pathfinder' schemes identifies cultural resistance as an issue in that prison discipline staff did not always cooperate with resettlement staff from voluntary sector organisations, they also identified a number of other practical obstacles which policy statements on resettlement do not appear to address. These include matters which the Prison and Probation Services might reasonably be expected to tackle such as a lack of trained staff, high staff turnover, mixed levels of support from prison managers and difficulties in sharing data across agencies. However, some of the problems lie well outside these services' purview as a later report on the same study notes:

> The projects were also hampered by the widespread inadequacy of post-release support. Gaps in provision and long waiting lists existed, typically in relation to securing accommodation, financial support or drug treatment. (Lewis *et al.* 2007: 39)

The combined effect of these problems led to only a fraction of those identified as having resettlement needs receiving help: 40 out of 526 who were described as having 'significant' drug problems, and 77 of the 535 who were known to have 'significant' accommodation problems. A more recent report on drugs throughcare and aftercare (Fox *et al.* 2005) catalogues a similar set of practical obstacles but also identifies inconsistent assessment practices and uncertainty about the long-term funding as issues which need to be addressed. These reports reiterate the point that most offenders have multiple problems and any resettlement work which deals with only one factor is unlikely to have any appreciable effect in terms of their reintegration into society or reduced reoffending.

Given these findings it seems unlikely that restructuring services will in itself improve resettlement in practice. This is especially so given that results from the first region to test out the Offender Manager concept found only limited evidence of Offender Managers taking a sentence planning role (PA Consultancy Group and MORI 2005). It concluded that their efforts to liaise effectively were inhibited by a now familiar list of practical problems including the distance, travelling time and cost of visiting prison establishments; inconsistent assessments; and difficulties sharing data between agencies. It may even be that restructuring the Probation Service yet again to fit into NOMS will simply serve to further distract and distress staff who have not had a settled work environment since the formation of the National Probation Service in 2001.

Another major cause of the gap between resettlement policy and practice is that while resettlement policy statements regret the lack of joined-up working at the level of practice, the policy itself appears to be formulated with scant regard to what is happening within other parts of the prison system. Although the numbers released on temporary licence for a few days for resettlement purposes (before parole) has increased over the last couple of years, efforts to resettle ex-prisoners into the community are being undermined by risk-averse parole release and recall decision-making. Predictably, the opprobrium suffered by the Parole Board because a very small number of offenders on licence have reoffended seriously has caused them to refuse more applications for release and to be more willing to endorse recalls even for 'technical breaches' (e.g. failing to attend) rather than reoffending. For example, the release rate for those on determinate sentences fell to 49 per cent in 2005–06, having been just over 50 per cent for the previous four years (Home Office 2006b). In 2005–6, 8,680 determinate sentence offenders were recalled to custody. This is an increase of 5 per cent on the number recalled in the previous year. Arguably, this means that those who could most benefit from the structure and support a period on a parole licence brings are the least likely to receive it, putting their longer-term chances of resettlement in jeopardy.

Finally, the latest Government statements on reducing reoffending (Home Office *et al.* 2005; Home Office 2006a) recast the seven forms of social exclusion the SEU (2002) identified as being most commonly experienced by ex-prisoners into 'pathways' to 'reduce reoffending and protect the public'. These are: accommodation; education, training and employment; health; drugs and alcohol; finance, benefit and debt; children and families; and attitudes, thinking and behaviour. The first four are regarded as the 'main pathways' (Home Office *et al.* 2005: 8), although the reasons for according them this status is not clear. While it may well be most productive to tackle some issues first, both their ordering and importance are likely to vary from one individual to another. Both documents also appear to assume that the pathways into the offending labyrinth are the same as the ones which lead out. That said, it is reasonable to assume that they are a good place to start. Unfortunately, advice is also absent on whether a reduction in reoffending will result if only some of offenders' problems are tackled, or if the help received ameliorates but does not solve the problem. Certainly providing advice on obtaining accommodation may be necessary, but surely only obtaining suitable accommodation will make a significant difference to the prospect of most homeless offenders' reoffending? And, even if benefits advice results in benefits being received immediately on release, will this be enough to stop offenders contemplating further offending unless they have also received help with their thinking skills before release?

Perhaps the most encouraging aspect of the Government's latest plans is its recognition that the pathways can only be navigated successfully with the active participation of a range of government departments other than the new Ministry of Justice, and an even broader range of statutory and voluntary sector agencies working on the social exclusion issues the pathways represent. The decision to regionalise the National Offender Management Service is also likely to improve the chances of policy pathways becoming real routes to assistance as there are signs in at least some regions' action plans (e.g. East Midlands Regional Offender Management Service 2006) that local agencies have genuinely attempted to engage in joint planning, and that the level of resources needed to deliver action plans to the required level has been understood even if it is not currently available. It is to be hoped that the spectre of 'contestability' will not jeopardise these developments.

Narrowing the gap between policy and practice

Although Government policy is not usually shaped in direct response to criminological theorising, it is usually informed by it. Resettlement has not generally been well-served in this respect. While theories explaining why people offend abound, and psychological explanations of desistence have gained some currency through the recent focus on 'What Works?', much of the criminological theorising about why people desist is relatively recent and has not yet had much impact on the formulation of either resettlement policy or practice, at least in the UK (see Raynor, this volume). This is important because both resettlement work and practice tend to focus on combating the factors which are associated with the onset and persistence of offending, but it may be, as some recent papers suggest, that this is a necessary but not sufficient condition for change (McNeill 2006). Both policy and practice would be better for being informed by this perspective.

The latest Government statements on reducing reoffending and protecting the public (Home Office *et al.* 2005; Home Office 2006a) describe how resettlement work will be improved and discuss who will be involved in its delivery, but neither describes what resettlement is or the purpose(s) it serves. Reading between the lines it is possible to identify two implicit objectives in the resettlement work the Government funds. First, resettlement supervision is expected to control and risk manage offenders at a time when they would otherwise be in prison. If this were the only aim of resettlement, success could be measured in terms of a saving in prison places set against the cost of supervision and the number and seriousness of offences committed while offenders would otherwise have been in prison. However, the second resettlement objective is to secure public protection in the longer term by tackling practical obstacles to resettlement such as drug misuse and unemployment. As things stand success in meeting this resettlement objective is being measured in much the same way as for the first objective, but over a longer period. This is clearly setting resettlement work up to fail. In the same way that measures of school performance now take account of the pre-existing features of its pupils, any measure of whether resettlement interventions foster reduced reoffending must include a notion of 'distance travelled'. Without this, there is a danger that reductions in the frequency of offending or in offence seriousness will be treated as unimportant, whereas when the pre-existing levels of social exclusion suffered by most offenders is taken into account, these achievements can sometimes seem little short of miraculous. A more realistic appraisal of what interventions can be expected to achieve in these circumstances would help to improve the policy/ practice dialogue.

There is no doubt that national standards for supervision steer practitioners to prioritise short-term risk control over longer-term reintegration aims, but whether this is in the public interest has gone unchallenged and undebated because the twin aims of resettlement are not being clearly distinguished. Practitioners do, of course, sometimes prioritise ex-prisoners' longer-term resettlement needs, but they risk censure for doing so when something goes wrong and get little reward, beyond a degree of personal satisfaction, when their work is successful.

It is important that the purposes of resettlement supervision are made explicit and the potential conflict between them acknowledged if supervision is to be fair, safe and effective in both the short and longer term.

The evidence-base is too weak for resettlement policy or practice to be entirely evidence-based. This is partly because some of the studies which have been conducted had weak designs, but many of the recent Pathfinder evaluations, including the one focused on resettlement, were also undermined by poor implementation (Clancy *et al.* 2006; Lewis *et al.* 2003). Indeed, the single clearest finding from most of the recent probation and prison Pathfinder evaluations conducted in England and Wales is that very little of what was planned was implemented as intended (Clancy *et al.* 2006; Lewis *et al.* 2003). As the evaluations discussed above make clear, this was not solely, or even mainly, down to practitioner resistance (although that played a part) but was a consequence of insufficient capacity within both the prison and probation services. The strain the expanding prison population has put on prison resources is probably generally recognised; however, probation numbers have also grown dramatically over the last decade. Unlike prison overcrowding, probation 'overcrowding' cannot be accommodated by 'doubling up' or spilling over into police cells; instead probation officers are taking on ever larger caseloads. What suffers in these circumstances is the quality and quantity of supervision, including that devoted to resettlement. This is by no means to deny the tremendous effort many practitioners and local managers devote to securing the resettlement of offenders, but to argue that it is unrealistic to expect new ways of working to be carefully developed and comprehensively delivered in such straitened circumstances.

Effective resettlement work is going to be expensive. What is clear from existing evaluations is that to stand a chance of success, resettlement work must be holistic. This means dealing with motivational and attitudinal problems as well as practical ones. It means responding effectively to *all* of the practical obstacles offenders will face on release, not just one or two of them; and responding intensively enough to yield practical improvements. It also means ensuring that comprehensive plans are in place and ready to be activated on release not several weeks later. As recent studies have pointed out delivering those plans is often hampered by a lack of capacity in the community, especially in relation to accommodation and drug treatment. It is encouraging that the latest reducing reoffending action plan (Home Office *et al.* 2005) acknowledges the importance of involving non-criminal justice agencies in the delivery of work with offenders, but this is tempered by the knowledge that:

> It will be for each agency to determine the specific arrangements that relate to their own locality considering such matters as staff responsibilities and resources to ensure there is wherever possible effective synergy between the criminal justice and welfare to work agendas. (Home Office *et al.* 2005: 37)

There may in fact be some comfort in the reference to resource decisions being made locally. The intention to devolve decisions about criminal justice priorities and resources to local Criminal Justice Boards and Regional Offender Managers offers a genuine opportunity to hold all local agencies to account for supporting the resettlement of offenders. Working at this more local level may also help to secure the support of the local communities into which offenders are resettling which is an essential ingredient if resettlement is to involve genuine reintegration.

Finally, for as long as success is to be measured in terms of simple reconviction rates, the most cost-effective way to tackle resettlement problems is to reduce the number of people going into prison, particularly on short sentences. These sentences have the highest reconviction rates partly because they cause people to lose their accommodation, employment and family support. This was acknowledged by the Social Exclusion Unit (2002) but has been downplayed in successive policy statements on resettlement. Another important research finding, which has been underplayed is that interventions work best in a community setting (see McGuire 1995, for example). So, while the policy (Home Office 1999) commitment to the concept that all work with offenders should be evidence-based is laudable, in practice it has fallen at the first hurdle by failing to take both the politically palatable and unpalatable results equally seriously.

Notes

1 Both the prison population and reconviction rates have continued to rise since 1997. The increase in reconviction over time suggests that the nature of the offenders received into prison had changed significantly and/or that prison was becoming less effective even as its use increased (see Hedderman and Hough (2005) and Hedderman (2006) for more detailed discussions).

2 As has been argued elsewhere, this is only one of several tough penal policy questions which have not been answered (or even acknowledged). See Hedderman (2006) for a discussion of those relating to the purposes of sentencing.

3 To be fair Carter (2003) recognised that if NOMS was to deliver better coordinated and more effective supervision in the community under sentence or on release this would require more resources. Unfortunately, his expectation that this could be paid for as demand for imprisonment decreased has not been realised. Instead, the total prison population has gone up by 6,000 since his report was published.

References

Andrews, D.A., Zinger, I., Hoge, R.D., Bonta, J., Gendreau, P. and Cullen, F.T. (1990) 'Does correctional treatment work? A clinically relevant and psychologically informed meta-analysis', *Criminology*, 28: 369–404.

Brody, S.R. (1976) *The Effectiveness of Sentencing: A Review of the Literature*, Home Office Research Study No. 35. London: HMSO.

Carter, P. (2003) *Managing Offenders, Changing Lives: A New Approach*. London: Home Office.

Chui, W.H. and Nellis, M. (2003) 'Creating the National Probation Service – new wine, old bottles?', in W.H. Chui and M. Nellis (eds), *Moving Probation Forward: Evidence, Arguments and Practice*. Harlow: Pearson Education.

Clancy, A., Hudson, K., Maguire, M., Peake, R., Raynor, P., Vanstone, M. and Kynch, J. (2006) *Getting Out and Staying Out: Results of the Prisoner Resettlement Pathfinders*. Bristol: Polity Press.

Crow, I. (2006) *Resettling Prisoners: A Review*. York: University of Sheffield and National Offender Management Service.

Davis, J. (1984) 'A poor man's system of justice: the London Police Courts in the second half of the nineteenth century', *The Historical Journal*, 27 (2): 309–35.

East Midlands Regional Offender Management Service (2006) *Changing Ways: Regional Reducing Re-offending Delivery Plan 06–07*. See: www.noms. homeoffice.gov.uk/news-publications-events/publications/strategy/em-rr-delivery-plan-0607?view=Standard&pubID=400328 (accessed 19 January 2007).

Folkard, M.S., Smith D.D. and Smith D.E. (1976) *IMPACT Volume II The Results of the Experiment*, Home Office Research Study No. 36. London: HMSO.

Fox, A., Khan, L., Briggs, D., Rees-Jones, N., Thompson, Z. and Owens, J. (2005) *Throughcare and Aftercare: Approaches and Promising Practice in Service Delivery for Clients Released from Prison or Leaving Residential Rehabilitation*, Home Office Online Report 01/05. London: Home Office. See: www. homeoffice.gov.uk/rds/pdfs05/rdsolr0105.pdf (accessed 19 January 2007).

Garland, D. (1985) *Punishment and Welfare: A History of Penal Strategies*. Aldershot: Gower.

Gendreau, P. and Ross, R.R. (1979) 'Effective correctional treatment: bibliotherapy for cynics', *Crime and Delinquency*, 25: 463–89.

Gladstone Committee (1895) *Report from the Departmental Committee on Prisons*. London: Parliamentary Papers, 1895.

Harper, G. and Chitty, C. (eds) (2004) *The Impact of Corrections on Re-offending: A Review of 'What Works'*, Home Office Research Study No. 291. London: Home Office.

Haslewood-Pocsik, I., Merone, L. and Roberts, C. (2004) *The Evaluation of the Employment Pathfinder: Lessons from Phase I, and a Survey for Phase II*. Home Office Online Report 22/04. See: www.homeoffice.gov.uk/rds/pdfs05/rdsolr2204.pdf (accessed 19 January 2007).

Hedderman C. (2006) 'Keeping a lid on the prison population – will NOMS help?', in M. Hough, R. Allen and U. Padel (eds), *Reshaping Probation and Prisons: The New Offender Management Framework*. London: Polity Press.

Hedderman, C. and Hough, M. (2005) 'Diversion from prosecution at court and effective sentencing', in A.E. Perry, C. McDougall and D.P. Farrington (eds), *Reducing Crime: The Effectiveness of Criminal Justice Interventions*. Chichester: Wiley.

Her Majesty's Inspectorates of Prisons and Probation (2001) *Through the Prison Gate*. London: Home Office.

Her Majesty's Prison Service (2006) *Resettlement*. See: www.hmprisonservice. gov.uk/adviceandsupport/beforeafterrelease/resettlement/ (accessed 19 January 2006).

Hollin, C.R. (1990) *Cognitive-Behavioural Interventions with Young Offenders*. New York: Pergamon.

Home Office (1992) *National Standards for the Supervision of Offenders in the Community*. London: Home Office.

Home Office (1995) *National Standards for the Supervision of Offenders in the Community*. London: Home Office.

Home Office (1999) *What Works: Reducing Re-offending: Evidence-Based Practice*. London: Home Office.

Home Office (2001a) *Probation Statistics England and Wales, 1999*. London: Home Office.

Home Office (2001b) *Making Punishments Work: Report of a Review of the Sentencing Framework for England and Wales* (The Halliday Review). London: Home Office.

Home Office (2003) *Prison Statistics England and Wales, 2001*, Cmnd 5743. London: HMSO.

Home Office (2004) *Reducing Crime, Changing Lives: The Government's Plans for Transforming the Management of Offenders*. London: Home Office.

Home Office (2006a) *A Five Year Strategy for Protecting the Public and Reducing Re-offending*. London: Home Office.

Home Office (2006b) *Offender Management Caseload Statistics 2005, England and Wales*, Home Office Statistical Bulletin 18/06. London: Home Office.

Home Office/DH/DfES/ODPM/DWP (2005) *The National Reducing Reoffending Action Plan*. London: Home Office.

Howard, M. (1993) *Prison Works*. Speech to the 110th Conservative Party Conference, 6 October 1993. London: Conservative Party Central Office.

Lewis, S., Maguire, M., Raynor, P., Vantstone, M. and Vennard, J. (2007) 'What works in resettlement? Findings from seven Pathfinders for short-term prisoners in England and Wales', *Criminology and Criminal Justice*, 7 (1): 33–53.

Lewis, S., Vennard, J., Maguire, M., Raynor, P., Vanstone, M., Raybould, S. and Rix, A. (2003) *The Resettlement of Short-term Prisoners: An Evaluation of Seven Pathfinders*, RDS Occasional Paper No. 83. London: Home Office.

Lipsey, M.W. (1992) 'The effect of treatment on juvenile delinquents: results from meta-analysis', in F. Losel, T. Bliesener and D. Bender (eds), *Psychology and Law: International Perspectives*. Berlin: de Gruyter.

McGuire, J. (ed.) (1995) *What Works: Reducing Reoffending*. Chichester: Wiley.

McNeill, F. (2004a) 'Desistance, rehabilitation and correctionalism: developments and prospects in Scotland', *Howard Journal*, 43 (4): 420–36.

McNeill, F. (2004b) 'Desistance-focused probation practice', in W.H. Chui and M. Nellis (eds), *Moving Probation Forward: Evidence, Arguments and Practice*. Harlow: Pearson Education.

McNeill, F. (2006) 'A desistance paradigm for offender management', *Criminology and Criminal Justice*, 6 (1): 39–62.

Maguire, M. and Raynor, P. (1997) 'The revival of throughcare: rhetoric and reality in Automatic Conditional Release', *British Journal of Criminology*, 37 (1): 1–14.

Martinson, R. (1974) 'What works? Questions and answers about prison reform', *Public Interest*, 10: 22–54.

Maruna, S., Immarigeon, R. and LeBel, T.P. (2004) 'Ex-offender reintegration: theory and practice', in S. Maruna and R. Immarigeon (eds), *After Crime and Punishment: Pathways to Offender Re-integration*. Cullompton: Willan.

PA Consultancy Group and MORI (2005) *Action Research Study of the Implementation of the National Offender Management Model in the North West Pathfinder*, RDS Online Report 32/05. London: Home Office. See: www.homeoffice.gov.uk/rds/pdfs05/rdsolr3205.pdf (accessed 19 January 2007).

Raynor, P. (2003) 'Research in Probation: from "Nothing Works" to "What Works"', in W.H. Chui and M. Nellis (eds), *Moving Probation Forward: Evidence, Arguments and Practice*, Harlow: Pearson Education.

Raynor, P. (2004) Editor's Introduction, *Vista*, 8 (3): 127–9.

Social Exclusion Unit (2002), *Reducing Re-Offending by Ex-Prisoners*. London: Office of the Deputy Prime Minister.

Trotter, C. (1999) *Working with Involuntary Clients: A Guide to Practice*. London: Sage.

UNHCR (1990) *Standard Minimum Rules for Non-custodial Measures (The Tokyo Rules)*, adopted by General Assembly Resolution 45/110 of 14 December 1990. Geneva, Switzerland: Office of the United Nations High Commissioner for Human Rights.

Underdown, A. (1998) *Strategies for Effective Offender Supervision: Report of the HMIP What Works Project*. London: Home Office.

Vanstone, M. (2004) 'Mission Control: the origins of a humanitarian service', *Probation Journal*, 51 (1): 34–47.

Vennard, J., Sugg, D. and Hedderman, C. (1997) *Changing Offenders' Attitudes and Behaviour: 'What Works'*, Home Office Research Study No. 171. London: Home Office.

Webster, R., Hedderman, C., Turnbull, P.J. and May, T. (2001) *Building Bridges to Employment for Prisoners*, Home Office Research Study No. 226. London: Home Office.

Chapter 2

Theoretical perspectives on resettlement: what it is and how it might work

Peter Raynor

Introduction

As the previous chapter points out, when people use terms like 'resettlement' they do not always mean the same thing, and often they do not realise this, which contributes to a good deal of vagueness and confusion. This chapter is about the meanings of resettlement, and particularly about its purposes and justifications: what is it for? What is it realistically meant to achieve? The answers to these questions might seem obvious, but even a small amount of exposure to official documents and statements is enough to dispel such confidence, and studies of practice reveal different assumptions about what kind of activities and practices should be involved in resettlement. These in turn reflect different assumptions or beliefs about imprisoned offenders' needs, and about how they come to be imprisoned offenders in the first place. This chapter traces some of the changing views and concepts of resettlement which have underpinned recent and earlier policies, drawing on the author's involvement in a series of Home Office funded evaluations of resettlement services extending over the past fourteen years in collaboration with Mike Maguire, Maurice Vanstone and others (see Clancy *et al.* 2006; Lewis 2004; Lewis *et al.* 2003; Maguire and Raynor 1997, 2006; Maguire *et al.* 1996; Maguire *et al.* 2000; Raynor 2004). In addition, the chapter explores some evidence of what resettlement *can* achieve, and points to areas of convergence between the thinking behind some apparently effective resettlement work and recent studies of desistance from offending. Such work can help to throw light on what models of resettlement can be regarded as realistic, in the sense that their goals might actually be achievable.

Our current concept of resettlement lacks clarity around two issues in particular. One concerns the goals of resettlement, or the state of affairs intended to result from resettlement activity. Is it, as the name rather implies, an attempt to restore people to the social environment and condition which preceded their prison sentence? The problem with this view is that it may have been an actively criminogenic environment, and even the main reason why they found themselves in prison in the first place. 'Reintegration', another currently popular term, makes little sense for those who were not integrated in the first place, and may not be the best outcome for others who were well integrated into communities or peer groups where offending was normal or accepted. If, on the other hand, the intended outcome is new social bonds and commitments which support a way of life in which offending is less likely (as suggested, among others, by Haines 1990), resettlement is not a very clear description of such a process.

The second area where there is a lack of clarity concerns the reasons for providing resettlement as a publicly funded service within the criminal justice system. Are such services provided simply because many ex-prisoners have social needs? If so, it is not clear why these welfare needs should be met by the criminal justice system rather than by other services which (at least in principle) are available to all. There is also a risk of perceived unfairness if ex-prisoners are believed to be receiving special help which is not available to people with similar needs who have not offended. (At one time it was argued by some criminal justice professionals that the development of the Welfare State would in due course make discharge grants obsolete (Home Office 1953: 11)). Or are resettlement services provided in order to meet particular needs which ex-prisoners have because they have served prison sentences? If so, are these special needs the result of damage done to prisoners by imprisonment, in which case the taxpayer is paying both to create the needs and to try to meet them, or are they a consequence of the *beneficial* impact of imprisonment, such as the need to continue and reinforce the work of rehabilitative programmes begun in prison? Or are resettlement services best understood as part of a range of work done with offenders, including those subject to community sentences, in an attempt to rehabilitate them and reduce their propensity to offend? If so, questions about the purposes and justifications of resettlement become subsumed under the broader question of why and how criminal justice systems try, or should try, to rehabilitate offenders. These are complicated questions (see, for example, Raynor and Robinson 2005). In this chapter, I attempt no more than some clarification of the history of the *concept* of resettlement and its predecessors, to supplement the history of policy and practice which is reviewed in the preceding chapter. I follow this with some suggestions about how it might be understood in current circumstances in the light of evidence about what it actually achieves.

Resettlement and its predecessors – the history of an idea

What we now call 'resettlement' has had various names through the last two centuries. In the nineteenth century it was called 'Discharged Prisoners' Aid'. It was provided on a charitable basis by voluntary associations linked to local prisons (the earliest clearly traceable examples, in Gloucester, Hampshire, Shropshire and Montgomery, went back to 1800 or before (National Association of Discharged Prisoners' Aid Societies 1956)) and by publicly funded associations such as the Central Association for the Aid of Discharged Convicts, which was founded in 1910. Its first President was Winston Churchill, whose views on resettlement are discussed later in this chapter. In addition, other specialist associations were set up to assist women prisoners (the Aylesbury Association) and Borstal boys (the Borstal Association). A representative example of early charitable thinking about the plight of ex-prisoners can be found in the work of William Booth ('General' Booth of the Salvation Army) who included criminal justice issues in his social investigation of 'Darkest England' (1890):

> Absolute despair drives many a man into the ranks of the criminal class, who would never have fallen into the category of criminal convicts if adequate provision had been made for the rescue of those drifting to doom. When once he has fallen, circumstances seem to combine to keep him there ... the unfortunate who bears the prison brand is hunted from pillar to post, until he despairs of ever regaining his position, and oscillates between one prison and another for the rest of his days. (Booth 1890: 58)

Booth was particularly conscious of the difficulties encountered by many ex-prisoners in securing accommodation and employment, and in staying sober: his book gives examples of successful help, sometimes in offenders' own words. His argument is that the punishment should end when prisoners are released, and further obstacles resulting from their ex-prisoner status prolong the punishment unfairly and prevent people who wish to maintain a crime-free life from doing so. He certainly does not see aid to the released prisoner as continuing the rehabilitative efforts of the prison: 'At present there seems to be but little likelihood of any real reform in the interior of our prisons. We have therefore to wait until the men come outside, in order to see what can be done' (Booth 1890: 174). However, anticipating many later authorities, he argued that successful help after release was made more likely if a relationship could be established by pre-release contact: 'We should seek access to the prisons in order to gain such acquaintance with the prisoners as would enable us the more effectually to benefit them on discharge' (Booth 1890: 175). The attitudes underpinning such relationships are clearly indicated: 'Our people ... have never learnt to regard a prisoner as a mere convict ... He is ever a human being to them ...' (Booth 1890: 174).

During the first half of the twentieth century this type of charitable and faith-based approach became more organised and began to adopt a more secular and professional guise. The separate Discharged Prisoners' Aid Societies came together as the National Association of Discharged Prisoners' Aid Societies (NADPAS) in 1936, and the associations linked to the convict prisons, the women's prison and the Borstals were merged into the Central After-Care Association in 1948. By this time the term 'after-care' was being preferred to earlier terms like 'aid' or 'relief', but the focus was still on what happened after release: the NADPAS Handbook for 1956 uses 'after-care' consistently. It also states that 'none should enter in, or remain in, this work who is not committed to the principle that every offender offers hope of reclamation' (NADPAS 1956: viii; William Booth would have agreed). However, more professional concerns about the best use of scarce resources also find their place in the Handbook, anticipating later concerns about the 'revolving door':

> In every local prison there are those serving short terms of imprisonment who are continually coming and going – some are discharged several times in one year after serving fresh sentences ... it is considered a waste of valuable time in seeing such cases ... (NADPAS 1956: 32)

In 1963 a report of the Advisory Council on the Treatment of Offenders (ACTO) proposed a major rationalisation of the provision of aftercare (Home Office 1963). Responsibilities for compulsory aftercare (provided by the Central After-Care Association and often in practice by probation officers) and voluntary aftercare (provided largely by NADPAS) were to be merged, and both were to be provided by the Probation Service, to be renamed the Probation and After-Care Service. Aftercare was seen clearly in this report as a professional service ('After-care is essentially a form of social casework' – Home Office 1963: ii) and

> to be fully effective, must be integrated with the work of the penal institutions in which the offender serves his sentence, and must be conceived as a process which starts on the offender's reception into custody, is developed during his sentence, and is available for as long as necessary after his release. (Home Office 1963: 4)

Here the prison is no longer simply punishment, but is seen as doing rehabilitative 'work' in its own right, with which the aftercare must be 'integrated'. This passage also introduces the idea of a process which is continuous from the start of the sentence, anticipating the term 'throughcare', which began to replace 'aftercare' in probation officers' terminology and literature during the late 1960s.

The next few decades involved rapid development in the work of probation services, and many of the important milestones in this have been described in the previous chapter. Those which most significantly affected the concept and meaning of throughcare and aftercare included the Statement of National Objectives and Priorities (Home Office 1984), which consigned voluntary aftercare to a low-priority residual role in a service redefined as a provider of non-custodial sentences. This began a process of withdrawal by the Probation Service from the voluntary aftercare responsibilities acquired as recently as the 1960s, and incidentally fulfilled a gloomy prediction made by Radzinowicz in his dissenting note to the 1963 ACTO report. 'Throughcare' now came to mean primarily the supervision of statutory licences. A few years later this was reinforced by the 1991 Criminal Justice Act and the innovative series of Green and White Papers which preceded it (Home Office 1988, 1990a, 1990b). These developments famously redefined probation as 'punishment in the community', less severe than custodial punishment but not different in kind; in addition, they introduced the concept of the 'seamless sentence', a single punishment to be served partly in prison and partly on licence in the community, under supervision by the Probation Service. In addition to the discretionary release arrangements which replaced parole for longer-sentence prisoners, all those serving sentences of at least one year but less than four years were to be subject to automatic conditional release (ACR) under supervision, normally at the halfway point. Strict new requirements relating to reporting and enforcement (Home Office 1992) emphasised the fact that this was a continuation of the sentence. Although these more punitive features were balanced by the 1991 Act's intention to bring about a significant reduction in custodial sentencing, the decarcerative elements in the Act were quickly undermined by new legislation as a crumbling Conservative administration lurched towards law and order populism. The enduring elements turned out to be the redefinition of probation service activities as punishments and the 'seamless sentence'. Interestingly, offenders subject to ACR during the first years of the new scheme clung to an earlier concept of aftercare and thought that its purpose was to help them rather than to punish them. Probation officers, however, thought that the main focus of supervision was to secure compliance with licence requirements (though they also recognised a need to address offending behaviour and offenders' problems), and probation managers stated that the primary aims of the scheme were to protect the public and to ensure compliance (Maguire et al. 1996). The early 1990s also saw the almost complete disappearance of voluntary aftercare for the short-term prisoners who were not included in the ACR scheme: voluntary arrangements no longer had a place in a probation service focused on coping with expanded caseloads and stricter requirements for contact and enforcement (Maguire et al. 2000). Although these offenders had many problems and a high risk of reconviction, they were no longer a priority.

As government policies increasingly assumed that there were strong similarities between the work of prisons and probation, with probation seen as offering lesser punishments rather than alternatives to punishment, it was a logical development to begin to think about unifying the 'correctional' services. The first major government report on this theme appeared in 1998, in the first full year of the New Labour government, with a foreword and endorsement by the then Home Secretary Jack Straw (Home Office 1998). It came to the conclusion that the two services should remain separate but should work more closely together, and that the Probation Service, locally managed until then, should become a national service for England and Wales run from the Home Office. (Those were the days when some people still believed that if you wanted something run properly, you should arrange for the Home Office to run it.) The 1998 report is also important for this chapter because it marks the definitive adoption of the term 'resettlement' into official discourse:

> 'Throughcare' is the term which lies at the heart of the two services' joint work. It is unlikely to be properly understood outside of the prison and probation worlds ... We think that public and sentencer confidence would be enhanced if the focus was on the ultimate goals of 'throughcare' – high quality sentence planning and successful resettlement in the community. Our preference is for this work to be called simply 'resettlement' ... (Home Office 1998: 9)

It is not known what evidence was available that the public and sentencers did not understand 'throughcare'; however, a rather different rationale for the change is spelled out in another section of the report:

> It is important that the names, language and terminology used by the services should give accurate and accessible messages about the nature and aims of their work. Some of the terms have been criticised, for example because ... they are associated with tolerance of crime ... or they are too esoteric to be understood outside the two services (e.g. 'throughcare' which sounds more associated with the 'caring' services). (Home Office 1998: 8)

'Resettlement' was the broadly accepted term by the time the experimental 'Pathfinder' projects were funded by the Crime Reduction Programme in 1999. One of these experiments, which concerned resettlement, is discussed in the second part of this chapter. However, before moving on to the empirical side of this exploration of the meaning of resettlement, there is one more terminological shift to be taken into account. In 2003 Patrick Carter, a businessman and Downing Street advisor, was asked to undertake a further review of the operation of the criminal justice system. His report was published at the end of 2003 (Home Office 2003) and recommended the establishment of a National Offender Management Service (NOMS) combining prisons and probation, and an extension of 'contestability' within the system to allow the voluntary and private sectors to compete with the public sector to provide 'offender management' services. Within a couple of weeks the government had committed itself to implementing most of the report's recommendations, though at the time of writing we are still waiting to see exactly how.

As far as resettlement was concerned, the Carter Report seemed to involve another change of language: both prisons and community-based services were doing 'offender management', a term which covered everything from secure incapacitative custody to supervision in the community, and which aimed to protect the public by reducing the risk of reoffending. This was to be achieved by individualised assessment, planning and case management which could include work to address offending behaviour, or could aim to manage and reduce risk through an appropriate set of controls and restrictions, or could combine these approaches in various ways (for example, personal supervision supported by an electronically monitored curfew). Offenders' needs were not ignored: in so far as they were criminogenic, the system should try to meet them in order to reduce risk. The notion of 'end-to-end' offender management promised a more coherent and planned approach to doing this, ideally with continuity of supervision from a known person, although it was difficult to see how the proposed 'contestable' structure of services would actually deliver such a high level of continuity (Raynor and Maguire 2005). Like the 1991 Act, the Carter Report had some very positive underlying purposes: for example, to limit the prison population to 80,000; to end the use of community penalties for low-risk offenders who could be fined; and to supply the missing resettlement services to the thousands of short-sentence prisoners through a new sentence, 'Custody Plus', which was introduced by the Criminal Justice Act 2003 and would ensure that every short prison sentence was followed by a period of supervision in the community. Sadly, at the time of writing, the prison target has already been abandoned and the cost of new prisons is to be found partly from the indefinite postponement of the implementation of Custody Plus. The focus instead has been on forcing through the structural reorganisation and 'contestability', against considerable resistance from the existing services.

Through all these twists and turns of policy the official notion of what services should be provided to released prisoners and the terminology used to describe them has changed beyond recognition, and changed far more than the realities of resettlement practice. It is now time to anchor this discussion in some of these realities. The way we think about and conceptualise resettlement should reflect what it actually can and does achieve, if our thinking is to serve as a useful guide to practice rather than a source of misleading or unrealistic expectations. The largest and most detailed empirical explorations of recent mainstream resettlement practice in England and Wales have been carried out in the series of studies mentioned at the beginning of this chapter, and in particular in the Resettlement Pathfinder evaluations. The next section of this chapter considers what can be learned from these studies about the nature of successful resettlement work.

What worked in the Resettlement Pathfinders

The Resettlement Pathfinders, which focused mainly on short-term prisoners, ran between 1999 and 2005 and were evaluated as part of the Crime Reduction Programme. Full accounts of the findings from these studies can be found elsewhere (Clancy et al. 2006; Lewis 2004; Lewis et al. 2003; Raynor 2004) and this summary concentrates on those aspects which are important for the purposes of this chapter. The first phase of the study, involving seven 'pathfinder' projects, was intended to improve the availability and take-up of appropriate post-release services for short-term prisoners and to help them to make a better transition back into the community. In addition, the first phase was designed to test and compare a number of different approaches to providing resettlement services. Three voluntary sector projects were to concentrate on 'welfare needs' while four probation-led projects would concentrate more on addressing offending behaviour. Although other differences between projects emerged in the course of the research, the main intended difference in approach remained and showed itself in a number of ways: for example, Offender Assessment System (OASys) assessments in the probation-led projects for male prisoners were more likely than in the voluntary sector projects to identify 'thinking' problems. The probation-led projects also attempted a considerable amount of work with individuals on problems of thinking and attitudes, and by the end of the study all four probation-led projects were using a form of group programme to address these issues.

In the three projects for male prisoners this was a cognitive-motivational programme, 'FOR – A Change', designed specifically for pre-release use with short-term prisoners (Fabiano and Porporino 2002). This programme was rather different in aims and content from the majority of accredited offending behaviour programmes. Designed for delivery in the weeks preceding release, FOR consisted of twelve group sessions and one individual session. The group sessions concentrated on developing motivation and setting goals, and included a 'marketplace' session attended by representatives of agencies likely to be of use to prisoners on the outside, in accordance with the long-standing observation that the appointments most likely to be kept on release are those arranged before release (see, for example, Maguire *et al.* 2000). The rationale of the whole programme was closely based on established principles of motivational interviewing (Miller and Rollnick 1991, 2002) and was designed to be followed up through continuing contact with resettlement workers after release. The 'motivational' approach can be summed up as attempting to 'develop discrepancy', in other words promoting awareness of gaps between what prisoners want or aspire to be and their current situations or behaviour. The assumption is that prisoners will face obstacles on release, and will need motivation, resourcefulness and determination to overcome them even with the assistance of available support and services: motivated prisoners are likely to make more and better use of whatever help is available.

In analysis of the results of the seven first-phase pathfinders, it was difficult to distinguish between the results of the programme itself and of other features of the services provided in the probation-led projects, and some offenders would have been exposed to both. However, it was possible to compare some outcomes of probation-led projects with voluntary organisation-led projects, and here the results were fairly clear (see Lewis *et al.* 2003). Probation-led projects achieved significantly higher levels of continuity of contact with offenders after release, and in most cases also achieved significantly higher levels of positive change in attitudes and beliefs and in self-reported life problems as measured by repeat administration of the CRIME-PICS II questionnaire (Frude *et al.* 1994). Although the numbers (1,081 prisoners divided among the seven projects and 2,450 comparison cases) were rather small for a comparative reconviction study, later analysis showed that when other factors were controlled for, participants in two of the probation-led projects had significantly lower reconviction rates than those in the other projects. In addition, continuity of contact with project workers (especially volunteer mentors) 'through the gate' was significantly associated with lower reconviction rates (Clancy *et al.* 2006). Obviously there are likely to be selection effects involved here, since those who choose to remain in contact may be those who are already more likely to avoid reoffending, but the different rates of continuity achieved with rather similar offender populations suggest that some projects were indeed motivating offenders rather more effectively than others. The importance of continuity lies not simply in the fact that offenders are more likely to keep appointments with and take advice from somebody they know and in whom they have some confidence:

the challenging of discrepancy and the maintenance of motivation are also easier in the context of a relationship. Put at its simplest, we mostly find it easier to break a promise to a stranger than to let down someone we know. Some projects achieved useful levels of continuity by using professional staff; others relied on volunteer mentors, who may have more time to offer and sometimes also a more unconditional commitment to helping.

Another discussion of this study (Raynor 2004) has explored the differences between these resettlement projects in terms of underlying assumptions about offending and desistance, which constitute the 'implicit criminologies' of resettlement work. In that paper a distinction is drawn between 'opportunity deficit' models, which regard offenders as victims of circumstances who offend because of lack of access to resources, and 'offender responsibility' models (perhaps better described as 'offenders' choice' models) which highlight the role of offenders' own decisions about how to respond to the circumstances in which they find themselves. Approaches based on 'opportunity deficit' tend to concentrate on welfare needs and on facilitating access to services, on the assumption that this will lead to desistance; approaches which emphasise offenders' own choices and their response to circumstances will also pay attention to thinking and motivation. (This does not mean that offenders are somehow held responsible for circumstances and deficits which are completely beyond their control, but simply that they often also need help in developing the motivation and resourcefulness which will give them a better chance to manage their lives without offending.) In the resettlement pathfinders, the projects led by voluntary organisations appeared more likely to operate on 'opportunity deficit' assumptions, and the greater success of the probation-led projects appeared to be due, in part, to their greater focus on thinking and motivation.

Resettlement and the process of desistance

These findings are also consistent with recent research on desistance from crime which has been concerned with the roles of structure and agency in the desistance process (see, for example, Farrall and Calverley 2005; Maguire and Raynor 2006). Opportunity deficits can be considered as part of social structure, and offenders' choices as an aspect of personal agency. Research on desistance shows that agency is as important as structure: for example, Zamble and Quinsey (1997: 146–7) concluded from their large study of released male prisoners in Ontario that 'factors in the social environment seem influential determinants of initial delinquency for a substantial proportion of offenders ... but habitual offending is better predicted by looking at an individual's acquired ways of reacting to common situations'. For many ex-prisoners, the latter include negative or pessimistic reactions to practical problems, which lead them to give up on attempts to avoid reoffending. Maruna's interview-based study of offenders in Liverpool added the insight that people may react differently depending upon their personal understandings or accounts of their situations and behaviour – what he calls different kinds of 'narrative', some of which support continued offending and some of which support desistance. A key element of desistance narratives was a belief that the offender had begun to take control of his or her own life: 'Whereas active offenders ... seemed to have little vision of what the future might hold, desisting interviewees had a plan and were optimistic that they could make it work' (Maruna 2000: 147). These ideas are also reminiscent of much earlier writing about resettlement, for example: 'The central object of after-care is to provide such guidance and moral support as will help the ex-prisoner to cope with his personal and peculiar difficulties, and to withstand the spirit of apathy and defeatism in which many are liable to drift back to crime' (Home Office 1953: 16).

Other findings of recent desistance research also have implications for resettlement: these are explored in more detail elsewhere (Maguire and Raynor 2006) and a summary must suffice here. One particularly important insight is that desistance is a process, not an event, and reversals and lapses are common: Burnett (2004) refers to a 'zigzag' rather than a linear process, and Maruna and Farrall (2004) refer to one involving complex progression from 'primary' to 'secondary' desistance. ('Primary' desistance is the achievement of an offence-free period; 'secondary' desistance is the adoption or consolidation of a non-offending identity and self-concept.) Different individuals may make progress at different times for different reasons, and motivation cannot be taken for granted but needs to be generated and sustained. As people change they also need new skills and capacities appropriate to their new lives, and opportunities to use them. Another way of putting this is that they need to acquire both 'human capital' (skills, personal resources, motivation) and 'social capital' (links, connections and relationships with other people, formal and informal social networks and organisations) (McNeill 2006). Both capacities and opportunities for change are needed. Also relevant here is the distinction between 'bonding' and 'bridging' social capital

(Putnam 2000): 'bonding' social capital links you to existing networks of relationships and resources, and tends to reinforce and stabilise current identities; 'bridging' social capital extends your contacts and opportunities and facilitates social mobility. Bonding social capital is good for 'getting by' and is described as 'a kind of sociological superglue', while bridging social capital is good for 'getting ahead' and is 'a sociological WD-40' (Putnam 2000: 23). One promotes security and stability while the other promotes change. This also suggests one possible resolution of the question raised at the beginning of this chapter about whether resettlement aims to restore ex-prisoners to the social situations which existed prior to sentence or to create new social bonds, attachments and opportunities. The answer might be that resettlement should aim to help in developing both bonding and bridging social capital as well as human capital.

All of these insights into the process of desistance have implications for 'offender management' practice, and McNeill (2006) has spelled out a number of them in his proposal for a 'desistance paradigm' for probation practice. In resettlement work, they point to a need for early individualised preparation for release; access to resources and advocacy; awareness of the importance of motivation and cognition; continuity of personal contact; empathetic support in the face of setbacks; help in acquiring relevant skills; a positive and optimistic approach; a genuine collaboration between resettlement worker and ex-prisoner, and a flexible and realistic approach to temporary lapses which does not equate them with long-term failure. It remains to be seen how far the National Offender Management Model can deliver this type of service: the impact of new structures and contestability is difficult to predict (Raynor and Maguire 2005) and the continuing preoccupation with rigid and inflexible enforcement simply recycles large numbers of ex-prisoners back into prison (Solomon 2005).

Regional plans for the reduction of reoffending are based on the 'Seven pathways' to desistance originally set out in the influential Social Exclusion Unit report on reoffending by ex-prisoners (Social Exclusion Unit 2002) and discussed in detail in the preceding chapter. The 'Pathways' are: accommodation; education, training and employment; mental and physical health; drugs and alcohol; finance, benefits and debt; children and families of offenders; and attitudes, thinking and behaviour. These pathways make the crucial point that reoffending is not just a criminal justice problem and its reduction requires collaboration between many different services and different parts of Government. The findings reviewed in this chapter also suggest that for many offenders, the seventh pathway ('attitudes, thinking and behaviour') is not just another item on a list of needs, but will play a critical role in determining how effectively they use resources designed to address any of the other six.

Conclusion: resettlement as rehabilitation

It will be clear from the foregoing discussion that successful resettlement has much in common with other forms of supervision intended to rehabilitate offenders. It belongs much more plausibly in the territory of rehabilitation than in the territory of punishment: at best, it helps offenders to help themselves to stop offending. It does not look like the final part of a seamless episode of punishment: on the contrary, pursuing it in a punitive style with trigger-happy enforcement is likely to undermine any rehabilitative effect. (This is not to argue that restrictive licence conditions do not have an important part to play, particularly in relation to public protection from dangerous offenders; however, an approach which is simply or primarily restrictive is perhaps better described as risk management than resettlement. Resettlement can and often does *include* monitoring of compliance, but monitoring alone is not the same as providing a resettlement service.) As with other forms of rehabilitation, the question then arises as to why the state should provide it. Why not leave released prisoners to their own devices? There is not space in this chapter to discuss this issue in any detail, but a number of recent commentators (Carlen 1994; Cullen and Gilbert 1982; Raynor and Robinson 2005; Rotman 1990) have argued that the most satisfactory answer is that the state is obliged, as part of a social contract with its citizens, to ensure that its expectation that we should obey the laws is matched by a duty to ensure realistic opportunities to maintain a crime-free life. This view, known as 'state-obligated' rehabilitation, resembles the social contract which underlies general welfare provision: the legitimacy of the state depends in part on guaranteeing the basic conditions of life for its citizens. To expect citizens to obey the law, and to punish them for not doing so, is fair and justified only in so far as reasonable provision is made to ensure that compliance is realistically possible. Resettlement services to reduce reoffending are part of this provision, and while they may be prepared for and begun during the prison sentence, they are not part of the punitive content of the sentence.

There is again little in these ideas which is completely new. For example, reference has already been made to Winston Churchill's personal interest in aftercare when he was Home Secretary in a Liberal government. His much quoted speech of 20 July 1910, in which he famously argued that 'the mood and temper of the public in regard to the treatment of crime and criminals is one of the most unfailing tests of the civilisation of any country' (Churchill 1910), also pointed to a state-obligated theory of aftercare:

> We cannot impose these serious penalties upon individuals unless we make a great effort and a new effort to rehabilitate men who have been in prison, and secure their having a chance to resume their places in the ranks of honourable industry.

He also spoke of:

> A calm and dispassionate recognition of the rights of the accused against the State, and even of convicted criminals against the State, a constant heart searching by all charged with the duty of punishment, a desire and eagerness to rehabilitate in the world of industry all those who have paid their dues in the hard coinage of punishment, tireless efforts towards the discovery of curative and regenerative processes, and an unfaltering faith that there is a treasure, if you can only find it, in the heart of every man.

How different from that later Home Secretary who was so anxious to avoid using language that might give an inappropriate impression of caring.

References

Booth, W. (1890) *In Darkest England and The Way Out*. London: International Headquarters of the Salvation Army.

Burnett, R. (2004) 'To reoffend or not to reoffend? The ambivalence of convicted property offenders', in S. Maruna and R. Immarigeon (eds), *After Crime and Punishment: Pathways to Offender Reintegration*. Cullompton: Willan, pp. 152–80.

Carlen, P. (1994) 'Crime, inequality and sentencing', in A. Duff and D. Garland (eds), *A Reader on Punishment*. Oxford: Oxford University Press, pp. 306–32.

Churchill, W. (1910) Speech to the House of Commons, 20 July. Reprinted in *Vista*, 10 (3): 155–61.

Clancy, A., Hudson, K., Maguire, M., Peake, R., Raynor, P., Vanstone, M. and Kynch J. (2006) *Getting Out and Staying Out: Results of the Prisoner Resettlement Pathfinders*. Bristol: Policy Press.

Cullen, F.T. and Gilbert, K.E. (1982) *Reaffirming Rehabilitation*. Cincinnati, OH: Anderson Publishing.

Fabiano, E. and Porporino, F. (2002) *Focus on Resettlement – A Change*. Canada: T3 Associates.

Farrall, S. (2004) 'Social capital and offender re-integration: making probation desistance focused', in S. Maruna and R. Immarigeon (eds), *After Crime and Punishment: Pathways to Offender Reintegration*. Cullompton: Willan, pp. 57–84.

Farrall, S. and Calverley, A. (2005) *Understanding Desistance from Crime: Theoretical Directions in Resettlement and Rehabilitation*. Milton Keynes: Open University Press.

Frude, N., Honess, T. and Maguire, M. (1994) *CRIME-PICS II Manual*. Cardiff: Michael & Associates.

Haines, K. (1990) *After-Care Services for Released Prisoners*. Cambridge: Institute of Criminology.

Home Office (1953) *Report of the Committee on Discharged Prisoners' Aid Societies*, Cmnd. 8879. London: HMSO.

Home Office (1963) *The Organisation of After-Care. Report of the Advisory Council on the Treatment of Offenders*. London: HMSO.

Home Office (1984) *Probation Service in England and Wales: Statement of National Objectives and Priorities*. London: Home Office.

Home Office (1988) *Punishment, Custody and the Community*, Cmnd 424. London: HMSO.

Home Office (1990a) *Crime, Justice and Protecting the Public*, Cmnd 965. London: HMSO.

Home Office (1990b) *Supervision and Punishment in the Community*, Cmnd 966. London: HMSO.

Home Office (1992) *National Standards for the Supervision of Offenders in the Community*. London: Home Office.

Home Office (1998) *Joining Forces to Protect the Public: Prisons–Probation*. London: Home Office.

Home Office (2003) *Managing Offenders, Reducing Crime – A New Approach: Correctional Services Review by Patrick Carter*. London: Prime Minister's Strategy Unit.

Lewis, S. (2004) 'What works in the resettlement of short-term prisoners?', *Vista*, 8 (3): 163–70.

Lewis, S., Vennard, J., Maguire, M., Raynor, P., Vanstone, M., Raybould, S. and Rix, A. (2003) *The Resettlement of Short-term Prisoners: An Evaluation of Seven Pathfinders*, RDS Occasional Paper 83. London: Home Office.

McNeill, F. (2006) 'Towards a desistance paradigm for offender management', *Criminology and Criminal Justice*, 6 (1): 39–62.

Maguire, M. and Raynor, P. (1997) 'The revival of throughcare: rhetoric and reality in automatic conditional release', *British Journal of Criminology*, 37 (1): 1–14.

Maguire, M. and Raynor, P. (2006) 'How the resettlement of prisoners promotes desistance from crime: or does it?', *Criminology and Criminal Justice*, 6 (1): 19–38.

Maguire, M., Perroud, B. and Raynor, P. (1996) *Automatic Conditional Release: The First Two Years*, Research Study No. 156. London: Home Office.

Maguire, M., Raynor, P., Vanstone, M. and Kynch, J. (2000) 'Voluntary after-care and the Probation Service: a case of diminishing responsibility', *Howard Journal of Criminal Justice*, 39 (3): 234–48.

Maruna, S. (2000) *Making Good*. Washington, DC: American Psychological Association.

Maruna, S. and Farrall, S. (2004) 'Desistance from crime: a theoretical reformulation', *Kölner Zeitschrift für Soziologie und Sozialpsychologie*, 43: 171–94.

Miller, W.R. and Rollnick, S. (1991) *Motivational Interviewing. Preparing People to Change Addictive Behaviours*. New York: Guildford Press.

Miller, W.R. and Rollnick, S. (2002) *Motivational Interviewing. Preparing People for Change*, 2nd edn. New York: Guildford Press.

National Association of Discharged Prisoners' Aid Societies (NADPAS) (1956) *Handbook of the National Association of Discharged Prisoners' Aid Societies*. London: NADPAS.

Putnam, R. (2000) *Bowling Alone: The Collapse and Revival of American Community*. New York: Simon & Schuster.

Raynor, P. (2004) 'Opportunity, motivation and change: some findings from research on resettlement', in R. Burnett and C. Roberts (eds), *What Works in Probation and Youth Justice*. Cullompton: Willan, pp. 217–33.

Raynor, P. and Maguire, M. (2005) 'End-to-end or end in tears? Prospects for the effectiveness of the National Offender Management Model', in M. Hough, R. Allen and U. Padel (eds), *Reshaping Probation and Prisons: The New Offender Management Framework*. Bristol: Policy Press, pp. 21–34.

Raynor, P. and Robinson, G. (2005) *Rehabilitation, Crime and Justice*. Basingstoke: Palgrave.

Rotman, E. (1990) *Beyond Punishment: A New View of the Rehabilitation of Offenders*. Westport, CT: Greenwood Press.

Social Exclusion Unit (2002) *Reducing Re-offending by Ex-Prisoners*. London: Office of the Deputy Prime Minister.

Solomon, E. (2005) 'Returning to punishment: prison recalls', *Criminal Justice Matters*, 60: 24–5.

Zamble, E. and Quinsey, V. (1997) *The Criminal Recidivism Process*. Cambridge: Cambridge University Press.

Chapter 3

Models of resettlement work with prisoners

Anthea Hucklesby and Emma Wincup

Introduction

A wide range of resettlement work is being undertaken currently with prisoners in England and Wales (some examples of which are discussed in Part 3 of this book). Recently, a large number of local and regional resettlement schemes have been set up as a result of the increasing emphasis on resettlement as a driver for reducing offending and the proposed introduction of contestability, enabling a range of organisations hitherto excluded from statutory funding to bid to provide such services. The resettlement schemes vary enormously in how they are created and operated. Some of these schemes are funded and run by statutory agencies while others are operated by voluntary sector organisations. Schemes can be entirely prison or community based or they may provide services both inside and outside prisons. They also differ in the type of services provided. This chapter scopes the range of resettlement activities taking place in England and Wales. In doing so it identifies and describes the different ways in which resettlement activity may be carried out and examines the issues each approach raises for policymakers and providers of resettlement services.

The chapter draws on our recent evaluations of three resettlement initiatives conducted over the past four years or so and it is from these that much of the evidence for what we are going to say has been derived. We do not aim to describe every possible way to organise resettlement work but instead to provide a broad overview of the most common ways it is arranged currently.[1] The lack of an evidence base for resettlement work has been commented upon before (Crow 2006). Yet it is still worthy of note that there is limited research which has studied how resettlement work is done, why it is done in the way that it is and the effectiveness of different models (with the exception of Lewis et al. 2003).

There is a consensus that the ideal model for the provision of resettlement services is that they are provided 'through the prison gate', meaning both in prison and in the community (Her Majesty's Inspectorates of Prisons and Probation 2001; Raynor 2004). This joined-up approach should provide continuity of service provision and support. Purely basing resettlement provision in prison is perceived to be inadequate because of the likelihood of prisoners relapsing into their old lifestyles, including offending, when they are released (Crow 2006). Additionally, poor services in prison result in low levels of contact after release (Clancy et al. 2006; Maguire et al. 1998, 2000). Similarly, community-based work does not allow preparations to be made for release while prisoners are in custody and may result in no support or services being available during the first few days of release. Consequently, prisoners may leave prison with significant unmet needs which may increase the likelihood of reoffending.

The officially adopted model of resettlement which involves 'case management' suggests that resettlement needs should be identified through the sentencing planning process and the issues worked upon while prisoners are incarcerated ensuring that concrete and realistic plans are made for their release (Carter 2003; Harper and Chitty 2004; Home Office 2006a, 2006b; PA Consulting and MORI 2005). After release, prisoners should continue to receive support and guidance. Under this model, a single case manager would be responsible for the whole of the process, coordinating various services for the prisoners in prison and in the community and referring them on to other services (Home Office 2006a; PA Consulting and MORI 2005). So, it is envisaged that their role should be as a coordinator of service provision and not a provider of services. This continuity of personnel appears to be an important contributory factor in success (Clancy et al. 2006; PA Consulting and MORI 2005). The extent to which this occurs will be covered in other chapters of this book. Suffice it to say here, that this model remains very much an ideal and challenges exist in terms of its implementation (PA Consulting and MORI 2005). It is also worth noting that there is little empirical evidence to support this model (Crow 2006). Rather it appears to have gained prominence through its recycling in official reports to achieve the label of 'evidence-based' policy as described by Boaz and Pawson (2005) in other contexts, notwithstanding that the model makes sense intuitively.

Despite the diversity of organisational, funding and management models, most resettlement activity in England and Wales follows a similar pattern. Resettlement workers assess prisoners to identify their needs and establish what services and/or support is required. The form that these assessments take varies considerably. The difference between assessment techniques is not so much about what they aim to find out, i.e. the needs of offenders, but *how* they do this. This ranges from utilising structured risk assessment tools such as OASys[2] as part of the formal sentencing planning process to unstructured 'conversations'. The focus of assessments is largely dictated by the aims of the project: some will consider a broad range of needs while others will concentrate on single or a small number of issues. Once an assessment has been completed a range of activities may occur. In prison, this involves activities in preparation for release including efforts to find accommodation, employment or education provision, accessing services and setting up appointments while in prison and on release. When prisoners are released or once they are in the community, other support may be offered including meeting prisoners at the gate on their date of release and transporting them to their accommodation, accompanying them to appointments, providing mentors, signposting them to other services or simply keeping in contact (Lewis *et al.* 2003).

Many of the problems faced by prisoners are deeply entrenched and require responses from agencies outside of the criminal justice process (Crow 2006; SEU 2002). Indeed, one of the themes running through recent reports on prisoners' resettlement (SEU 2002) is the difficulties faced by prisoners who try to access services relating to housing and benefits despite these services being technically available to them. Prisoners are rarely priorities for these services and as a result face considerable barriers to accessing them (SEU 2002). So the ability of resettlement schemes to build and sustain links with agencies and to smooth the way for offenders to access services is an important measure of effectiveness (Clancy *et al.* 2006; Harper and Chitty 2004).

Most commentaries on resettlement focus on the paucity of services and the gaps in provision. However, there is also the potential for overlap. The most significant area of overlap is with the Counselling, Assessment, Referral, Advice and Throughcare Service (CARATS). Its principal purpose is to provide throughcare for drug-using prisoners by promoting continuity of provision. To this end it aims to coordinate and arrange drugs assessment and treatment both in prison and in the community. However, tackling drug use cannot be dealt with in isolation and CARATS often provide more generalised assistance to prisoners leaving prison particularly in relation to accommodation and employment. Research has shown that CARATS have been failing to provide drug services through the prison gate (Burrows *et al.* 2000; Harman and Paylor 2005a, 2005b; Turnball 2004). Nevertheless, our research suggests that they do provide generalised assistance to prisoners within prisons, which results in overlaps with generic resettlement provision, notwithstanding that CARATS are also an important source of referrals for resettlement services. However, there also appears to be an apparent lack of liaison between CARATS and other agencies involved in resettlement (Senior 2004). CARATS appear to be reluctant to share information or work in conjunction with other agencies/individuals and this can result in duplication of effort. These issues arise partly as a result of the lack of information sharing between health-related staff and others which appears to be routed in the tight definition of confidentially operationalised by some health professionals. These and other issues relating to multi-agency working such as confidentially and the need to sustain income and market share are likely to be barriers to 'mixed economy provision' under contestability (McSweeney and Hough 2006).

Currently a large proportion of resettlement work is being undertaken locally. Joint working and communication between different projects is often non-existent or weak even when their funding is from the same source. This means that provision is often ad hoc and fragmented resulting in overlaps and significant gaps in provision. This has also given rise to considerable issues in terms of continuity of provision. In the current climate of high levels of overcrowding in prisons, transfers of prisoners between prisons are commonplace. Unless prisoners happen to be transferred to prisons where the same project is working, and it is not guaranteed that work will continue even then, this is likely to result in resettlement activities stalling or stopping completely (Hucklesby and Wincup 2005a; Lewis *et al.* 2003). The introduction of Offender Managers is unlikely to deal with these issues in the short term as contestability will ensure that locally provided services remain territorial and aware of the competitive rather than cooperative environment they are working in (McSweeney and Hough 2006). The proposed scheme also will not deal with an important structural constraint of resettlement services. Prisons receive funding from one source and house prisoners who will be returning to wide geographical areas covered by several probation areas and voluntary sector services. Who provides and pays for the services offered to prisoners has always been a moot point and will continue to be so as will coordination between prison and community services when such large numbers of agencies are involved spread over large areas.

Prison-based resettlement initiatives

Under this model resettlement teams are based within prisons. In most cases, teams are based in only one prison (although they may be part of a large project and linked to teams in other prisons) but occasionally they can work in two prisons usually because they share a site and movement between the two is relatively easy. They provide services to prisoners who are being released from the specific prison. They may also restrict their caseload to prisoners who are returning to specific geographical areas, which are usually local to the prison establishment. There are two ways in which this model may work. Resettlement workers may be based exclusively in the prison undertaking assessments, working with prisoners towards release and making appointments for when prisoners are released. In some prisons, resettlement workers also arrange for representatives of outside agencies such as accommodation, education or employment providers to come into the prison, A second prison-based model is that workers are primarily located in the prison but they undertake outreach work providing services and support to prisoners once they are released.

There are a number of advantages to prison-based models. One, they are dealing with a captive audience so it is likely that they will be able to contact and speak with prisoners, although this does not necessarily equate to full engagement. Two, resettlement workers usually have unrestricted access to the prison and to the prisoners housed there. Normally, workers have enhanced security clearance and are key holders, which makes moving around the prison relatively easy. Three, workers can foster relationships with prison staff and links with other prison-based services and become fully integrated into the prison environment. This facilitates referrals to and from other individuals or services within the prison. Four, preparations can begin prior to release and as early in the sentence as possible. Time is key to the provision of resettlement services as many problems facing prisoners may take significant periods of time to resolve, for example the provision of accommodation or negotiations over the repayment of debts or rent arrears. Other issues caused by entering prison which may result in considerable problems on release as well as anxiety while prisoners are in custody can be dealt with early such as the dissolving of tenancies to prevent rent arrears accumulating and possessions being destroyed and sorting out the payment of fines and other debts. Timing of interventions to prepare for release is particularly important for short-term prisoners who may spend a very limited time in custody (Lewis *et al.* 2003). Five, prisoners can be prepared for release while still in prison. Any arrangements may be made for them and particular or pressing concerns addressed prior to their release.

While prison-based teams have a number of advantages there are also a range of disadvantages. Resettlement work within the prison may be appropriated (Cohen 1985). This term has been used by Hannah-Moffat (2002) and others to describe how critical discourses are silenced by institutions such as prisons and to explain the gap between the intentions of penal reformers and the reality of change (Carlen 2002; Hannah-Moffat 2002). The process which they describe is one where discourses, and for our purposes projects, are 'appropriated, redefined and adapted to concur with the managerial and political priorities of an organisation' (Hannah-Moffat 2002: 205). So, the process we are interested in is how the Prison Service reconfigures and adapts the focus of resettlement projects to achieve its own aims, including key performance targets, rather than the original goals of the project. Consequently, resettlement workers operate to Prison Service and National Offender Management Service (NOMS) agendas and targets rather than towards the original aims of the resettlement programme or initiative.

Appropriation is an increasing concern as resettlement becomes a higher priority for the Prison Service and individual prisons' performance is measured by key performance targets (KPTs) such as the number of prisoners who have accommodation arranged on release (HM Prison Service 2006). The concern is that the work undertaken by resettlement workers becomes narrow in focus and target driven thus militating against its effectiveness (Tilley 1995). An example might be that a resettlement programme which was originally intended to have a broad remit, working on any resettlement needs brought to their attention by prisoners, is asked to refocus by the host prison on accommodation provision in order to achieve their KPT. Further, as the KPT only deals with immediate accommodation needs, the danger is that resettlement service providers concentrate on meeting this target by sourcing short-term and/or inappropriate accommodation rather than good quality, sustainable long-term accommodation. Meanwhile, other needs which may militate against the sustainability of any accommodation found remain unmet as resources are limited. Another consequence of working in a target-driven environment is what Tilley (1995) terms 'tunnel vision', which results in emphasising the quantifiable aspects of work at the expense of the unquantifiable. Consequently, there is a danger that resettlement service providers focus on quantity not quality (Tilley 1995). An example of this is that projects concentrate on signing up prisoners in order to meet enrolment targets and then fail to provide assistance and services to the prisoners which results in dashed expectations and the loss of prisoner confidence in the service. There is also some evidence that promising and not delivering services can cause more damage to prisoners (Crow 2006). These issues may be also relevant to resettlement initiatives which have set their own targets whether for internal management reasons, wider organisational goals or as a condition of their funding.

A further disadvantage of prison-based resettlement work is that access to prisons and the facilities available are at the discretion of the Governor. There are examples of funded resettlement projects being prevented from working in particular prisons and workers being denied security clearance. Currently there is no requirement on prisons to provide reasons for these exclusions. One factor which makes the exclusion of projects more likely is if they intend to work only with a proportion of prisoners confined in a particular prison because its remit is restricted to working with prisoners from specific geographical areas or a particular age or ethnic group(s) or if they refuse to work with the prison in order to meet its targets. Access to the prison may be denied at any time during the duration of the project. Permission to use even the most basic equipment such as computers and particular software, prison records, telephones and so on is also up to the discretion of the prison and in some circumstances these have been refused leaving workers unable to undertake their work, communicate with agencies and individuals outside the prison and record their work effectively (Hucklesby and Wincup 2005a; Lewis *et al.* 2003). Gaining access and the necessary permissions to commence work in prison can be a lengthy process and these issues may be ongoing throughout the lifetime of a project. For example, when new workers are appointed to replace workers who have left they require security clearance before being able to work in the prison but this is often delayed because of the lengthy process, which means that posts remain unfilled for several months. Similarly, if staff are unavailable for work due to illness, other workers cannot step in to cover at short notice.

Prisons are also difficult places to work particularly if workers are employed by an outside, typically voluntary organisation. Prisons are regimented places and adjusting to this can be tough. Working in a prison may also be stressful and dealing with the culture of prisons and prison officers may be difficult (Lewis *et al.* 2003). Not all staff can adjust and it may cause significant problems for initiatives including staff taking periods of sick leave sometimes for significant lengths of time. Some of these problems may be prevented by clearer recruitment objectives and close supervision.

Prison-based workers may also be unaware of the services available in the areas in which prisoners will be resettling. In order to provide a comprehensive service schemes have a wide range of organisations to access (SEU 2002). They are less likely to have personal contacts with agencies or individuals who may be able to assist in the provision of community services. This is more likely to be the case where prison-based schemes deal with all prisoners leaving custody rather than to discrete geographical areas as prisoners are likely to be dispersed over a wide area when released. Similarly, prison-based resettlement teams may have to familiarise themselves with many different forms and procedures as these vary considerably between areas (SEU 2002). Prison-based services are less likely to be familiar with service provision which is geographically removed from the prison. High population levels in the prison system make contacting and setting up services and appointments in the community more difficult as prisoners are more likely to be held away from their resettlement areas.

Finally, as exclusively prison-based services do not take prisoners through the prison gate, this results in a lack of continuity of services provision. This is a particular issue as it is well documented that good intentions on the part of prisoners to 'go straight' often dissolve as soon as they leave prison (Burnett 2004).

Community-based resettlement initiatives

Under this model resettlement services are based in particular geographical areas and provide services for any prisoners returning to that area irrespective of which prison they have been released from. There are two ways of working under this model. One, resettlement workers go into local prisons to recruit and assess prisoners themselves and start working with them prior to release and continue into the community. Two, workers do not go into prisons themselves but rely on receiving referrals from other agencies such as the Prison Service and voluntary sector agencies or prisoners may self-refer.

This model has a number of advantages. Potentially, all prisoners returning to an area may be seen and supported by resettlement workers. Community-based workers may have a better knowledge of and working relationship with other organisations and agencies based in the community. They can build up local knowledge and relationships with providers and become familiar with their procedures and forms. This should make ongoing referrals easier and perhaps quicker. Community-based workers have the potential to provide a wider range of post-release supervision because they are working solely in the community. Further, it could be argued that post-release support is of more value than prison-based support as this is likely to be when prisoners' resolve and any preparations and planning start to unravel. So, community-based resettlement work provides support at a time when it is most needed. They are also able to provide or signpost prisoners to emergency support when necessary.

The community-based model can mean that certain categories of prisoners are missed. Some prisoners returning to an area may be overlooked because they are released from prisons situated some distance away from their resettlement area, especially if workers concentrate on collecting or receiving referrals from local prisons. This is a particular issue in relation to women because of the small number of prisons which accommodate them. Prisoners who are excluded from the project because they are returning to an area not covered by the initiatives may feel aggrieved because the service is unavailable to them.

Community-based resettlement work can mean that some prisoners receive little or no support because they lose contact before they get help. Additionally, prisoners who want support may not seek it as they are either reluctant to do so, do not know how to or do not have the financial or personal resources to do so. For community-based work to exist it is vital that prisoners are provided with clear instructions about how to access the service before leaving prison. There is some evidence that Freephone numbers and drop in sessions in an easily accessible location may facilitate post-release contact (Clancy et al. 2006; Hucklesby and Wincup 2005a). For community-based staff the realities of trying to keep in contact with prisoners post release may bring about its own problems. It is well known that offenders can be very elusive once released and disappear without warning (Lewis *et al.* 2003). This can impact upon staff morale and result in their enthusiasm diminishing over time.

Other potential problems relate to the Prison Service. Access to prisons and Prison Service records may be denied if the service is not available to all of the prisoners housed in the prison and/or the prison does not have ownership of the resettlement initiatives. Referrals may be limited. Prisons, prisoners and other agencies may be unaware that an initiative exists or lack confidence in its ability to deliver. In order to counter this, significant investment needs to be made in publicising the project to potential users and referral agencies.

A critical question for community-based resettlement initiatives is how long support and supervision should continue. Few community-based resettlement initiatives appear to have tackled this issue. While this is understandable given that efforts are focused on engaging prisoners in the first place, a well thought-out exit strategy is vital for the prisoners, albeit a small number, who become reliant on the services and support provided. Some initiatives propose an arbitrary cut-off time but often with no strategy to achieve this while others appear to continue support despite the workload and other issues which this potentially creates.

Hybrid model

Resettlement work which is undertaken exclusively in prison or in the community is unlikely to provide the same continuity of services 'through the prison gate' as those models which encompass workers operating in both the prison and the community, wherever the teams are based. Consequently, many resettlement initiatives operate a hybrid model which encompasses elements of both prison and community work and this would be seen as the 'gold standard' service.

This model involves both prison and community working with members of the team based in both situations. But within this there are a number of ways in which it can be organised. Workers based in the prisons may refer cases on to community-based workers on release. Alternatively, prison-based workers may continue to work with prisoners in the community after release or community-based workers may go into the prison to undertake assessments and plan for prisoners' release.

This model potentially allows all the advantages of both prison- and community-based initiatives to be gained while minimising any disadvantages. However, any initiative which utilises both prison and community workers is only likely to be effective if the two teams work together, are flexible and are fully integrated (Clancy *et al.* 2006). The foundations of effective community work are often laid down in prison (Clancy *et al.* 2006; PA Consulting and MORI 2005). Yet this model is not a panacea and has its own disadvantages. Principally, these relate to the severing of relationships and trust between workers and prisoners when they are released as different individuals may work with prisoners in the community to those which have been working with them in prison. This may be particularly important as it is suggested that prisoners are less likely to engage with community services if they are not familiar with the personnel (Clancy *et al.* 2006). To overcome this, projects may use the same workers in prison and in the community. This has the disadvantage of workers having to deal with the problems of both environments and never getting to grips with the working practices and cultures of either or gaining a thorough knowledge of the range of services available. Further, such working may result in work overload, particularly if workers are covering a large geographic area. Certainly, this model has resource implications, particularly in relation to the time taken to travel to prisons which may be considerable distances from the resettlement area (PA Consulting and MORI 2005). By contrast, it may improve job satisfaction as it provides variety, enables workers to see cases through to the end and offers respite from working in the prison environment.

Many resettlement initiatives strive to implement a hybrid model with services provided both in the prison and in the community. Yet in reality many do not achieve this balance. In practice, work is often concentrated in prison. In many cases, this contradicts the original aims of the project but may be driven by the need to meet enrolment targets. Often it occurs as a result of the practicalities of dealing with prisoners on release and the fact that services have a captive audience in the prison and become overloaded with cases in prison leaving little time or resources to provide community-based services. However, it is also a function of the differential resources which are often put in place with prison-based workers being seen as a priority to capture and engage prisoners prior to release. Sometimes workers concentrate on prison-based work to the exclusion of community work simply because of the pressures of working in the prisons and finding it almost impossible to leave the prison to undertake any work in the community. Finally, community workers may choose to provide comprehensive help and support to a small number of prisoners rather than seeking to work with a larger range of offenders which would inevitably impact upon the depth of support provided. Consequently, the number of prisoners receiving help with their problems post release is relatively small (Hucklesby and Wincup 2005a; Lewis *et al.* 2003).

Focus of resettlement initiatives

Maruna and LeBel (2002, 2003) make a useful distinction between risk-, needs- and strengths-based resettlement work. It is suggested that nearly all resettlement initiatives, except formal supervision under licence, are based currently on the needs model. It is widely acknowledged that prisoners have multiple needs and these can be a barrier to effective resettlement and desistance (Crow 2006; SEU 2002). Nevertheless, resettlement initiatives often focus on single needs whether by accident or design and take little or no account of other needs which impact upon the success of any interventions (McSweeney and Hough 2006). Where interventions attempt to work on multiple needs, there is often no clear understanding of how the needs interact and impact upon each other or the sequence in which they should be dealt with (McSweeney and Hough 2006).

According to Maruna and LeBel (2002), the risk-based model is premised on the assumption that prisoners are dangerous and that they need to be controlled when released through a series of surveillance strategies, including drug testing and electronic monitoring. These sorts of measures are more likely to be used during statutory licence periods, be policed by statutory services, most notably the Probation Service, and used for prisoners who are deemed to be high risk. However, many short-term prisoners are released on Home Detention Curfew (HDC) which can also be conceptualised as a risk-based resettlement strategy.

There is little evidence that risk-based strategies alone lead to effective resettlement (Maruna and LeBel 2002). Indeed, it may be counterproductive as increasing the number and restrictiveness of conditions and/or increasing surveillance heightens the likelihood that breaches will occur and be detected resulting in higher failure rates and increased numbers of prisoners being recalled to prison (Crow 2006; Hedderman and Hough 2004). This has contributed significant numbers to the prison population recently (Maruna 2004; Padfield and Maruna 2006).

Often conceptualised as being the opposite of a risk-based system, needs-based resettlement strategies focus on dealing with the needs of offenders (Maruna and LeBel 2002, 2003). Offenders are perceived as people with multiple needs which militate against resettlement and desistance. Needs which are commonly identified as criminogenic include homelessness, unemployment and substance use and the majority of the seven resettlement pathways set out in the Reducing Re-offending National Action Plan (Home Office 2004) are based on these needs. According to this model dealing with prisoners' needs will produce conformity and resettlement. This model resembles closely much of the resettlement work currently undertaken. Yet it may be of limited effectiveness (Maruna and LeBel 2002). It is recognised that the approach taken may be sensible and pragmatic, especially in the limited time available, and it enables initiatives to meet performance targets. Nevertheless, its effectiveness is compromised by focusing on immediate practical needs such as housing and benefits at the expense of more entrenched needs, which militates against effective long-term desistance. Another danger of needs-based approaches is that they deny prisoners agency as they are people whose needs are catered for by others rather than taking responsibility for their own resettlement (Maruna and LeBel 2002). As a result, needs-based approaches do not take account of much of the research evidence on desistance and may militate against desistance because prisoners become dependent upon the support provided so that when it is withdrawn they simply revert to their previous lifestyles. Additionally, research suggests that resettlement initiatives, which engage in trying to increase prisoners' agency, are more effective (Lewis *et al.* 2003).

Raynor (2004) identifies two models which both derive from this needs-based model. These are the 'opportunity deficit' model and the 'offender's responsibility' model (see Chapter 2). The first of these models is based on the assumption that offenders have been deprived of opportunities and resources. It usually relies on offenders' assessments of their own needs and puts them in touch with agencies which may be able to help them. So, under this model, resettlement is about identifying needs and ensuring that offenders access services to deal with them (Maguire and Raynor 2006). As Raynor (2004) points out, one disadvantage of this approach is that it enables offenders to see themselves as victims of circumstances rather than taking responsibility for their actions. By contrast, the 'offender's responsibility' model requires offenders to take responsibility for their actions while recognising that they may have considerable needs. Here, offender behaviour has its roots in the attitudes, beliefs and responses to problems. Initiatives based on this model usually require offenders to set clear goals and work on problem-solving and motivation to reduce offending.

> Responsibility models recognise obstacles, disadvantage and exclusion faced by offenders, but also see that offenders have some choices about how to respond to circumstances, and may need to focus on habits of thinking, beliefs and motivation in order to make more successful choices. (Maguire and Raynor 2006: 31)

While this model may underestimate the needs of offenders it is also clearly recognised that offending is avoidable and that offenders can desist (Raynor 2004). Initiatives which focus on dealing with offenders' attitudes and beliefs are more effective than those which concentrate exclusively on dealing with offenders' 'welfare' needs (Clancy *et al.* 2006; Lewis *et al.* 2003; Maguire and Raynor 2006).

All of the models discussed so far are 'deficit' models where offenders lack something, either practical things such as accommodation or a job or thinking skills and/or motivation (Burnett and Maruna 2006). By contrast the third model concentrates on 'repair, reconciliation and community partnership' and derives from restorative justice (Burnett and Maruna 2006; Maruna and LeBel 2002). The 'strengths-based' model is more conceptual rather than descriptive as few initiatives practise this model presently (Maruna and LeBel 2002; for exceptions see Burnett and Maruna 2006). This model focuses on the contribution that prisoners can make to society. In short 'how can their lives become useful and purposeful' (Maruna and LeBel 2002: 165). It asserts that prisoners will be reintegrated when they make amends through reparation and are subsequently destigimatised (Burnett and Maruna 2006). So, it aims to actively engage prisoners. As Toch (1994: 71) explains, 'they need to do something to get something'. Yet, the nature of engagement and reparation may be important. Drawing on evidence from desistance research, a key determinant of successful desistance appears to be making offenders responsible for others either financially or in a caring capacity (Barry 2006; Farrell and Calverley 2006; Maruna 2001; Sampson and Laub 1993). Yet, few resettlement initiatives presently provide a 'responsibilisation' strategy for prisoners and it is not envisaged that this will form a central part of resettlement policy. Of course, any form of responsibilisation requires that prisoners are in a position to take on the tasks and it is recognised that many may not be and that assistance will be required to get them to a stage where they are.

Another way in which resettlement initiatives can be distinguished is by whether they deal themselves with issues raised by prisoners or whether they simply signpost prisoners to relevant services. On the one hand, doing things for prisoners obviously is more resource-intensive and raises issues about whether it is appropriate and/or whether workers have suitable skills to undertake such work. On the other hand, referring prisoners to other agencies enables problems to be dealt with by specialists. However, these services may not prioritise or deal with offenders (SEU 2002) and prisoners may not turn up for appointments. Some initiatives have tackled this issue by resettlement workers or volunteers accompanying prisoners to appointments. In practice, it is unlikely that resettlement initiatives do one or the other but rather provide some services themselves while referring others to specialist agencies. The challenge here is to ensure that the correct balance is struck between generic and specialist providers. The key issues for initiatives are to have the contacts to enable prisoners to access services, to put mechanisms in place to ensure that prisoners attend appointments and to check that missed appointments are followed up.

The management of resettlement work

The proposed introduction of contestability and the increased priority of resettlement have resulted in many different management models of resettlement being implemented. In turn, these models are linked partly to the source of the funding. However, most resettlement initiatives are funded by 'soft money', i.e. short-term projects with time-limited funding, which raises a range of issues such as continuity of provision, staff retention and so on which are discussed in more detail in Chapter 8. This section describes and evaluates the various management models currently operating within the resettlement arena.

A limited number of initiatives are managed by the statutory sector. This includes projects such as PS Plus, which is discussed in this volume, and Connect, which is an initiative managed by the Probation Service in the West Midlands area (Staffordshire, Warwickshire, West Mercia and West Midlands probation areas). Yet neither of these projects have received statutory funding as they were financed by the European Social Fund. Initiatives which are managed by statutory agencies have the advantage that they are more likely to be prioritised within their own organisations and this may contribute to the smooth running of the project. Nevertheless, such initiatives may still have to overcome significant barriers within the organisations themselves and may be marginalised because they are not seen as the core business of the agency. Importantly, there is some evidence that initiatives managed by the statutory sector are more effective in terms of reducing reoffending, providing continuity of service and changing attitudes and problem levels in custody (Clancy *et al.* 2006; Lewis *et al.* 2003). Projects run by the statutory sector have the potential to be scaled up more easily and effectively but they may lack flexibility and vision. The statutory sector usually has greater power and levels of resources to call upon when necessary.

Alternatively, many resettlement projects are managed by the voluntary sector. It is this sector where the speed of growth has been greatest as a direct result of the future funding opportunities which are likely to become available under the proposals for contestability. Generally, voluntary sector projects do not receive statutory funding but are funded by a variety of sources such as charities and trusts. The benefits and challenges of voluntary sector involvement in the management of projects are discussed in more depth in Chapter 8. The main advantages of the voluntary sector are its flexibility, enthusiasm and experience. One of the main disadvantages is that it is necessary to work with statutory agencies, most notably with the Prison Service, to gain access to prisons and prisoners. Voluntary sector projects may face many barriers to effective working in prisons including limited access to resources and information as well as dealing with the prejudices of prison staff. Further, voluntary sector organisations are generally reliant on short-term funding which may result in a lack of continuity. They may also overstretch themselves in order to be competitive and bring in funding which may have consequences for resourcing levels of particular projects. Voluntary-sector projects usually cover local or regional areas and the potential for expansion can be limited by the lack of a nationwide infrastructure and personnel.

In practice, rarely do resettlement projects conform exactly to either of these management models. While they are usually managed and operated by either the statutory or voluntary sector they involve partnerships with other agencies often from within the other sector. These partnerships may be contractual and involve funding such as voluntary sector organisations providing community-based mentoring services for a statutory-sector-managed project. Conversely, partnerships may be based on more informal protocols and service level agreements such as prisons providing access and space to voluntary-sector organisations. Finally, there may be no formal agreements between two agencies but users of the resettlement project may access other agencies' resources. Contractual agreements are clear and for this reason may be preferable. However, they are not necessarily inherently more stable as they can also break down (Hucklesby and Wincup 2005a). Contractual agreements may lock organisations into services that are failing to provide value for money. For example, mentoring services are usually contracted and funded on anticipated levels of use but they may deal with considerably less offenders in practice. By contrast, mentoring agencies may be out of pocket and under-resourced if demand is greater than planned. Mentoring services may also provide an ineffective mentoring service.

Volunteer workers

Resettlement initiatives can also been distinguished from one another by whether, and to what extent, they use volunteers. Most projects employ paid workers to perform the core duties of resettlement work such as enrolling and assessing prisoners' needs. Many projects, however, also rely on volunteers, particularly to provide mentoring services. The ways in which mentoring is organised varies from paid workers employed by resettlement projects coordinating activities including the training and management of mentors through to services being contracted out to completely different voluntary mentoring service providers such as SOVA (Supporting Others through Volunteer Action).

Mentoring is an integral part of most resettlement projects. It has been defined as 'a relationship between two strangers, instigated by a third party, who intentionally matches the mentor with the mentee according to the needs of the ... [prisoner] as part of a planned intervention programme' (Freedman 1993, in Newburn and Shiner 2005: 46). Maguire (2004) suggests that their role is akin to the traditional role of probation officers of 'advise, assist and befriend'. These definitions and mentoring in practice are very broad and encapsulate a wide range of activities between mentor and mentee from directed work towards agreed goals to simply providing informal unstructured support over the telephone, or face to face once prisoners are released.

Mentoring is often perceived to be an antidote to many difficult situations and has been referred to as a 'golden bullet' (Newburn and Shiner 2005). However, there are problems of definition, a lack of theoretical underpinning and scant systematic research evidence to support the enthusiasm for it (Newburn and Shiner 2005). Lewis *et al.* (2003) found limited evidence of their effectiveness in resettlement services and concluded that their work was less effective than that undertaken by probation officers. Newburn and Shiner (2005) agreed, demonstrating that mentoring does not reduce offending or drug use among disaffected young people. Mentoring research has also been used as a case study to show how research evidence, and more specifically systematic reviews, can distort evidence of effectiveness (Boaz and Pawson 2005; Pawson 2006). This work demonstrates how mentoring has become an integral part of criminal justice policy and specific interventions when only limited evidence exists about its impact and efficiency.

Mentoring is a process which may be undertaken by paid workers or volunteers. Generally in resettlement work, mentors are volunteers who are managed and trained by paid staff. Within this, there is a range of ways in which mentoring services operate. Mentors may work alongside paid staff to provide additional guidance and support to mentees. Conversely, mentors may be the only community-based workers and have a greater role in assisting prisoners to deal with their resettlement needs such as helping them to access services such as accommodation, employment and education. Commonly, mentors transport prisoners from prison to their accommodation and accompany them to appointments, yet they are just as likely to have unstructured meetings in public places which facilitate contact and provide general support.

Many resettlement projects would be unable to provide services in the community if they did not use volunteers and for this reason they are vital. Volunteers also bring high levels of commitment and enthusiasm to the job. However, this can quickly drain away when the realities of working with prisoners with entrenched and multiple needs become apparent. Voluntary workers may be closer to the community and they can be matched closely with mentees (Maguire 2004). However, using volunteers involves considerable management and has been described as similar to managing a workforce without the same level of leverage and authority (McGonigle 2002). One of the main challenges facing mentoring services is the recruitment of mentors. Working with offenders is probably not high on the list of priorities for people seeking to do voluntary work and this limits the available pool. Indeed, many mentors who are recruited by resettlement projects want to pursue careers in criminal justice and volunteer on this basis (Hucklesby and Wincup 2005a; McGonigle 2002). This may result in problems with the medium- and long-term retention of mentors as they quickly pursue their career ambitions. Further retention problems can arise due to the nature of the work involved and the lack of engagement with mentees. Mentors can soon become demotivated because they are not matched with mentees and/or mentees do not turn up for appointments (McGonigle 2002). Retention problems mean that many projects have few mentors on their books at any one time and are continually having to recruit and train new mentors, which has resource implications as well as operational implications in terms of the accumulation of experienced mentors. Ensuring that mentors have realistic expectations of what can be achieved is, therefore, important.

A further challenge for mentoring services is matching the availability of mentors with caseload and mentees' needs. Mentors have other commitments including work and family and this limits their availability, which may not coincide with mentees' routines nor with prison visiting times. Further, there is often an age, social and economic as well as geographic distance between mentors and mentees which sometimes cannot be bridged. However well prepared mentors may be they may also struggle with the realities of their role, particularly in terms of the prison environment and the backgrounds and circumstances of offenders.

Using volunteers to provide mentoring in criminal justice presents challenges in terms of health and safety and the potential risks involved. These can be heightened when mentoring services are contracted out as important information may not be shared between agencies so that mentoring agencies or mentors remain unaware of potential risks. It is for this reason that clear protocols are vital to ensure that relevant information is passed on to mentoring coordinators and mentors when appropriate. Mentors have to be trained to be risk aware and to avoid risky situations and also to ensure that they are aware of the boundaries of their role. Clear procedures need to be in place to ensure that mentors contact coordinators when meetings are taking place. This may raise issues for mentoring coordinators in terms of working hours as many of the contacts between mentors and mentees may occur outside of normal hours.

Ideally, prisoners will have met their mentors before leaving prison so that a relationship has already been built up. Yet this may not happen for practical reasons. These include ensuring that all mentors are security cleared to enter prisons; the expense of having mentors going into prison for a short time and usually only for one meeting; and the often long distances between the prison where the mentor is located and the mentor's and mentee's home (Hucklesby and Wincup 2005a). Consequently, some schemes have compromised on this ideal by using a small pool of mentors or paid workers to meet with mentees in prison. Consequently, the continuity of personnel is reduced which may result in contact between mentors and mentees after release being less likely to occur.

Volunteers are unlikely to make record-keeping a priority and they do not operate under the same constraints or accountability mechanisms as paid employees. Consequently, much of the work they undertake may not be recorded and therefore not available for monitoring purposes. This makes it difficult to ensure that contacts between mentors and mentees are appropriate and within set limits. As a result it can be difficult to make an accurate assessment of mentoring activities, particularly in relation to their effectiveness.

Conclusion

This chapter has scoped the various models of practice in prisoner resettlement which exist currently. In common with all models, they are ideal types and most initiatives will not conform wholly to one type or another; rather they will mix elements of different models. Consequently, differences between resettlement schemes are often measured in degrees, particularly as they are inevitably moulded by extraneous factors, are pushed in alternative directions by circumstances and evolve over time. At this relatively early stage in the re-emergence of resettlement policy it is extremely useful to have different models operating because it allows them to be tested out in order to assess their effectiveness in terms of implementing projects, providing services and measures of success. In some cases, projects have been set up exactly for this reason (Hucklesby and Wincup 2005b). This should enable the ingredients of effective resettlement work to be identified and explored.

The downside, however, is that the enormous range of initiatives has resulted in a lack of consistent provision with some areas having access to large-scale, relatively well-funded projects while others have none. Further, it has resulted in gaps and overlaps in provision in particular prisons. For example, in some prisons there is more than one resettlement initiative, and this can lead to territory issues and also to initiatives limiting their work in order to operate alongside each other. In other prisons/communities there are no provisions. Additionally, many projects operating currently only deal with prisoners who fit certain criteria whether in terms of age, prison that they are located in, gender, ethnic origin or resettlement area. This limits their potential. Nevertheless, projects which are more generic and have no specific target group may not provide adequate support for some individuals as their services may not meet the specific needs of individuals or certain groups.

Most initiatives involve an evaluation of their work and this is often a requirement of the funders. However, there is also a lack of consistency and coordination of research and the evidence it is producing. Consequently, the evidence base about what works in resettlement work is limited, particularly as research is often undertaken locally and for particular projects. Often it is not shared, partly as a result of the project needing to be portrayed as effective. The prospect of contestability has contributed to this situation with agencies becoming increasingly territorial and competitive in order to ensure that they are in the running to receive funding when it becomes available. Consequently, much of the evidence about which models work and which do not is not widely known and the opportunity to implement a truly evidence-based policy is being lost.

Notes

1 For this reason we do not consider the resettlement work undertaken routinely by prison staff.
2 This is the standardised process for the assessment of offenders introduced by the National Offender Management Service.

References

Barry, M. (2006) *Youth Offending in Transition*. London: Routledge.

Boaz, A. and Pawson, R. (2005) 'The perilous road from evidence to policy: five journeys compared', *Journal of Social Policy*, 34 (2): 175–94.

Burnett, R. (2004) 'To reoffend or not to reoffend? The ambivalence of convicted property offenders', in S. Maruna and R. Immarigeon (eds), *After Crime and Punishment: Ex-offender Reintegration and Desistance from Crime*. Cullompton: Willan.

Burnett, R. and Maruna, S. (2006) 'The kindness of prisoners: strengths-based resettlement in theory and in action', *Criminal Justice*, 6 (1): 83–106.

Burrows, J., Clarke, A., Davison, T., Tarling, R. and Webb, S. (2000) *The Nature and Effectiveness of Drugs Throughcare for Released Prisoners*, Research Findings No. 109. London: Home Office.

Carlen, P. (2002) 'New discourses for justification and reform of women's imprisonment', in P. Carlen (ed.), *Women and Punishment*. Cullompton: Willan.

Carter, P. (2003) *Correctional Services Review*. London: Home Office.

Clancy, A., Hudson, K., Maguire, M., Peake, R., Raynor, P., Vanstone, M. and Kynch, J. (2006) *Getting Out and Staying Out: Results of the Prisoner Resettlement Pathfinders*. Bristol: Polity Press.

Cohen, S. (1985) *Visions of Social Control*. Oxford: Polity Press.

Crow, I. (2006) *Resettling Prisoners: A Review*. Sheffield: University of Sheffield.

Farrall, S. and Calverley, A. (2006) *Understanding Desistance from Crime*. Maidenhead: Open University Press.

Hannah-Moffat, K. (2002) 'Creating choices: reflecting on choices', in P. Carlen (ed.), *Women and Punishment*. Cullompton: Willan.

Harman, K. and Paylor, I. (2005a) 'An evaluation of the CARAT Initiative', *Howard Journal*, 44 (4): 357–73.

Harman, K. and Paylor, I. (2005b) 'Throughcare of drug-using prisoners in Britain: a clinical report', *Journal of Offender Rehabilitation*, 40 (1): 61–83.

Harper, G. and Chitty, C. (2004) *The Impact of Corrections on Re-Offending: A Review of 'What Works'*, Home Office Research Study No. 291. London: Home Office.

Hedderman, C. and Hough, M. (2004) 'Getting tough or being effective: what matters?', in G. Mair (ed.), *What Matters in Probation*. Cullompton: Willan.

Her Majesty's Inspectorates of Prisons and Probation (2001) *Through the Prison Gate: A Joint Thematic Review*. London: Home Office.

Her Majesty's Prison Service (2006) *Annual Report and Accounts April 2005 – March 2006*. London: Home Office.

Home Office (2004) *Reducing Re-offending National Action Plan*. London: Home Office.

Home Office (2006a) *Offender Management Model 1.1*. London: Home Office, National Offender Management Service.

Home Office (2006b) *A Five Year Strategy for Protecting the Public and Reducing Re-offending*. London: HM Government.

Hucklesby, A. and Wincup, E. (2005a) 'Connect Resettlement Initiatives: Final Report'. Unpublished report to the West Mercia Probation Board.

Hucklesby, A. and Wincup, E. (2005b) 'Pyramid Project: Implementation Report'. Unpublished report to Depaul Trust and Nacro.

Lewis, S., Vennard, J., Maguire, M., Raynor, P., Vanstone, M., Raybould, S. and Rix, A. (2003) *The Resettlement of Short-term Prisoners: An Evaluation of Seven Pathfinders*, RDS Occasional Paper No. 83. London: Home Office.

McGonigle, T. (2002) 'The contribution of volunteers to work with children in a criminal justice organisation', *Child Care in Practice*, 8 (4): 262–72.

McSweeney, T. and Hough, M. (2006) 'Supporting offenders with multiple needs: lessons for the "mixed economy" model of service provision', *Criminal Justice*, 6 (1): 107–26.

Maguire, M. (2004) 'Resettlement of short-term prisoners: some new approaches', *Criminal Justice Matters*, 56: 22–3.

Maguire, M. and Raynor, P. (2006) 'How resettlement of prisoners promotes desistance from crime: or does it?', *Criminal Justice*, 6 (1): 19–38.

Maguire, M., Raynor, P., Vanstone, M. and Kynch, J. (1998) *Voluntary After-care*, Research Findings 73. London: Home Office.

Maguire, M., Raynor, P., Vanstone, M. and Kynch, J. (2000) 'Voluntary after-care and the Probation Service: a case of diminished responsibility', *Howard Journal*, 39, 234–48.

Maruna, S. (2001) *Making Good: How Ex-convicts Reform and Rebuild Their Lives*. Washington, DC: American Psychological Association Books.

Maruna, S. (2004) 'Californa Dreamin': are we heading toward a national offender "waste management" service?', *Criminal Justice Matters*, 56, Summer: 6–7.

Maruna, S. and LeBel, T.P. (2002) 'Revisiting ex-prisoner re-entry: a buzzword in search of a narrative', in S. Rex and M. Tonry (eds), *Reform and Punishment: The Future of Sentencing*. Cullompton: Willan.

Maruna, S. and LeBel, T.P. (2003) 'Welcome home? Examining the "Re-entry Court" concept from a strengths-based perspective', *Western Criminology Review*, 4 (2): 91–107.

Newburn, T. and Shiner, M. (2005) *Dealing with Disaffection: Young People, Mentoring and Social Inclusion*. Cullompton: Willan.

PA Consulting and MORI (2005) *Action Research Study of the Implementation of the National Offender Management Model in the North West Pathfinder*, Online Report 32/05. London: Home Office.

Padfield, N. and Maruna, S. (2006) 'The revolving door at the prison gate: exploring the dramatic increase in recalls to prison', *Criminology and Criminal Justice*, 6 (3): 329–52.

Pawson, R. (2006) 'Digging for nuggets: how "bad" research can yield "good" evidence', *International Journal of Social Research Methodology*, 9 (2): 127–42.

Raynor, P. (2004) 'Opportunity, motivation and change: some findings from research on resettlement', in R. Burnett and C. Roberts (eds), *What Works in Probation and Youth Justice*. Cullompton: Willan.

Sampson, R. and Laub, J. (1993) *Crime in the Making: Pathways and Turning Points through Life*. Cambridge, MA: Harvard University Press.

Senior, P. (2004) 'Tackling social exclusion through positive pathways to resettlement', *Criminal Justice Matters*, 56: 14–15 and 45.

Social Exclusion Unit (SEU) (2002) *Reducing Re-offending by Ex-prisoners*. London: Office of the Deputy Prime Minister.

Tilley, N. (1995) *Thinking about Crime Prevention Performance Indicators*, Crime Detection and Prevention Series Paper 57. London: Home Office.

Toch, H. (1994) 'Democratising prisons', *Prison Journal*, 73: 62–72.

Turnball, P. (2004) 'Drug treatment: the importance of aftercare', *Criminal Justice Matters*, 56: 28–9.

Chapter 4

Researching and evaluating resettlement

Emma Wincup and Anthea Hucklesby

As Hedderman argues in the first chapter of this edited collection, resettlement has been rediscovered. This policy renaissance has created plentiful opportunities for criminologists to become involved in researching the raft of new initiatives which have been developed, ranging from national projects such as the resettlement pathfinders launched under the Crime Reduction Programme (Clancy *et al.* 2006; Lewis *et al.* 2003) through to more localised schemes such as the South West Integration project (see Chapter 5 of this volume). Generally, researchers have not been given carte blanche to suggest research designs which would both contribute to relevant academic debates, for example around desistance, and add to the evidence base for policy development. Instead, the opportunities afforded to researchers have tended to take the form of issuing invitations to tender in which, to a greater or lesser extent, the research questions, research design and methodology have already been specified. Inevitably these require researchers to evaluate projects. Evaluation can be defined as 'the systematic identification and assessment of effects generated by treatments, programmes, policies, practices and products' (Tilley 2006: 104).

This chapter draws predominantly upon our experiences of evaluating three resettlement projects: two managed by voluntary sector agencies and one managed by one probation area in partnership with three other areas and HM Prison Service. Collectively this has involved research in 12 prisons in the Midlands and the North East accommodating male and female prisoners of different ages, ethnic backgrounds and sentence lengths. These projects have deployed varying models of resettlement (see Chapter 3). At the time of writing (Spring 2007), we have completed one evaluation and are nearing completion of the data collection phase of the remaining two. We supplement our own experiences by referring to other published evaluations of resettlement projects, particularly the resettlement pathfinders. However, as we noted in our concluding remarks in the previous chapter and we will develop later here, the political context does not encourage the dissemination of the findings of evaluative studies so information on the research designs and methods used and problems encountered is somewhat limited.

The remainder of our discussion is divided into three parts. The first deals with issues of research design and the challenges of putting ideal research designs into practice, the second focuses on the particular issues which arise when conducting evaluations in prison and the third focuses on the politics of evaluation with specific reference to resettlement projects. Throughout the chapter we draw attention to the ethical issues which evaluating resettlement projects present.

Evaluating resettlement: what is the best approach?

The rapid development of opportunities to evaluate new interventions is not peculiar to resettlement policy and practice. Rather there have been plentiful opportunities for researchers to evaluate different aspects of the criminal justice process and social interventions more generally, especially those designed to tackle social exclusion. As opportunities for evaluation have developed, they have been accompanied by debates about the most appropriate research design and methods to deploy to judge effectiveness. New Labour came to power in May 1997 and made explicit at the outset its commitment to evidence-based policy. For criminologists, this provided ample opportunities in the shape of the Crime Reduction Programme, which made available £25 million for evaluating criminal justice interventions as diverse as CCTV, drug treatment and youth work. The intention was to establish 'what works' by evaluating small-scale 'pathfinder' projects, which would be 'rolled out' nationally if they proved to be effective both in terms of outcomes and cost. The successes and failures of the programme have been debated elsewhere (Hough 2004; Morgan and Hough 2007) and we need not revisit them here. Instead, we will focus on the considerable discussion the programme generated in terms of the most appropriate research design for evaluating criminal justice interventions and identify the implications for resettlement research. Before we do so, it is important to note that these lively and, at times, heated discussions among criminologists and commissioners of criminological research took place against a backdrop of a long-standing academic debate about the best approach for conducting evaluations.

The importance of longitudinal research

Ideally all evaluations of resettlement projects should be longitudinal in design to ensure that questions about the impact of participation can be answered adequately. This is particularly important for research on resettlement since the literature on desistance from offending suggests it is best conceived as a lengthy process rather than a sudden event with individuals often moving back and forth between crime-free lifestyles and pursuing criminal careers (Bottoms *et al.* 2004; Burnett 2004; Maguire and Raynor 2006). Despite the apparent advantages of a longitudinal design spanning a number of years, it can be difficult to incorporate into an evaluation for two main reasons. The first is due to the resource intensive nature of longitudinal work. Rarely is the budget allocated for evaluation sufficiently large to cover the high financial costs involved. The second relates to the eagerness of project managers to obtain 'results' quickly, especially if funding applications need to be submitted to allow the project to continue. Consequently, there are no UK-based studies of resettlement which span a period of several years and involve continued contact with the original participants beyond a period of the first few months following their release from prison. Evaluators seeking to maintain contact with ex-prisoners over a lengthy period of time need to look elsewhere for guidance. Farrall and Calverley's (2006) study of 199 offenders subject to probation supervision in the late 1990s provides a detailed account of the challenges of maintaining contact with this group over a seven-year period and the strategies they used to achieve a response rate of 26 per cent in the fourth sweep of their study.

It would be misleading to describe them as longitudinal studies but a number of researchers have sought to incorporate a longitudinal dimension into their work. In our three evaluations of resettlement projects we have attempted to make contact with the prisoners we interviewed while they were in custody three months after their release. While we have conducted face-to-face interviews, mainly with ex-prisoners continuing to receive support in the community or those who have returned to prison, mostly we have interviewed ex-prisoners by telephone. Widespread mobile phone ownership has made it easier to maintain contact and conduct telephone interviews with ex-prisoners who often do not have stable accommodation (Social Exclusion Unit 2002). Similarly, the evaluation of the resettlement pathfinder projects included telephone interviews with participants they had previously interviewed six months after their release (Lewis *et al.* 2003). In order to boost their sample size, the evaluation team interviewed ex-prisoners in the community who they had not previously spoken to in prison. We have also adopted this approach.

The main problem faced by evaluators seeking to conduct post-release interviews is a low response rate. At the time of writing we have completed one of our three resettlement project evaluations and managed to secure a response rate of just under 50 per cent for our follow-up interviews. This compares favourably with the 16 per cent response rate achieved by the pathfinder evaluation team although their lower response rate may reflect the fact that they waited for a longer period of time (six rather than three months) before attempting to make contact with those they had interviewed in prison (Lewis *et al.* 2003). Following up ex-prisoners in the community is both challenging and time-consuming but acceptable response rates can be achieved through forward planning. In our experience asking prisoners to sign a consent form so we have their permission to contact them again is essential, particularly if they are unable to provide their release address or telephone number and it is likely that we will need to request their details from the resettlement project or another organisation. Many prisoners we have interviewed were still preparing for release and unsure where they would be living. As a result, we asked them to provide contact details for family and friends they would definitely remain in touch with and individuals (for example, probation officers and leaving care workers) or organisations (for example, drug treatment providers) they intended to keep in contact with. In practice, we found family members to be the best people to help us trace ex-prisoners, although inevitably some were initially suspicious of us and our motives. Perseverance is the key to success and some of the interviews we completed with ex-prisoners took place after numerous attempts to make contact. Along the way we have also learnt that Sunday afternoons is one of the best times to telephone ex-prisoners! Finally, we are in no doubt that the use of incentives in the form of high-street vouchers worth £15 (£10 for the first evaluation) had a positive impact on our response rate, a strategy also utilised in the resettlement pathfinder evaluation, which rewarded participation with a £15 postal order (Lewis *et al.* 2003). Lack of space precludes discussion of the debates surrounding their use, which relate to ethical and moral considerations as well as practical ones (see Noaks and Wincup 2004, for a discussion).

Evaluators need to pay attention to the representativeness of the achieved sample. It is important to recognise that ex-prisoners who participate in follow-up community interviews may have different post-release experiences from the larger sample interviewed in custody. As with all research studies, there is a selection effect because participants have to give their consent to be involved and they might represent those with the strongest views on the research topic, both positive and negative. We have found that most ex-prisoners we have managed to contact have been willing to be interviewed. Given that ex-prisoners are more likely than the general population to be homeless or living in transient accommodation (Social Exclusion Unit 2002) and consequently may be difficult to contact, a greater concern is that the sample achieved consists largely of those participants with the most 'settled' lives. However, at the other extreme ex-prisoners who have been recalled to custody or remanded in custody/reconvicted for a new offence were also relatively easy to contact. Care therefore has to be taken when interpreting the findings of post-release interviews because the achieved sample is unlikely to be representative. This, of course, does not mean the data are without value but it does mean that the characteristics of the achieved sample have to be noted, compared to the original sample and the possibility of bias recognised. It is also helpful to note any information gathered about ex-prisoners who could not be contacted, for example the number no longer living at their release address.

We have emphasised the importance of longitudinal research but recognise that this research design can only be adopted if there are sufficient resources available: human, financial and time. If not, an alternative approach would be to develop a study based upon a cross-sectional design and choose one of the following possible ways forward. The first is to interview ex-prisoners in the community and to collect retrospective data about their experiences of resettlement and the help and support they receive from the project being evaluated. The second is to build up a sample of individuals at different stages in the resettlement process. This form of staggered cohort sampling has been used in previous studies of imprisonment because it proved impractical to track a single cohort (for example, Casale's (1989) study of women remanded in custody). When selecting between the two options evaluators need to weigh up the value of collecting complete accounts of an individual's journey through the prison gate against the limitations of retrospective data, which will provide an account of the past through the lens of the present (de Vaus 2006b).

Measuring outputs and outcomes

A challenge for those engaged in evaluating resettlement projects is how best to define effectiveness. Following Chapman and Hough (1998) effectiveness can be defined as what prisoners do as a result of participating in a resettlement programme and conceptualised in terms of whether prisoners have achieved what is expected of them. Effectiveness needs to be operationalised through the development of a series of output and outcome measures. Outcomes are distinct from outputs although the two are often conflated. Outputs can be defined as 'the products of a programme, narrowly defined in terms of what the organisation has done' and outcomes as 'the outcome of a programme as measured against its objectives' (Chapman and Hough 1998: 9). Outcomes can therefore be viewed as the effects of the outputs but 'the boundaries between them are not always hard and fast' (1998: 9).

Output measures for resettlement projects are likely to include the numbers participating in the project as a whole and, where relevant, different components within it such as groupwork programmes or mentoring schemes. They might also include details of actions undertaken with prisoners such as securing a place in a hostel, finding employment or reducing levels of debt. They provide a measure of whether the project is being implemented as intended and, in many cases, whether targets originally specified in the funding application are being met. While these measures are in themselves straightforward, to calculate them data need to be made available to evaluators in an accessible format. Our experiences in this respect have been extremely varied. We evaluated one project which employed a team of information officers to enter data from files consisting of profomas completed by project staff and volunteers into a Microsoft Access database. This project was funded by the European Social Fund and the project managers were required to provide evidence that they had met the targets specified in the bid and that HM Prison Service and the National Probation Service had contributed 'matched' funding in the form of completing pre-sentence reports, risk assessment and so on. While we raised some concerns about data quality in our final report, it proved easy to convert the database into our chosen statistical package (Statistical Package for the Social Sciences (SPSS)) and conduct the necessary analyses. In contrast we have encountered numerous difficulties with the two other projects. These range from technical difficulties such as using individually designed databases which are incompatible with the usual data analysis packages and Microsoft applications or recording information as 'free text' (which cannot be easily quantified) rather than using standard categories through to more fundamental problems such as the lack of central and/or standardised record-keeping, the absence of key data and expectations that evaluators should design information systems for the project as a whole not just the evaluation. For evaluators such difficulties can often only be resolved, if resources allow, by re-entering data from hard-copy printouts or extracting the relevant information from paper files: activities which are time-consuming and somewhat laborious. We cannot emphasise enough the importance of specifying data collection needs at the outset and repeating it regularly.

Even if databases provide complete data on a wide range of variables ultimately they are produced for a different purpose, usually to record case histories of clients and the activities undertaken. Consequently they are there primarily to monitor rather evaluate the work of the project. Chapman and Hough (1998: 9) describe monitoring as keeping track of inputs (i.e. resources – staff, financial, skills – invested in a programme) and outputs and refer to it as 'a rudimentary form of evaluation'. Evaluation is defined in terms of whether 'the programme is achieving its objectives' (1998: 9). Monitoring requirements are often different to evaluation requirements and influenced by the requirements of the funder of the project and the organisation managing the project. Monitoring and evaluation should complement each other to minimise the burden of data collection on project staff but evaluators should not be expected to monitor the project unless this was agreed at the outset.

Commissioners of evaluation studies will inevitably want to know the impact of the intervention on levels of reoffending. This is unsurprising given the fact that many prisoners released from custody return in a relatively short space of time. The latest figures available based on prisoners who left custody in the first quarter of 2003 state that 66 per cent of adults were subsequently convicted in a court in the two years following their release (Shepherd and Whiting 2006). Projects in receipt of statutory funding, or those which hope to receive it in the future, must demonstrate that they contribute to the Home Office target to reduce reoffending by 5 per cent as part of its overall aim to build a safe, just and tolerant society (HM Treasury 2004).

Reconviction measures are typically used as a proxy for reoffending and the difficulties of interpreting reconviction rates have been explored in detail elsewhere (Lloyd *et al.* 1994; Mair *et al.* 1997). To summarise here, the main issue raised is that they provide an under-estimate of involvement in offending because only a small proportion of offences lead to a conviction. These problems aside, reconviction rates remain a plausible measure of effective practice, which have been used widely to evaluate the success of new methods of working with offenders. Researchers have moved beyond looking at the crude measure of whether offenders have been reconvicted. The Home Office has recently adopted the approach of comparing predicted and actual reconviction rates (Solomon *et al.* 2007). Reconviction studies need to use multivariate statistical techniques and build theoretically informed models when analysing the reconviction data. While overall reconviction rates are important, the type and seriousness of offence at reconviction and the time period to reconviction need to be explored. Reductions in the severity of offending and the adoption, albeit short-lived, of a crime-free (or at least conviction-free) lifestyle for prolific offenders are important measures of success.

Reconviction rates were used in the evaluation of the resettlement pathfinder (Clancy *et al.* 2006). In this instance, data were collected one year after release and actual scores were compared to predicted scores generated using the Offender Group Reconviction Scale (OGRS2). This was also done for a comparison group of offenders who had been in the prisons which hosted the resettlement pathfinders but had not participated in them. It was intended that the use of a local comparator group would allow factors which could distort the data such as changes in conviction patterns to be taken into account. External factors should apply equally to both groups so that any differences between them could be attributed with confidence to participation in a resettlement pathfinder. Although it is worth noting that the overall conclusion reached was that the pathfinders 'had no immediately obvious impact on reconviction rates "across the board"' (Clancy *et al.* 2006: 68), for our purposes the methodological lessons are more important than the findings. First, they suggest the need for sophisticated analyses of reconviction data using bivariate and multivariate analyses so an extensive range of variables which could influence outcomes can be taken into account, for example the nature and extent of post-release contact. Second, this experience reveals that it can be difficult to find a matched comparison group. The achieved comparison group was dissimilar in the sense that the mean risk of reconviction score was higher. While this provided evidence of effective targeting of those most in need of intervention it required the evaluators to take this into account when comparing the two groups. Thirdly, some cases could not be located on the Offenders Index so that approximately one-fifth of the pathfinder sample and one-quarter of the comparison sample had to be excluded: a figure which would have been higher if a careful verification process had not been undertaken. Finally, the difficulties of analysing the reconviction rates of females should be noted. Clancy *et al.* (2006) note that OGRS2 is less reliable for females and, as a result, analyses were conducted separately for males and females.

For evaluators of resettlement projects it is not always possible to provide data on reconviction rates using official data sources. Researchers need to apply to the Home Office to obtain data from the Offenders Index and this can be a time-consuming process. It requires evaluators to supply Police National Computer (PNC) numbers, which uniquely identify each individual on the database, and these may not be available from resettlement projects, particularly if it is managed by voluntary sector organisations. Additionally, organisations may not have access to or record the offence(s) which led to offenders' imprisonment, which makes comparisons of levels of offending before and after interventions impossible. These problems make it difficult for organisations to prove that their work is effective when preparing bids for commissioners of offender management services.

An alternative approach to using reconviction data is to ask ex-prisoners via interview schedules or questionnaires to provide details of their involvement in offending, if any, following their release from custody. Self-report data have their limitations because they are dependent on respondents answering honestly questions about their offending behaviour, which may be a particular concern if offenders are on licence (see Coleman and Moynihan 1996, for a more detailed appraisal of their strengths and weakness).

These considerations aside, there remains the key question as to whether reconviction or reoffending rates are the most appropriate measure of effectiveness. There are two main considerations in this respect. First, prisoners targeted by resettlement projects are likely to have a wide range of needs, many of which will be criminogenic because they are linked, albeit not in a direct manner, to offending. For example, participants in the seven resettlement pathfinders had an average of four criminogenic needs (as identified using the Offender Assessment System (OASys) tool), most commonly relating to accommodation, drugs, thinking skills and employment (Lewis *et al.* 2003). Second, resettlement projects are rarely focused explicitly on offending behaviour; rather, they aim to address the criminogenic needs already highlighted. Outcome measures therefore have to be selected carefully to ensure they can identify whether the objectives of a programme have been achieved.

The evaluation of the resettlement pathfinders (Lewis *et al.* 2003) used three measures of success which it termed interim outcomes measures. The first of these was reconviction rates. The second measure was 'continuity of service', assessed through analysing attrition rates as prisoners moved through the different stages of the projects in prison and in the community. The third measure was changes in self-reported attitudes to crime and in social and personal problems determined using CRIME-PICS II, a questionnaire and problem inventory. These measures were also used in the evaluation of the second phase (Clancy *et al.* 2006).

In our own evaluations we have used a wide range of outcome and output measures. For example, we evaluated one resettlement project which was focused on enhancing employability among short-sentence prisoners. An important outcome measure was whether participants had found employment or embarked upon the process of seeking employment, for example through enrolling on an education or training course. However because our data revealed participants in the project were far from 'job ready', we also looked for evidence that barriers to employability had begun to break down, for example that levels of drug and alcohol use had decreased and that accommodation, even if only temporary, had been found. We also used a series of output measures, for example to measure participation in the various components of the project such as groupwork and mentoring or to calculate the success of the project at maintaining contact with prisoners after they went 'through the prison gate'. In our final report we also included a lengthy analysis of the views and experiences of all the stakeholders (project managers, project staff, volunteer mentors, partner agencies and mentors) and explored in considerable detail whether the project was implemented as envisaged. As we will explore in the next section, it is important to examine processes as well as outcomes.

We have emphasised in this section that the outcome measure should reflect the objectives of the project but one of difficulties we have encountered in our own evaluations is that the objectives of initiatives are not always clearly defined. Additionally objectives may make reference to terminology such as employability and homelessness which can be understood in multiple ways. We should also emphasise that through interviews with different stakeholders in the various resettlement projects we have evaluated we have become aware that their objectives often differ from each other and the officially stated ones.

Unravelling complex relationships: linking outcomes to participation in individual resettlement projects

A major, and perhaps even impossible, challenge for evaluators of resettlement projects is to link outcomes to participation in an individual project. To illustrate, we are currently evaluating two resettlement projects run in five prisons in the North East and are aware that in two prisons, prisoners may be participating in both the projects we are evaluating. Additionally, they may be participating in other services such as educational classes, job clubs, and the Counselling, Advice, Referral, Assessment and Throughcare Service (CARATS) programme for drug users. Current theorising on desistance suggests that it stems from a variety of complex developmental, sociological and psychological processes (Laub and Sampson 2001). While resettlement programmes may be influential in terms of motivating offenders to change and overcoming structural barriers, there may be further explanations for desistance. Summarising the literature on desistance, Farrall and Calverley (2006) identify a wide range of other factors, at least for men, which are not directly related to participating in a resettlement programme such as forming a stable relationship or becoming a parent. Given all these potential influences on outcomes, evaluators can find themselves wrestling with issues of 'validity of explanation' or 'internal validity' (Jupp 2006). This concept refers to 'the extent to which an explanation of how and why a social phenomenon occurs is the correct one' (2006: 311).

For some researchers, it is possible to arrive at a definitive answer to the question 'what works?' through the use of randomised controlled trials. As the name suggests, this involves the random allocation of individuals to experimental and control groups and the taking of measurements both before and after the 'treatment' has been given to the experimental group. To their advocates, they represent the 'gold standard' in social research because they are high in internal validity. This claim is based on the belief that the experimental and control groups are initially equivalent and the only variation between the two groups is the application of the 'treatment'. Accordingly, differences between the two groups in terms of the outcome variables are attributed to differences in their exposure to the 'treatment' because other possibilities have been ruled out. The causal hypothesis can be tested and the results interpreted as evidence of success of the treatment with confidence.

Randomised controlled trials, or RCTs as they are often referred to for brevity, are rare in criminological research but there are proposals for them to be used more widely in government-funded research (Chitty 2005). This plan has attracted fierce criticism with considerable debate taking places at conferences and seminars organised by the British Society of Criminology. Wilcox et al. (2005: 39) argue RCTs 'are frequently dogged by methodological weaknesses' and, even in the absence of these, 'are often unable to provide unambiguous, policy-relevant answers'. De Vaus (2006a: 108) neatly summarises these as the history, maturation and selecting and testing effects which threaten the internal validity of RCTs and thus the whole basis of their claim to be a superior approach to evaluation. His argument centres on the view that it is impossible to control for all factors: other things happen, people get older and the very fact that they are aware they are participating in an experiment can be influential. Further threats to internal validity in criminological evaluations are discussed in Losel (2007).

In the UK, a randomised controlled trial of a resettlement project has yet to take place. This is unsurprising given that there are numerous reasons why it is neither possible nor desirable to conduct this type of evaluation. Leaving aside ethical considerations, one of the main barriers to conducting RCTs of resettlement projects is generating a sufficiently large sample. In a recent report prepared by researchers from the Home Office Research, Development and Statistics Directorate (Friendship et al. 2005), minimum sample sizes for RCTs are provided which vary according to the anticipated impact on reconviction. Designers of resettlement projects are rarely bold enough to state this upfront but given the high reconviction rate among released prisoners, it would be overly optimistic to expect this to be of any great magnitude. One of the key messages conveyed in the report is that the greater the anticipated impact on reconviction rates, the smaller the sample required. It therefore follows that RCTs of resettlement projects where the best that might be hoped for is a reduction of 5 per cent requires a sample size of 1,273 in the experimental and control groups.

To put this into perspective, the evaluation of the resettlement pathfinders (Lewis et al. 2003) – likely to be the most generously funded evaluation of a resettlement project to date – had an experimental sample size of 1,081. It was anticipated at the outset that each of the seven resettlement pathfinders would recruit 400 prisoners resulting in an overall sample of 2,800. The shortfall was significant although, as the evaluators note, they found it difficult to identify who had participated in a project because of the lack of consistent record-keeping. We have experienced similar problems in our own evaluations and can add to this the difficulty of determining what participation entails. For example, one of the projects we evaluated had just over 4,000 participants and their thorough record-keeping led us to believe this was a 'true' figure. However, participants in this instance sometimes referred to those who had done little more than complete the initial induction stage. More generally, evaluative studies in the UK fail to achieve sufficient sample size, which Friendship *et al.* (2005) attribute to pressures to evaluate interventions at the outset before a critical mass of participants has built up and insufficient numbers commencing and completing interventions. These explanations square with our experiences but we would caution against arguing that evaluations should not be set in motion at the outset. They should, but their focus initially should be two fold: to study the implementation process and operational processes rather than outcomes. Both of these exercises can usefully take the form of action research to allow emerging findings to shape the direction of the project and any planned expansion.

Evaluators have also objected to RCTs on moral and ethical grounds because it involves denying one group access to an intervention which, in theory, should have a positive impact on them. Critics of this position might argue that employing untested approaches is equally unethical. In an article which cautions against the use of RCTs, Gelsthorpe and Sharpe (2005/6: 8) note 'that many argue that the vicissitudes of justice do not preclude randomised allocation to interventions'. For example, Losel (2007: 147) argues that 'it is not true that random assignment of participants to a specific project or to a control condition is unfair'. He goes on to argue the contrary case, that 'randomisation is the fairest procedure if a programme is a limited resource, which is not available to everybody who would need it' (2007: 147). Losel concludes by arguing there are no legal barriers to pursuing RCTs in criminology and randomisation can be justified for reasons of knowledge enhancement.

While the classic experimental design is difficult to implement in social research, it has been suggested that this model provides a useful logic for developing alternative designs (de Vaus 2006a). These involve the use of comparison or control groups which have been selected by evaluators. On the Maryland Scale of Methodological

Rigour (Sherman *et al.* 1997), these studies can be placed at levels three and four (RCTs are at level five). What distinguishes these levels is whether the sample is well matched on theoretically relevant factors which are related to the outcome being measured. If comparability to the experimental group can be demonstrated, it is a level four study.

While it has been argued that it is essential to have a comparison group (Friendship *et al.* 2005), often this is not possible because of the resource implications and the logistical difficulties of locating an appropriate comparison group. Compared to the costs of the intervention, only a small proportion of the budget is allocated to evaluation and including a comparison group increases the costs considerably. Indeed, we were unable to incorporate comparison groups into our own evaluations given the resources allocated to the evaluation and for this reason they would be placed at level one on the Maryland Scale. Given the wide range of factors which might influence an outcome, it can be difficult to match the 'experimental' and 'comparison' groups and thus eliminate the influence of other external factors. Often the relevant information (for example, data on risk) is unavailable to allow the two groups to be matched appropriately.

Even if an experimental or quasi-experimental design is implemented as intended, it may not provide sufficient detail to answer key policy questions. It would reveal whether a resettlement project had successfully reduced reconviction rates; however, this is not sufficient. For example, the reconviction rate among the sample of participants as a whole might be lower than expected or there may be important differences between subgroups in the sample. Hence questions need to be asked about the project's differential impact on prisoners who may vary in terms of age, gender, ethnic origin, sentence length and other characteristics. Similarly, a finding that projects have had little impact on reconviction rates reveals little about the reasons why, which might include theoretical deficiencies, implementation failure and inappropriate targeting. As a result, an alternative approach to experimentalism has been advocated by realists.

The differences between realist and experimental approaches to evaluation are neatly summarised by Tilley (2005/6: 106).

> Experimentalists try to establish what works and what does not work. Realists try to establish what works for whom, in what circumstance and how.

The main proponents of realist evaluation in the UK – Ray Pawson and Nick Tilley (Pawson 2006; Pawson and Tilley 1997) – have raised fundamental objections to the experimental orthodoxy, although they are not critical of experiments per se but rather of those that take the form of RCTs (Tilley 2005/6). Instead they adopt a more inclusive approach to research design and methods. For a realist evaluation to be successful it requires theoretical sophistication, the ability to design studies appropriate to the theory and a willingness to use the full range of methods available and accordingly different types of data (Tilley 2005/6). The emphasis on theory is welcomed by evaluators dissatisfied with the tendency to perceive evaluation as a technical exercise. Realists emphasise the need for evaluations to look at both processes and outcomes. In this instance, processes refer to both mechanisms and context: the latter refers to the conditions which need to be in place for the mechanisms to work effectively. While none of the evaluations of resettlement projects which have taken place have been described as realist evaluations, they have included many aspects of the realist approach. Indeed the resettlement pathfinder projects, like other New Labour 'pilots', were established in order for them 'to be tested, evaluated and adjusted where necessary, before being rolled out nationally' (Cabinet Office 2003: 3) and this involved looking at both the process of the resettlement pathfinder projects and their impact.

Making compromises: conducting research in prisons

As one of us has argued elsewhere (King and Wincup 2007), all research designs are ultimately a compromise between what one would like to do and what is possible within the inevitable constraints. While researchers should begin by outlining the best research design possible, the next stage must be to reflect upon what *actually* can be done. Further refinements may need to be made once the research is underway if it becomes evident that the selected approach can no longer be pursued. We have already documented some of the general difficulties of putting particular research designs into practice. In this section we focus on the realities of conducting research in prison. As we are acutely aware and others have noted (King 2000; King and Liebling 2007), conducting research in prisons creates considerable challenges. Access issues are paramount and in the remainder of this section we explore the difficulties of negotiating access to prisons and prisoners.

A successful bid for evaluating a resettlement project already operating in a prison is not always accompanied by unproblematic access to prisons. This still needs to be negotiated and evaluators must be willing to comply with the security clearance procedures each prison insists upon. This can involve as little as providing a full name plus date and place of birth through to completing a lengthy form, supplying personal documents and consenting to a criminal record check. The inevitable time delays, inconsistent practices and the lack of information sharing between prisons are sources of frustration. Access arrangements can be precarious and we have experienced having to renegotiate access to prisons we had been conducting fieldwork in for some time. If a researcher leaves, no research in prisons can take place until a replacement researcher is security cleared.

In our experience the relationship between the resettlement project and the prison is highly influential for facilitating access. If the relationship is poor, evaluators can find themselves without the degree of access they need to conduct their fieldwork effectively. For example, in a number of prisons we have not been able to conduct interviews with prisoners in the main part of the prison but instead have been required to use the legal visits area. There are many reasons why this is unsatisfactory. First, while in any area of the prison it can be difficult to create an atmosphere which encourages interviewees to talk with ease, this is particularly challenging in an area designed for formal meetings where prisoners are used to meeting legal and criminal justice professionals including police officers. Normally, the legal visits area comprises a corridor of small rooms with basic furniture. This provides some privacy although prison officers are able to observe with ease through large glazed panels. However, in two prison establishments we discovered that legal visits took place in the main visits hall. In one we found ourselves interviewing prisoners in close proximity to their peers and in the other during normal domestic visits. Second, prisoners may be reluctant to come to legal visits because they may be accused of 'grassing' to the police in some prisons. In a prison setting, rumours about the reasons for prisoners having official appointments can easily spread. Third, the legal visits may not take place throughout the week and on the days that they do are restricted to certain times of the day, which are very short. Researchers will find themselves being asked to leave the prison in the middle of the day so that the maximum time available for interviewing is four hours. The reality is that far less time than this will be spent talking to prisoners. It can take time to go through the security checks and be escorted to legal visits. Prisoners who have agreed to be interviewed may not be available at the time agreed for reasons we will discuss shortly. A further complication is that appointments are normally restricted to 30 minutes, which is insufficient time to conduct an in-depth interview so permission has to be sought for an interview room to be made available for longer periods of time.

Once physically in the prison, evaluators are unlikely to be given keys – a practice which in any case may not be seen as desirable and would be resisted by many prison researchers although there are exceptions (see King and Liebling 2007, for a discussion). Consequently, they may need to be escorted by project staff if, for example, they need to go to a wing to interview prisoners, and in some instances prisons may require project staff to remain close by. These duties can be time-consuming for project staff who may have already spent substantial amounts of time organising a visit, potentially leading to resentment about the impact of the demands of the evaluation on their workload. Providing guidance for would-be prison researchers, King (2000) outlines ten nostrums for doing field research in prisons, which include 'you must always remember that research has costs for staff and prisoners'.

Even if evaluators have full access to the prison, it can still be complicated to arrange interviews with prisoners, which relates more to practical considerations than high refusal rates among prisoners. What is often termed 'the prison day' is one of the main constraints. Evaluators will find it impossible to conduct interviews at certain points of the day. Evaluators have no choice but to adhere to the institutional timetable. While long lunch breaks and early finishes might be welcomed, the number of days within the project set aside for interviewing prisoners, or indeed conducting any fieldwork within the prison, has to be increased. Ensuring sufficient numbers of prisoners are available to be interviewed can be challenging. Interviews with prisoners have to be pre-booked and prisoners are supposed to be kept back from their usual activities. Nevertheless, prisoners may not be available as planned because of more important commitments such as a visit from their probation officer or legal representative. They may also be unavailable because they have been moved to another part of the prison (for example, the hospital wing or the segregation unit) or to another prison altogether. Short-sentence prisoners, in particular, may be released earlier than expected. To ensure that a visit to a prison is productive, one strategy is to follow the approach of the airlines and to 'overbook', predicting that some prisoners will not be available for interview. This runs the risk that more prisoners than expected will turn up and interviewers will have to rush through their questions and compromise the quality of the data they collect. There is also the risk that prisoners will be reluctant to wait.

Conducting research in prisons can also create ethical dilemmas. Prisoners may state they are willing to participate in a research study with only scant knowledge about what participation may entail. Often potential interviewees have been provided with some basic information about the evaluation in the form of a letter from the evaluation team and/or by project staff talking to prisoners. The former can be problematic given that many offenders have poor literacy skills (McMahon *et al.* 2004) and the latter because staff may not have a full understanding of the evaluation. The desire to spend time out of their cell and to talk to someone interested in them from the outside world is a compelling reason for agreeing to participate. A further consideration is that in the coercive environment of the prison, prisoners may agree to participate because they feel they should participate or interpret the request as a requirement. Sometimes prisoners may confuse the evaluation team with the project team and arrive for a research interview expecting to receive help and support with their problems.

There are a number of ways in which these difficulties can be overcome. The most important approach is to spend time at the beginning of an interview informing prisoners about the evaluation and what is required so that any consent they give is informed. At this stage prisoners should be aware that they have the right to refuse. The issue of confidentiality is a thorny one. We never promise complete confidentiality but prisoners are told that no information will be passed on unless it relates to risk of serious harm to themselves or to others. In our first evaluation of a resettlement project, the importance of this was brought into sharp focus when a prisoner informed one of us that he intended to commit suicide upon release. We ask prisoners to sign consent forms to confirm they are willing to be interviewed in prison and in the community. Increasingly these are required by research ethics committees and, despite the reservations that have been expressed (Coomber 2002), their use has had little apparent impact on participation rates.

A further difficulty researchers face relates to sampling. The reality of conducting research in prison makes the sample a convenience one. While different sampling strategies may be favoured, there are numerous practical reasons why compromises have to be made.

Participants in a resettlement project are likely to be accommodated in different wings of the prison making it difficult for researchers to invite them personally to participate in the evaluation. Even if the logistics of moving around the prison could be overcome, prisoners selected as suitable interviewees may not be easily located. Prisoners are often referred to as a 'captive population' implying they are easy to reach but at particular times of the day they may be participating in different activities in a prison and difficult to trace. Indeed, our interviews with resettlement project workers have revealed that a significant proportion of their day is spent on this task. As a consequence of these practical difficulties, staff working on resettlement projects are usually asked to select suitable interviewees who meet the criteria specified by the research team. This runs the risk of 'cherry picking' taking place so that evaluators hear the 'success stories', a further reminder that evaluation is not a politically neutral activity.

The politics of evaluating resettlement projects

As Taylor and Balloch (2005) argue, evaluation research is inherently political. Within the methodological literature there are competing definitions of the term 'political' (see Noaks and Wincup 2004, for an overview). We use it here in two distinct but closely related ways: first, in recognition that we are researching a social problem which politicians seek to explain and control, and second, because research involves engaging with the micro-political processes of human interaction.

Since New Labour came to power in May 1997, one of its main priorities in terms of crime reduction has been the reduction of reoffending (Solomon *et al.* 2007). Earlier chapters in this volume have charted the rediscovery of resettlement and there is no need to revisit this journey here. Instead it is important to emphasise that the policy context has encouraged the development of resettlement projects, especially for prisoners serving sentences of less than 12 months, a group which are not supervised upon release unless they are aged under 21. Without core statutory funding, these projects are largely dependent upon securing funding from alternative organisations. The European Social Fund has been a major source of financial support for projects which aim to develop employability and human resources but funding has also been obtained from charitable trusts such as the Northern Rock Foundation. While many of the projects may have chosen to engage in monitoring and evaluation in order to discover 'what works' anyway, evidence of success is required not only to secure future funding but sometimes to ensure payments are made for the original project. These requirements influence the micro-political context in which both the project and the evaluation take place.

During the relatively short period we have been evaluating resettlement projects (2004–7) there have been major changes to the political context in which work to resettle prisoners operates, and these in turn have had implications for our evaluations. The two most significant developments are the introduction of Custody Plus and the development of the National Offender Management Service (NOMS). Proposed in the Halliday Report (Home Office 2001) and provided for in the Criminal Justice Act 2003, Custody Plus refers to a new order, which involves a period in custody followed by a period of supervision on licence in the community subject to conditions specified by the court at the sentencing stage in the criminal process. It replaces the current system of sentencing prisoners to custody for a period of less than 12 months and releasing them without statutory supervision. As we write, the Home Office's position is that no decision has been taken about the implementation of Custody Plus (Hansard 27 February 2007) and it is commonly understood that it has been put back indefinitely. The National Offender Management Service, initially recommended in the Carter Report (Carter 2003) and established by the Home Office in 2004 (Home Office 2004), brings together HM Prison Service and the National Probation Service to provide end-to-end offender management to bridge the divide between prison and the community. Emphasising contestability in the commissioning process, NOMS intends to commission offender management services from the private, public and voluntary sectors. The statutory framework (Offender Management Bill 2006) to permit this is currently progressing through Parliament. The net effect of these two developments is the potential it creates for current providers of resettlement services to seek statutory funding but only if they can provide evidence of effective practice when competing for limited resources.

In our experience the main implications of the political context we described above are the pressures placed on the evaluation team to produce results quickly, to focus on outcomes of the project rather than the processes by which outcomes are secured and to provide 'good news'. Expectations of both the evaluation and the project might be unrealistic, and, finally, there may be additional problems if the evaluation has been commissioned by an organisation with little or no experience of managing research contracts. All this takes place against a backdrop where evaluators are engaged in a 'customer-contract' relationship with funders. We elucidate these issues in the remainder of the chapter.

As others have noted (Losel 2007), evaluators are typically confronted by demands from policymakers for quick answers. The sense of urgency often stems from the need to apply for additional funding prior to the evaluation being completed. Such applications require evidence of success and thus evaluators are pressured into providing 'hard' evidence. Quantitative data are favoured, presented in a way so that they offer definitive statements about the success of a project. While qualitative data plays a key role in evaluations, particularly for representing the views of stakeholders, they are accorded a far lower status. In our first evaluation of a resettlement project we found ourselves defending the use of such data after it was dismissed by a senior project manager as 'anecdotal'.

We emphasise success because so much is at stake that evidence of failure, even if carefully presented in a way which emphasises the challenges of resettlement work, is unwelcome. Without evidence to support a future funding application, employment contracts may not be renewed and aspirations for developing the project may be quashed. The evaluation occupies an instrumental role in securing the continuation of the project. Understandably staff whose future employment is dependent in part on the final report of the evaluation may be suspicious and steer researchers towards the 'success' stories or be reluctant to cooperate at all. Invariably the reaction to evidence of failure is a defensive one. In our own evaluations we have become aware of attempts to hide difficulties, even major ones, from us.

In our experience, individuals with little knowledge of commissioning research may have unrealistic expectations about what the evaluation can deliver and research teams seeking to be the successful bidder may not state as forcefully as they should the limits to evaluation research for fear they may not secure the contract. Commissioners of research hope that the final report will include definitive statements relating to the impact of the project, which need no further explanations. They remain either unaware or blinkered to the view that findings are inevitably imperfect, contested and provisional (Mair 2005) and in need of careful interpretation.

For Balloch and Taylor (2005) there is no other option than to acknowledge the politics of evaluation and they propose a four-fold approach to doing so. Firstly, they argue that all evaluations should include the viewpoint of the central actors. Second, they propose that prescribed indicators should be challenged. Third, they suggest that the overall approach adopted should be positive, exploring both processes and outcomes. Finally, they suggest that learning should be shared. Applied to evaluations of resettlement projects, adopting their approach would mean developing a research design which gives a voice to prisoners and ex-prisoners, challenging the orthodoxy of reconviction rates as a measure of success, identifying what supports effective practice and how existing barriers can be overcome and a willingness to disseminate the findings to allow learning to be transferred to other projects. This is close to our own approach although we should point out that we have been unable to disseminate the findings from our first evaluation. In a contractual relationship, decisions about dissemination rest ultimately with the contractor rather than evaluators and their interests may not be best served by allowing the findings to reach a wide audience. As a result, no evidence base is established to allow project developers to learn from others and avoid making the same mistakes.

Concluding comments

In this chapter we have argued that the evaluation of resettlement projects requires a research design to be developed which is theoretically informed, methodologically sophisticated and ethically sound. Faced with considerable barriers – practical and political – evaluators often find that the research design utilised is far removed from this ideal and there are further compromises to be made when confronted by problems such as incomplete data and small sample sizes. While encountering numerous challenges reflects the realities of doing criminological research – and especially so when it involves engaging in evaluations in prisons – we would like to end by offering some possible ways forward.

One solution to some of the problems we have discussed in this chapter is to allow interventions to 'bed down' before commencing the outcome evaluation so that the most appropriate research design can be developed. At the beginning, the evaluation should focus on processes and determining the feasibility of different research designs for the outcome evaluation. This early stage might take the form of action research involving collaboration between researchers and designers of the intervention with the intention of developing it based on the emerging research findings. The later stage should focus on measuring what works, for whom, why and at what cost using a wide range of measures of effectiveness.

The political nature of evaluation is inescapable and we argue that it is important to take on board Balloch and Taylor's (2005) advice and acknowledge the politics of evaluation. The strategies they suggest which we described earlier in this chapter need to be placed in what Losel (2007: 141) describes as a 'survival kit' for evaluators which contain research tools which are methodologically sound and can be used flexibly, realistic expectations regarding the role of evaluation in policymaking and practice and coping skills such as patience and sensitivity. In possession of such a kit, evaluators are well equipped, but as Balloch and Taylor (2005: 252) argue, evaluation 'is definitely not for the faint hearted'!

References

Balloch, S. and Taylor, D. (2005) 'What the politics of evaluation implies', in D. Taylor and S. Balloch (eds), *The Politics of Evaluation*. Bristol: Policy Press.

Bottoms, A., Shapland, J., Costello, A., Holmes, D. and Muir, G. (2004) 'Towards desistance: theoretical underpinnings for an empirical study', *The Howard Journal*, 43 (4): 368–89.

Burnett, R. (2004) 'To reoffend or not to reoffend? The ambivalence of convicted property offenders', in S. Maruna and R. Immarigeon (eds), *After Crime and Punishment: Pathways to Offender Reintegration*. Cullompton: Willan.

Cabinet Office (2003) *Trying It Out: The Role of 'Pilots' in Policy-making*. London: Cabinet Office.

Carter, P. (2003) *Managing Offenders: Reducing Crime: A New Approach*. London: Strategy Unit.

Casale, S. (1989) *Women Inside: The Experience of Women Remand Prisoners in Holloway*. London: Civil Liberties Trust.

Chapman, T. and Hough, M. (1998) *Evidence Based Practice: A Guide to Effective Practice*. London: HM Inspectorate of Probation.

Chitty, C. (2005) 'The impact of corrections on re-offending: conclusions and the way forward', in G. Harper and C. Chitty (eds), *The Impact of Corrections on Reoffending: A Review of What Works'*, 3rd edn, Home Office Research Study No. 291. London: Home Office.

Clancy, A., Hudson, K., Maguire, M., Peake, R., Raynor, P., Vanstone, M. and Kynch, J. (2006) *Getting Out and Staying Out: Results from the Resettlement Pathfinders*. Bristol: Policy Press.

Coleman, C. and Moynihan, J. (1996) *Understanding Crime Data: Haunted by the Dark Figure*. Buckingham: Open University Press.

Coomber, R. (2002) '"Signing your life away?" Why research ethics committees (REC) shouldn't always require written confirmation that participants in research have been informed of the aims of a study and their rights – the case of criminal population', *Sociological Research Online*, (7) 1. See: www. socresonline.org.uk/7/1/coomber.html.

de Vaus, D. (2006a) 'Experiment', in V. Jupp (ed.), *The Sage Dictionary of Social Research Methods*. London: Sage.

de Vaus, D. (2006b) 'Retrospective study', in V. Jupp (ed.), *The Sage Dictionary of Social Research Methods*. London: Sage.

Farrall, S. and Calverley, A. (2006) *Understanding Desistance from Crime: Theoretical Directions in Resettlement and Rehabilitation*. Buckingham: Open University Press.

Friendship, C., Street, R., Cann, J. and Harper, G. (2005) 'Introduction: the policy context and assessing the evidence', in G. Harper and C. Chitty (eds), *The Impact of Corrections on Reoffending: A Review of 'What Works'*, 3rd edn, Home Office Research Study No. 291. London: Home Office.

Gelsthorpe, L. and Sharpe, G. (2005/6) 'Criminological research: typologies versus hierarchies', *Criminal Justice Matters*, 62: 8–9 and 43.

Her Majesty's Treasury (2004) *2004 Spending Review: New Public Spending Plans 2005–2008*. London: HM Treasury.

Home Office (2001) *Making Punishments Work: Report of a Review of the Sentencing Framework for England and Wales*. London: Home Office.

Home Office (2004) *Reducing Crime, Changing Lives*. London: Home Office.

Hough, M. (2004) 'Special Issue: evaluating the Crime Reduction Programme', *Criminal Justice*, 4 (4).

Jupp, V. (2006) 'Validity of explanation', in V. Jupp (ed.), *The Sage Dictionary of Social Research Methods*. London: Sage.

King, R. (2000) 'Doing research in prisons', in R. King and E. Wincup (eds), *Doing Research on Crime and Justice*. Oxford: Oxford University Press.

King, R. and Liebling, A. (2007) 'Doing research in prisons', in R. King and E. Wincup (eds), *Doing Research on Crime and Justice*, 2nd edn. Oxford: Oxford University Press.

King, R. and Wincup, E. (2007) 'The research process', in R. King and E. Wincup (eds), *Doing Research on Crime and Justice*, 2nd edn. Oxford: Oxford University Press.

Laub, J. and Sampson, R. (2001) 'Understanding desistance from crime', in M. Tonry (ed.), *Crime and Justice: A Review of Research*, Volume 28. Chicago: University of Chicago Press.

Lewis, S., Vennard, J., Maguire, M., Raynor, P., Vanstone, M., Raybould, S. and Rix, A. (2003) *The Resettlement of Short-Term Prisoners: An Evaluation of Seven Pathfinders*, RDS Occasional Paper 83. London: Home Office.

Losel, F. (2007) 'Doing evaluation research in criminology: balancing scientific and practical demands', in R. King and E. Wincup (eds), *Doing Research on Crime and Justice*, 2nd edn. Oxford: Oxford University Press.

Lloyd, C., Mair, G. and Hough, M. (1994) *Explaining Reconviction Rates: A Critical Analysis*, Home Office Research Study No. 136. London: Home Office.

McMahon, G., Hall, A., Hayward, G., Hudson, C., Roberts, C., Fernandez, R. and Burnett, R. (2004) *Basic Skills Programmes in the Probation Service: Evaluation of the Basic Skills Pathfinder*, Home Office Online Report 14/04. London: Home Office.

Maguire, M. and Raynor, P. (2006) 'How the resettlement of prisoners promotes desistance from crime: or does it?', *Criminology and Criminal Justice*, 6 (1): 19–38.

Mair, G. (2005) 'Electronic monitoring in England and Wales: evidence-based or not?', *Criminal Justice*, 5 (3): 257–78.

Mair, G., Lloyd, C. and Hough, M. (1997) 'The limitations of reconviction rates', in G. Mair (ed.), *Evaluating the Effectiveness of Community Penalties*. Aldershot: Ashgate.

Morgan, R. and Hough, M. (2007) 'The politics of criminological research', in R. King and E. Wincup (eds), *Doing Research on Crime and Justice*, 2nd edn. Oxford: Oxford University Press.

Noaks, L. and Wincup, E. (2004) *Criminological Research: Understanding Qualitative Methods*. London: Sage.

Pawson, R. (2006) *Evidence-based Policy: A Realist Perspective*. London: Sage.

Pawson, R. and Tilley, N. (1997) *Realistic Evaluation*. London: Sage.

Shepherd, A. and Whiting, E. (2006) *Reoffending of Adults: Results from the 2003 Cohort*, Home Office Statistical Bulletin 20/06. Available online only – see: www.homeoffice.gov.uk/rds/pdfs06/hosb2006.pdf.

Sherman, L., Gottfredson, D., MacKenzie, D., Eck, J., Reuter, P. and Bushway, S. (1997) *Preventing Crime: What Works, What Doesn't, and What's Promising*. Washington, DC: US Department of Justice.

Social Exclusion Unit (2002) *Reducing Re-offending by Ex-prisoners*. London: Office of the Deputy Prime Minister.

Solomon, E., Eades, C., Garside, R. and Rutherford, M. (2007) *Ten Years of Criminal Justice under Labour: An Independent Audit*. London: Centre for Criminal Justice Studies.

Taylor, D. and Balloch, S. (2005) 'Introduction', in D. Taylor and S. Balloch (eds), *The Politics of Evaluation*. Bristol: Policy Press.

Tilley, N. (2005/6) 'Asking the right questions in criminal justice evaluations', *Criminal Justice Matters*, 62: 12–13.

Tilley, N. (2006) 'Evaluation research', in N. Tilley (ed.), *The Sage Dictionary of Social Research Methods*. London: Sage.

Wilcox, A. with Hoyle, C. and Young, R. (2005) 'Are randomised controlled trials really the "gold standard" in restorative justice research?', *British Journal of Community Justice*, 3 (2): 39–49.

Part 2

Issues in resettlement practice

Chapter 5

The SWing model of resettlement: some reflections

Kirsty Hudson

Introduction

This chapter gives an account of a unique experience of regional partnership. It provides details of an initiative that was designed to bring together a variety of public, private and voluntary service providers to deal with the resettlement needs of short-term prisoners (those sentenced to less than 12 months imprisonment). The chapter presents examples of new approaches to the resettlement of short-term prisoners that prefigured the creation of the National Offender Management Service (NOMS), Regional Offender Managers (ROMS) and the Government's resettlement agenda as set out in the National Action Plan (Home Office 2004). Key aspects of the project include the 'tracking' of offenders through the system as well as a strong emphasis on the evaluation of outcomes.

South West Integration (SWing) was established in April 2003 though a partnership between South West prisons and South West Probation Areas, and was principally funded through the Invest to Save Budget. It was created to offer a structured resettlement plan to every short-term prisoner in the region who requested it. SWing thus sought to create a regional partnership framework in order to integrate the efforts of prisons, probation and voluntary, private and public sector partners. The project officially came to an end in September 2006 (although it has secured funding for several of its projects as well as associated evaluations to continue for up to another year). While there is not enough space to document all of SWing's experiences since its inception, this chapter looks at how this project has helped to deal with three issues surrounding the broader topic of resettlement and, more specifically, the resettlement of a group of prisoners who have repeatedly been identified as having acute resettlement needs. The issues that will be addressed are:

• partnership work;
• information gathering and dissemination; and
• assessment and offender management.

The chapter also presents preliminary findings from the national pilot of the Going Straight Contract, in which offenders are supported through the transition from custody to community in terms of practical needs and the improvement of thinking skills and motivation to change. Finally, the chapter outlines the contributions that SWing has made to the provisions for prisoners' children and their families in the South West. The above all represent examples of new approaches to the resettlement of short-term prisoners, all of which have had to respond to some extent to the 'modernisation' agenda that is driving current rapid changes in the correctional services. The chapter thus first provides a brief account of these changes in light of the problems faced by short-term prisoners and SWing's aims and objectives.

Meeting the needs of short-term prisoners

The problems experienced by short-term prisoners have been extensively documented elsewhere.[1] In short, they typically have entrenched personal and social problems around the basic needs of accommodation, finances, substance misuse, health, relationships, education and employment (SEU 2002). These problems are often exacerbated by being sent to prison, for example in the loss of existing accommodation due to the failure to pay rent while inside, and by the rejection and the social stigma that are often experienced by ex-prisoners (NACRO 2000). In addition, although short-term prisoners constitute about half of all those released from prison each year – over 61,000 in 2004 (Home Office RDS NOMS 2005) – they are less likely than other prisoners to undertake any programmes or receive substantive services or preparation for release while in custody. Nor are they subject to statutory supervision upon release. Consequently, short-term prisoners become trapped in what has been coined the 'revolving door' of frequent, but usually minor, offending and repeat imprisonment. Indeed, 67 per cent of short-term prisoners are reconvicted within two years (Home Office RDS NOMS 2005).

The Government recently appeared to have responded to the problems faced by this group of prisoners, primarily due to the implications their neglect was having on reconviction rates, with the proposed introduction of Custody Plus. Originally recommended by Halliday (2001) and legislated for in the Criminal Justice Act 2003, Custody Plus proposed that all adult prisoners serving less than 12 months would receive between 2 and 13 weeks of custody followed by a period of at least 26 weeks' supervised licence. The introduction of this sentence would have meant that short-term prisoners would, for the first time, have been offered systematic help 'through the prison gate'. Such supervision would have also brought short-term prisoners in line with the new National Offender Management Service's (NOMS) system of so-called end-to-end 'Offender Management' (as set out within the framework of the National Offender Management Model (NOMM)) (NOMS 2005). It too, would have offered short-term prisoners greater opportunity to access resettlement initiatives developed within the 'pathway' arrangements (as outlined in the Reducing Reoffending National Action Plan (Home Office 2004) and regional strategies).[2] However, a decision was made in July 2006 to defer (indefinitely) the introduction of Custody Plus, leaving a needy and risky group still almost entirely without guidance or support. Nonetheless, recent developments within the South West of England hold some promise in this regard (Maguire 2004a).

A regional resettlement model

As stated earlier, South West Integration (SWing) was specially developed to encourage innovation and partnership work throughout the public, private and voluntary sectors, in order to improve the level and quality of resettlement provision offered to short-term prisoners. To achieve this, the project set out to coordinate all available services in the South West for this group of offenders into a regional framework, to identify untapped provision for short-term prisoners to be accessed in custody and in the community, to systematically identify gaps in service provision and then to generate income to fund projects where gaps were found. The rest of this chapter therefore explores areas in which promising developments have been made which could eventually be absorbed into the NOMS system.

Partnership work

The Government's new resettlement strategies and initiatives in England and Wales clearly recognise the potential of multi-agency partnerships in dealing with the high levels of social need found among ex-prisoners. In summary, the report by the Social Exclusion Unit (2002), *Reducing Re-offending by Ex-prisoners*, which provided the key stimulus for the Government's revived interest in resettlement, adopted a cross-departmental approach, whereby service agencies that had previously regarded ex-prisoners as of low priority (and in some cases excluded them from their services) were brought together to devise solutions. This resulted in the Government's Reducing Re-offending National Action Plan (Home Office 2004) and the systematic development of seven strategic service pathways – accommodation; education, training and employment (ETE); mental and physical health; drugs and alcohol; finance, benefit and debt; children and families of offenders; and attitudes, thinking and behaviour (Home Office 2004) – at both national and regional levels. The intention was for different partnership agencies to each play their part in tackling the problems faced by ex-prisoners in order to reach the central goal of reduced levels of reoffending.

Prior to pathway development SWing was engaged in the establishment and sustainability of multi-agency partnership work. Since its inception in April 2003, the project worked along 'pathway activity' in the first Regional Resettlement Strategy (Home Office 2003). SWing worked primarily along four pathways – accommodation; education, employment and training; finance, benefit and debt; and children and families of offenders – as the remaining pathways were, to some extent, already embedded within the region through mainstream activity. In doing so, considerable inroads have been made in joining up the work of different government departments, public sector agencies, and private and voluntary organisations within the region.

To provide an example, SWing invested time, energy and effort into attempting to build strategic alliances and accommodation forums in each of the five probation areas in the South West. Partnership work was undertaken with district council housing authorities, Supporting People, Rough Sleepers, private and social landlords, voluntary sector agencies and private investors, as well as the Prison and Probation Services. SWing essentially met with potential partners to try and influence their thoughts and perceptions about ex-prisoners in the hope that they would then incorporate work with this client group into their strategic development.[3] The project's involvement also stimulated cross-authority working between district and unitary authorities. Indeed, due to the work undertaken by SWing, the South West has become the site of the National Accommodation Pathfinder, involving the establishment of 'gateways' and 'one-stop-shops' for offenders with accommodation problems in Bristol, Plymouth and Dorset (see Maguire and Nolan, this volume).

The project's success at building and sustaining partnership capacity can be explained by a number of factors, not least due to the expertise of those involved.[4] For example, the 'SWing team' were all experts in their field, with a high level of knowledge and practical experience of working within the resettlement arena. Critically their knowledge and expertise was both local and regional. The project therefore had direct contact with local areas and issues which it used to help mould the shape of its plans to local circumstances. SWing then essentially took on a brokerage role, using its local expertise to bring the right people together to discuss new ways to deal with the problems faced by short-term prisoners. For example, as well as the work highlighted above, SWing set up a number of information and support networks with various service agencies working across all the different pathways, both in prison and the community. The aims of this were to identify both effective and ineffective practice and to identify existing methods and strategies that had been found to 'work best'. This was to ensure that lessons were learnt so that existing and new strategies avoided recurrent problems and increased their effectiveness. SWing thus recognised that in order to win commitment to partnership work they had to listen to, and build upon, current expertise and practice in both prisons and the community rather than impose a strategic master plan across the region from above.

SWing also ensured that communication channels were in place for ongoing partner involvement. This helped to sustain joint understanding, allay confusion and encourage shared learning across the region. To provide an example, SWing helped to secure the funding for a number of employment projects including 'Opening the Gates to Employment' in partnership with Jobcentre Plus, the Learning and Skills Council and Cygnet Training (together with a range of voluntary sector organisations and private sector partners); and the 'Warbath Cornwall Employability Project' ('warbath' meaning 'together' in Cornish) in partnership with Working Links. Both projects aimed to increase employment opportunities for offenders and provide an intermediate labour market provision for those not yet 'job ready'.[5] In addition, funding was secured in partnership with the private sector to train prison leavers in an identified skill gap area, place them in employment prior to their release and help ensure that this employment is retained on release. In light of these initiatives, SWing initially facilitated a meeting to provide some early coordination of these projects and shared learning across the region. This was then developed into a Regional Employment Forum which SWing led.

Partnership work: inherent tensions

However, despite achieving major inroads in building partnership capacity within the South West, this task also posed SWing's most daunting challenge. The multiple problems associated with partnership work are anything but new. The principle in itself relies heavily on:

> an assumed flexibility in professional cultures, whereby practitioners will be willing, or at least persuaded, to work in new ways, not only within their own organisation, but in the context of new forms of partnership between agencies unfamiliar with, and sometimes hostile to, each other's aims, assumptions and practices. (Maguire 2004b: 217)

Arguably five main factors hampered SWing's ability to build and secure successful partnerships. These were: regional versus local initiatives, cultural differences, competition versus collaboration, a shortage of resources and changing political climate. All five are implicitly interlinked and will now be discussed.

Regional versus local initiatives

While this chapter has suggested that SWing's local knowledge played a key part in their success at initially building partnerships within the region, SWing's wider remit was essentially to drive forward the implementation of a regional resettlement strategy. Its overall aim was therefore to craft a number of initiatives into a coherent whole across a region. However, different agencies have wider interests and responsibilities. Tensions thus arose when local tailoring and implementation was seen to be threatened by an externally imposed project with regional strategic targets. The partnership approach adopted by SWing (i.e. to listen to, and build upon, current expertise and practice and to keep communication channels with partners open) clearly helped to win commitment from their partners and encouraged ownership of a regional plan. However, tensions remained due to differing agendas and cultures.

Cultural differences

The Prison and Probation Services, for example, are highly performance driven. Both agencies exist within a culture of 'performance targets' which at various times during SWing's implementation had to take priority over new resettlement initiatives. Limits on the capacity available and the bureaucratic procedures that both services operate within also presented further barriers to successful partnership work. This was evidenced in work undertaken to develop video links in custody and the community to bridge the physical distance between prisoners and their families. In this example, a distinct clash of cultures between the private sector and the public, in terms of the immediacy of the decision and implementation became evident.

The project involved the installation of a total of 20 video links in seven prisons in the South West and national community sites. SWing successfully identified a private company who would provide, install and pay for all necessary equipment. It was also agreed that the Prison Service would incur minimal cost and that there would be no demand on the prison staff in terms of delivery of the video conference service, as a private sector call centre would be responsible for organising the visits and operating the equipment remotely. SWing thus essentially tried to develop a new partnership model between the public and the private sector in order to utilise private sector investment. However, this new and innovative partnership approach did not materialise. Instead, due to the regulations of SWing's parent organisations (namely the Prison and Probation Services) the project had to enter a national tendering process. Ultimately this placed restrictions on the type and nature of partnership work that could be developed. In addition, the advent of NOMS, and the changes that this brought led to staffing issues, which meant that sufficient resources could not be provided to facilitate the writing of a specification that was, in all sense and purposes, not bespoke.[6] Consequently, although SWing started to drive this project in the latter part of 2003, at the time of writing the project had still not reached fruition (although it had received backing from the South West Regional Offender Manager (ROM) and had also been adopted as a target for the South West Children and Families of Offenders pathway, which will be discussed later in this chapter).

Within the public sector there are inevitable systems and bureaucracy to overcome which slow down the pace of implementation and seem to impose unnecessary barriers. Arguably, it is only because of SWing's perseverance and resilience that this project will eventually be implemented. However, SWing has identified a real problem with regard to work in this area. The evidence suggests that the Prison and Probation Services have lost the ability to react speedily to opportunity. Arguably this can be attributed to the risk-averse culture in which they are embedded, for example their desire to avoid risk at all cost, thus reflecting wider shifts (and criminological debates) in the management of offenders in crime policy. (The growing prominence of the concept of risk in contemporary criminal justice and penal policy has been widely discussed and debated – see Hudson (2002) and Kemshall (2003) for an overview).

Competition versus collaboration

In terms of local community projects and individual prisons, both have a powerful commitment to their own developments and decision-making. Community projects, for example, face problems of short-term working contracts. Consequently their priority is to protect their own arena and sustainability. (The issue of contestability in the NOMS structure added to this tension and will be discussed later in the chapter.) This has a number of implications for the success of partnership work. In the first instance, where partnerships have already been built, all too often the voluntary or community project's funding period will come to an end, although the project will not have been mainstreamed. As a consequence, all partnership work will be dissolved and new ones will have to be made. Where this occurs, considerable care needs to be taken to ensure that the new agency does not revert to a traditional 'competitive' stance, causing other 'partners' to regress to similar patterns in order preserve their position.

It was also found that short-term projects, due to the very nature of their funding, will routinely prepare exit strategies before they even begin to implement their project plan. Added to this, they may have to contend with an exodus of staff, prior to the possible end of contracts, due to a realistic need to find alternative and more secure employment. These factors all, to differing degrees, have the potential to weaken naturally fragile partnership arrangements. They also instil a level of competitiveness that is not conducive to successful partnership activity.

A shortage of resources

A shortage of skilled labour and/or resources in all partner organisations undeniably hampered SWing's attempts to develop and/or sustain innovative and new partnership work. However, much of what has been documented above reflects the difficulties experienced by short-term resettlement projects to secure additional or mainstream funding. Indeed, this was a recurrent problem in the South West. One of SWing's targets was to build resettlement capacity 'through the prison gate' within the various strategic 'pathways'. However, while they were successful at securing funding for new innovative projects, funding bodies and managers who initially reacted to the projects with enthusiasm were reluctant to offer further funding or resources for the same product. The expectation is that investment will be obtained to test new products and then, if they prove effective, it is expected that the work will be mainstreamed. However, as this chapter has already suggested, this was seldom the case. While SWing placed strong emphasis on the evaluation of outcomes, no mechanism existed to effectively evaluate the project within the required time frame; therefore no decision was made as to its value. Consequently, there appeared to be little alignment between the proven effectiveness and the allocation of funding. This clearly needs to be recognised within the NOMS system of 'contestability', whereby Regional Offender Managers (ROMs) will be responsible for commissioning interventions from a variety of organisations, including the Prison and Probation Services, but also public, private and voluntary agencies that bid successfully.

Changing political climate

In light of the above, it must be noted that problems associated with partnership work were also exacerbated by the changing political climate. For example, the government's decision not to proceed with Custody Plus meant that the project's vision and focus on short-term prisoners became noticeably outside the government's new order of priorities. In addition, the new directives of NOMS brought a degree of vulnerability, confusion and uncertainty to professionals working within the criminal justice and resettlement arena.

However, while the advent of NOMS had the ability to threaten partnership work, in reality this did not happen. In fact, it had very little impact on existing partnership arrangements, specifically those between SWing and the voluntary and community sector. In these instances, the initial confusion and insecurity that staff faced was predominantly due to a lack knowledge regarding the local delivery of an integrated criminal justice service. Consequently, while the SWing team were involved in a number of discussions with regard to the issues, developments and potential impact of these changes, the creation of NOMS itself had no real effect on partnership activity. Partnerships thus continued to work efficiently, albeit through an additional level of bureaucracy. There was some evidence, however, that the major organisational change and staff redeployment that NOMS proposed had more impact on SWing's parent organisations (the Prison and Probation Services) who felt particularly threatened with regard to their roles and purpose within the new structure. As a consequence they lacked the drive and/or confidence to adopt, or partner, innovative projects.

Tracking offenders through the prison gate

Despite the multiple risks and tensions associated with partnership work, as this chapter has already shown, considerable inroads have been made in developing and sustaining new forms of partnerships within the South West. A further factor that has helped this process was SWing's emphasis on 'tracking' offenders through their involvement with the criminal justice system. This was attempted in two different ways, with varying levels of success: firstly, through the compilation of data on all prisoners released from South West prisons; and secondly, with the introduction of a regional 'offender management record', intended to capture and produce a formal assessment of risk and need on which to base decisions about the allocation of services and resources to all short-term prisoners in the South West. These will now be discussed.

Information gathering and dissemination

Since January 2004 SWing, in partnership with the 13 male prison estates in the South West, recorded information on all discharged male prisoners. These regional data have been used to provide a picture of the number and circumstances of male prisoners being released from South West prisons. For example, the data present basic profiles of prisoners, including details regarding their age, ethnicity and offending behaviour. The data also capture the problems faced by this subgroup of prisoners on release in relation to accommodation and employment. Additionally, it identified where these prisoners intended to resettle on release from prison. For example, the information was broken down into regions, counties and where possible unitary authorities.

Overall, data were captured on 16,842 prisoners who were discharged from the 13 male prisons in the South West of England from 1 January 2004 up to and including 31 March 2006.[7] Over half of all the prisoners released during this time intended to remain in the South West. Of these, over two-thirds were released into some form of employment (this includes full- and part-time work, temporary and casual employment and self-employment), while over a third of prisoners were released with no fixed abode (NFA). In terms of SWing's target population, just over half (51 per cent) of prisoners who intended to settle in the South West had been sentenced to less than 12 months (30 per cent of the total number of prisoners released).

SWing's regional data were sent to partners and stakeholders on a quarterly basis. As a result these data enabled partner organisations to command and commit sufficient resources to specific areas of resettlement in order to be able to deliver services more effectively. Consequently, it has been recognised as good practice in the Reducing Reoffending National Action Plan (Home Office 2004) in helping to build strategic partnerships and to progress joint resettlement planning and collaborative strategies between agencies working within the region (for further information on SWing's regional data go to: www.rrpsouthwest.org.uk).

However, these data only captured information on male prisoners released from South West prisons. Consequently, they did not capture data on offenders who intended to settle in the South West when released from prisons outside the region. Secondly, no data were collected on a systematic basis for female prisoners released from HMP Eastwood Park, the one female estate within the South West region.

Capturing data from the women's estate

Research studies have shown that female prisoners face immense practical problems on release from prison (see Gelsthorpe and Sharpe, this volume). However, developments in terms of prison-based and pre-release initiatives for women are clearly lagging behind the opportunities available to male prisoners. In light of this, SWing made considerable attempts to work alongside the female estate to help create a database (similar to that being used in the male estates) in order to identify existing gaps in provision for female prisoners within the South West. However, a number of organisational and delivery problems transpired which meant that this did not proceed. This was primarily due to limited resources available to the prison to capture information on female prisoners (see Hudson 2006a, for a more detailed overview).

Arguably these types of data would have identified the nature and the volume of criminogenic need of female prisoners released from HMP Eastwood Park. It could therefore have helped to build strategic partnerships, and perhaps more importantly ensure that partnership growth and strategic development occurred in the right areas. However, it is also recognised that these data would need to be collected nationally to have had the same impact because of the small number of female establishments and the fact that female prisoners are more likely to be imprisoned further away from their home areas than male prisoners (Home Office 2001; SEU 2002).

Assessment and offender management

Another practice growing in importance within the resettlement arena is a requirement to effectively assess risk and need, which can then be used as a basis for decisions about the allocation of services to individual offenders. While the Offender Assessment System (OASys) is used nationally to produce formal assessments of risk and need on prisoners sentenced to over 12 months, no tool has been developed for short-term prisoners. One of SWing's early targets was therefore to design an offender management record to be used to identify and address offending-related needs of all short-term prisoners.

SWing's approach to the introduction of this tool presents another example of its partnership style. For example, while SWing was the driving force behind its implementation, it set up a management board consisting of prison governors, prison officers working within resettlement and a researcher. As a result the offender management tool was adapted from existing risk assessment tools that were being used currently in each of the four local prisons and a case management record used in the Pathfinders Evaluation (Clancy et al. 2006; Lewis et al. 2003). Consequently, it was generally well received across the prisons within the region as a tool that would assist rather than duplicate or add extra work to those supervising prisoners in custody and after release. Furthermore, the tool was amended following feedback from prisons in its first four to six months operational period.

It was envisaged that the offender management tool would be implemented in three primary stages: firstly, into the four local prison establishments within the region; secondly, into the training estates – whereby the six male prisons would use and update offender management records that had been sent on by the local prisons at the point of transfer; and finally, the tool would travel 'though the prison gate' for use by partner agencies. It was therefore envisaged that the tool would coordinate joint working with individual prisoners both in prison and in the community, as well as chart the progress and outcomes across a range of partnership interventions. Finally, as part of this initiative, rapid assessment and target intervention units were established in all four local prisons within the South West. The aim of these units was to enable and facilitate the assessment of short-term prisoners and allocate space and resources to the delivery of partnership interventions.

The offender management record was initially used successfully within the four local prisons to capture information about prisoners at the point of reception and about their expected circumstances when released. In addition, some linkage between the local and the training estates as well as with community agencies had begun to take place whereby the offender management record was passed on to either the training estate following a transfer or community agency following release. Nonetheless, there was no single process in terms of how this document was shared between each of the parties. However, its implementation clashed with the introduction of the National Offender Management Model (NOMM), which clearly defined the framework of offender management within the NOMS system (NOMS 2005). SWing initially engaged with the Regional Offender Management group (established to oversee the implementation of the NOMM) in terms of integrating and agreeing developments and, at that time, with the aim of encompassing all the issues that short-term prisoners, and the proposed sentence Custody Plus, would bring to offender management. However, despite SWing's attempts to ensure linkage with mainstream developments, commitment to the use of the offender management record declined in the face of the decision not to proceed with Custody Plus and the high workload and financial restraints that many of the NOMS reforms threatened.

It should also be noted that the South West's offender management tool faced further obstacles in meeting its aims and objectives, aside from those mentioned above. For example, a primary function of the tool was to provide a single document which recorded offenders' risk and need assessments, any work that had already been done and any initiatives offenders were currently involved with. In theory, the document would be shared between all partners involved in offenders' resettlement therefore avoiding duplication and freeing up time and resources. It also prevented offenders having to repeatedly answer the same questions, a factor which has been to shown to diminish an offender's motivation to engage with resettlement initiatives (see, for example, Clancy *et al.* 2006). Finally, the tool captured the work of various partner agencies on one document to enable different interventions to be coordinated. In this way, it took account of the fact that offenders may need several resettlement services; for example, evidence suggests that it is important to link up drug intervention with supported accommodation, as often failure to deal with the former may lead to eviction (see Maguire and Nolan, this volume).

However, as this chapter has already argued, agencies working within the resettlement arena from all sectors (public, private and voluntary, both working in prison and through the prison gate) have different cultures and agendas. Each therefore had their own assessment tool, which reflected their project's individual interests and responsibilities. Consequently, there was a general unwillingness to adopt the tool as it was intended to be used. Instead, where it was used by partner agencies, it was done so alongside their own assessment tools. In addition, much of the relevant data was drawn together by resettlement officers working with offenders in prison, in terms of contacting partner agencies to find out the outcomes of a referral.

The adoption of the tool by partner agencies was certainly hampered by the fact that it was a paper document. In the prisons, the master copy was stored within the resettlement units (see above) with the expectation that partner agencies working within the prison would access and update it as and when needed. In the instances where the tool went through the gate,[8] the procedure was to photocopy the document to send to the service providers. SWing had nonetheless commissioned the development of an electronic offender management record which could pass 'though the prison gate' to a number of partner agencies simultaneously through a joint web-based data, information and offender management system. However, this was superseded by the NOMS system of end-to-end offender management, which includes provision for the systematic assessment and referral of offenders to a variety of interventions (NOMS 2005). While questions remain with regard to the effectiveness of the NOMS process in coordinating all the services involved in an offender's resettlement (Hudson *et al.* 2007), what is already apparent is that short-term prisoners will be exempt from offender management, due to the decision not to proceed with Custody Plus.

The Going Straight Contract

Nonetheless, one of SWing's core tasks was to pilot a model of offender management within the region. SWing was thus commissioned to run the Going Straight Contract (GSC) in October 2004. The GSC was first mentioned in the Social Exclusion Unit's report *Reducing Re-offending by Ex-prisoners* (2002), in which it was recommended that an 'end-to-end' resettlement approach that involves both an offender manager and a prisoner who 'buys in' or engages as an 'active collaborator' in the delivery of their own rehabilitation programme should be tested. A subregional GSC Pilot was thus developed by SWing in partnership with the NOMS Delivery Team in the Home Office and Her Majesty's Prison and Young Offender Institution Guys Marsh (HMP & YOI Guys Marsh).

The pilot project

As part of the GSC Pilot, each prisoner is assigned an Intensive Support Worker (ISW). The role of the ISW is to engage with prisoners both in custody and in the community, and through the use of motivational work, facilitate a relationship that includes offenders in their own resettlement programme. In relation to the NOMS Offender Management Model, the ISW undertakes all tasks relating to the Offender Supervisor role, and also some that are part of the Offender Manager role (NOMS 2005). However, the pilot has also drawn on insights from theory and research about how and why most offenders eventually desist from crime, especially in the context of 'through the prison gate' work and the value of 'continuity' (see, for example, Clancy *et al.* 2006; Lewis *et al.* 2003; Maguire and Raynor 2006), but also in recognising how important the notion of generating and sustaining motivation is to the process of change (see for example, Farrall 2002; Maruna 2000; Maruna and Immarigeon 2004). For example, the ISW, through the use of motivational interviewing (MI) techniques, targets a wide range of resettlement issues as well as attitudinal and behavioural issues. Thus the 'Going Straight' approach is to intervene not only to help with the social and practical needs of offenders, but also to help these offenders to develop as a person, to improve their attitudes, thinking and behaviour, and their motivation to change both personally and with regard to their involvement with anti-social elements within their local community (Hudson and Haines 2005).

Interim findings

Findings from the pilot's interim evaluation (Hudson and Haines 2005), at which time 78 prisoners were engaging with the ISW, indicate that one of the key successes of the GSC Pilot was the use of MI techniques. For example, the research showed a positive shift in the way prisoners perceived their problems and needs immediately prior to release due to increased self-confidence and motivation to change (as measured by the CRIME PICS II Instrument (Frude *et al.* 1994), the offender management record and interview data). The evaluation also identified wider recognition of the benefits of using MI techniques with offenders. For example, the pilot's implementation team decided that all staff working with prisoners needed to use the same motivational techniques in order to ensure consistency in resettlement work and a better response from prisoners in engaging in the process. In light of this, training was designed to help prepare staff (aside from the ISW) in the skills of motivational interviewing. Further commitment was shown from the prison, with the use of cascade training, i.e. workshops, in order to continue developments in MI techniques.

The interim evaluation also provides some provisional figures relating to levels of post-release contact (Hudson and Haines 2005). However, these should be treated with caution given the small number of offenders that had engaged with the project at this time. Nonetheless, of the 78 prisoners who were engaging with the ISW, only 44 had been released. Of these, 17 (39 per cent) had made face-to-face contact with the ISW at least once following their release and a further 20 (45 per cent) offenders had made some contact with the ISW either by telephone or e-mail since their release from prison. Furthermore, interviews with offenders indicated that the vast majority of participants reported needing practical assistance with issues such as accommodation, substance abuse and employment. The capacity to build close working relationships with local service providers able to address these resettlement needs is therefore of paramount importance to the success of the post-release phase of the pilot. Early indications show that the ISW had been successful at 'signposting' offenders to relevant agencies to aid in their resettlement, with some two-thirds (62 per cent) of the 37 offenders still in some form of contact with the ISW having accessed resettlement services that the ISW had referred them to. The GSC Pilot came to end in September 2006. A full evaluation will be published later this year. Evidently, lessons learnt from the implementation of the GSC Pilot could provide some insights into the roll-out of the NOMS end-to-end offender management system.

Children and families of offenders

The rest of this chapter outlines the contributions for the provisions for prisoners' children and families in the South West. While there has been much research into the needs and experiences of prisoners' families, it is only recently that strong family ties and community links have been recognised as an important factor in promoting effective resettlement and reducing reoffending by ex-prisoners (see, for example, Home Office 2001; Niven and Stewart 2005a, 2005b; SEU 2002). Recent research has provided strong evidence that friends and family are crucial to the resettlement process. Ditchfield (1994) found that prisoners without active support during their imprisonment were between two and six times more likely to offend in the first year after release than those who demonstrated or received active family interest. Mills and Codd (2007) point to the importance of social and psychological support that family ties offer offenders both during imprisonment and after release, which may help to reduce the risk of reoffending (see also Paylor and Smith 1994; Visher and Travis 2003). Other research shows a link between the role that friends and/or family play during an offender's period in custody and the prisoner's education, training and employment (ETE) outcomes on release (Niven and Stewart 2005a, 2005b).

Previous research has also highlighted the benefits of involving prisoners' families in the resettlement process. For example, evidence suggests simply involving the family in the process enables them to get a better understanding of what prisoners are going through (Mills and Codd 2007). Similarly, it can help prisoners to cope with changes that have taken place in the family home during their imprisonment. Additionally, family members can offer a unique insight into the circumstances that are likely to lead to reoffending. This information could be used by the prison to aid both sentence planning and the resettlement process (Home Office 2001).

Despite their importance to resettlement, families of prisoners are very rarely involved in this process.[9] In order to address this, 'Children and Families of Offenders' has become one of the seven strategic pathways identified for systematic development through the Government's Reducing Reoffending National Action Plan (Home Office 2004). However, it too has been recognised by the NOMS implementation team as being one of the most underdeveloped pathways.[10]

As this chapter has outlined, SWing was committed to drawing on existing practices and expertise working within different areas of the resettlement agenda. Data were therefore captured on the current provision for children and families within the region to identify untapped provision and gaps in the existing service for prisoners and their families. This included the mapping and collation of children and family provision across the 13 South West prisons and five probation areas, as well identifying organisations working directly with the families of offenders within the voluntary sector. Questionnaires were also administered to prisoners from four different prisons (which included the female estate and young offender estate) and 70 families visiting prisoners in the South West. These data were then used to identify how the South West region could support and possibly strengthen family ties during offenders' imprisonment and maintain these family ties on release. The findings pointed to the difficulties experienced by prisoners' families to remain in touch with a family member during their incarceration, the lack of provision available to families if they are able to visit and opportunities in which families can be involved in the resettlement process. This section will now discuss recent developments which hold some promise within these areas.

Maintaining family ties

In England and Wales, each prison establishment has a statutory obligation to allow prisoners to receive visits from friends and family (HM Prison Service 1999). Visits for convicted prisoners should last at least one hour, prisoners have an entitlement of two visits a month (HM Prison Service 2002) and up to three people can come to visit prisoners at any one time (however, children under ten years of age can come in addition to this limit). While visits are generally the preferred method of contact among both prisoners and their families (Murray 2003; Noble 1995), research has shown that despite the growing prison population, prison visits have declined in recent years, with two-thirds of convicted prisoners in local prisons and over half of those in training prisons receiving less than the minimum statutory requirement (SEU 2002).

As with previous research (Home Office 2001; SEU 2002), data gathered from questionnaires administered to prisoners in the South West[11] showed that the main challenge families faced in visiting their loved ones was the geographical location of prisons (Hudson 2006b).

Travelling time to prisons had a major impact on whether visits took place. Prisoners who lived less than an hour away from the establishment were approximately nine times more likely to receive visits than those who lived further away. In addition, only a third of prisoners that had dependent children[12] had been visited by them while in prison. When visits did take place, they were often reported to be time-consuming and expensive. Other factors which discouraged visits included a lack of information about visits, visiting facilities and security rules and procedures. This was consistent with other research in this area (see Mills and Codd 2007, for an overview). Indeed, as with previous research, the evidence suggested that prisoners would themselves actively discourage friends and family, and particularly children, from visiting them due to the 'ordeal' of visiting (Broadhead 2002; Home Office 2001; Mills 2005).

Video-conferencing

This chapter has already outlined the work undertaken by SWing to develop video links in custody and the community to bridge the physical distance between prisoners and families. To reiterate, the aim of the project is to address the difficulties that some families face in travelling to prisons (particular those in rural areas) by installing a total of 20 video links in seven prisons in the South West and national community sites. Prisoners will then be able to receive 'virtual visits' from their families via video-conferencing sessions, thereby providing cost-effective face-to-face contact between prisoners and their families. In order to ascertain the provision of need and expected service uptake of video-conferencing technology, questionnaires were administered to a random sample of prisoners and domestic visitors from three prison establishments in the South West.[13] Each respondent (prisoners and domestic visitors) was asked whether they would use video-conferencing technology to communicate with their families if it was made available. The majority (77 per cent) of respondents stated that they would (Hudson 2006b).

Visitor centres

The data obtained by SWing also captured the current provision for children and families across the South West prison estate. While each prison had a visitor centre, the facilities within the different establishments varied considerably. In an attempt to both increase and improve the quality of family contact with prisoners, the South West has developed a visitor centre 'specification' to make the facilities available to prisoners' families more welcoming. This should encourage families to visit thus strengthening relationships which will help to reduce reoffending. It therefore provides an opportunity for families to be involved in the resettlement process.

The scope of the South West's specification goes beyond the visitor centre and requires that changes take place in relation to domestic visits, transport and the offender assessment processes. In short, it addresses the need for cultural change and a shift of emphasis in terms of the way the prison service works with families. In doing so, visitor centres (to be renamed 'Family & Friends Centres') will contribute to developing child-friendly prisons. For example, the aim is to provide children's visits consistently across the South West prison area, to enable children to maintain relationships and regular contact with their imprisoned parent. The specification also seeks to imbed 'Family & Friends Centres' into the offender assessment process.

The developments in the South West aim to imbed visitor centres into the offender assessment process. For example, it is proposed that the centres themselves will be used to facilitate the involvement of prisoners' families in resettlement and sentence planning. Consequently, the proposal seeks to embrace the dual goals of working with families, namely to provide interventions which strengthen family ties and build resilience, while also implementing policies which protect and safeguard family members where appropriate, as well as using the maintenance of family ties to help reduce rates of reoffending.

In terms of progress, the specification has received substantial backing from the South West Regional Offender Manager (ROM). Furthermore, three areas from the specification have been prioritised and at the time of writing work had begun in these areas. The areas prioritised are:

- the recruitment of a Visitor Centre Manager in each prison;
- the development of effective transport to each prison;
- early and effective information for prisoners' families.

Furthermore, work had begun to guarantee that visitor centres could provide 'beginning to end' family support services. Measures were being implemented to ensure that visitor centres across the region would provide bridges to mainstream provision and community services working in this area, to which prisoners and their families could be referred and signposted. In summary, therefore, the South West has begun to make major improvements in one of the most underdeveloped pathways.

Conclusion

SWing officially came to an end in September 2006, although as stated earlier funding had been secured for several of its projects as well as associated evaluations to continue for up to another year. This chapter has clearly shown that SWing had begun to improve the level and quality of resettlement provision offered to short-term prisoners. For example, the project made genuine attempts to join up prison and probation systems as well as private and voluntary organisations. In many of SWing's key successes, it took on a brokerage role, successfully bringing people together from diverse organisations across the public, private and voluntary sectors, thereby enabling and facilitating partnership bids in order to build capacity within the region.

It has been argued that it did so through a partnership approach in which a trust was developed and maintained. This was achieved by ensuring that communication channels were in place for ongoing involvement and to build on current expertise and practice, as well as upholding a commitment to the sharing of information and expertise on work undertaken on all short-term prisoners in the South West both in prison and 'through the prison gate'. Added to this, SWing's regional data proved a vital tool for all partners to work productively on the regional reoffending agenda. Partnership activity thus became central to all aspects of SWing's work, from target setting to the design of local interventions and bidding for funds, as well as project management and delivery. Coupled with a commitment to evidence-based practice and research, it can be argued that SWing was ideally positioned to adapt established and proven approaches to crime reduction to local circumstances.

Indeed, the chapter has shown that SWing's vision fitted neatly within broader 'what works' initiatives, especially in the context of through the gate work with prisoners, the value of continuity and the importance of generating and sustaining motivation to change. SWing thus set their sights higher than merely providing short-term prisoners with help with immediate practical problems. For example, the project's commitment to evidence-based research and practice clearly helped to shape and mould the delivery of the Going Straight Contract Pilot. In addition, findings from the Pilot's interim evaluation suggest that the 'Going Straight' approach represents both practical improvements to the resettlement of prisoners involved in the project and attitudinal change in their motivation to desist from crime (Hudson and Haines 2005).

The chapter has, however, also identified a number of problems experienced by SWing during its implementation. These relate principally to operational issues surrounding partnership arrangements but also to factors associated with the changing political environment. Evidently SWing initially fitted neatly within the Home Office's interest in the crime reduction potential of multi-agency partnership resettlement drives. Its focus on short-term prisoners also chimed well with the government's renewed proposals to deal with the problems faced by short-term prisoners. It would therefore have been ideally placed to throw some light on issues of principle and practice that were likely to emerge if Custody Plus had been introduced. However, the decision not to proceed with the new sentence meant that the project's vision became noticeably outside the government's new order of priorities.

While much of SWing's work within the Pathways has generally been absorbed into the NOMS structure, concerns about the lack of services for short-term prisoners have been put to one side. The decision to defer indefinitely the introduction of Custody Plus has meant that short-term prisoners will not benefit from the NOMS agenda and its associated 'seamlessness'. Furthermore, the partnership-based resettlement agenda (which arguably stemmed from concerns about the lack of services for short-term prisoners), now clearly embedded within NOMS, is neglecting the offenders it set out to help. While SWing had a number of identified problems, it at least had begun to consider questions with regard to the operational arrangements involved in the coordination of services for short-term prisoners. The project's end therefore offers both opportunities and risks. The opportunities have to some extent already been discussed, in as much as the South West has clearly capitalised from SWing's experiences. The risk is that the progress made will not be built on and short-term prisoners will remain little better off than they were prior to SWing's intervention.

Finally, there are notable differences between SWing and NOMS. Although SWing was established through a partnership between South West prisons and South West probation areas, this was not how it was generally viewed. The project's perceived independence (perhaps due to the fact that it did not have the power of a formal organisation) may have contributed to its success (as well as its downfall). For example, as a project, it had more entrepreneurial freedom than its parent organisations. This enabled it to be more innovative and to cut across bureaucracies. In addition, where in the past there has been a genuine reluctance of voluntary participation from agencies across all sectors (particularly non-criminal justice agencies, such as health and accommodation services) to be set into some sort of government 'audit' or 'framework', SWing successfully pursued partnership activity through genuine collaboration rather than top-down managerial pressure. It remains to be seen whether NOMS will achieve the same level of compliance from organisations within a framework of enforcement.

Notes

1 For a full review of the problems faced by short-term prisoners and the part these play in reoffending see, for example, Banks and Fairhead (1976), Corden *et al.* (1978, 1979), Fairhead (1981), Home Office (1992, 2001), NACRO (1993, 2000), Maguire and Raynor (1997), Social Exclusion Unit (2002), Lewis *et al.* (2003, 2007), Clancy *et al.* (2006), Hudson *et al.* (2007).

2 For further information on NOMS and the NOMM see NOMS (2005). For a more critical perspective, see Hough *et al.* (2006). Peter Raynor's chapter in this volume also provides a descriptive overview of NOMS, the NOMM and the 'Pathway' arrangements.

3 SWing's regional data on prison leavers (which will be discussed later in this chapter) proved vital in identifying ex-offenders as a vulnerable and priority group, but also in directing spend and resources to this client group.

4 SWing recruited two Operational Directors: a previous prison Governor and an Assistant Chief Probation Officer. In addition, SWing's Director had worked as a Chief Probation Officer for Avon and Somerset before taking up an innovative and jointly salaried post between Bristol prison and Avon and Somerset Probation Areas.

5 For example, offenders may not have sufficient qualifications for particular jobs, or may be mentally or physically unable to work full time in their desired occupation at that time.

6 The impact that the advent of NOMS had on SWing will be discussed later in this chapter.

7 This figure includes data from HMP The Weare up until its closure in 2005.

8 As this chapter has already stated. Although SWing had not set up any formal information-sharing protocols to deal with the problem of prisoners being transferred, or to share information with community agencies involved in a prisoner's rehabilitation on release, two of the local prisons had begun to share this tool with community partners.

9 Prison governors are required to ensure that prisoners' families are given the opportunity to contribute to the sentence planning process for under 18s and offenders given Detention and Training Orders; in all other cases,

family involvement is left to the Governor's discretion (Mills and Codd, 2007).

10 The Finance, Benefit and Debt pathway is the other to be considered by the NOMS implementation team as being the most underdeveloped.

11 The questionnaire was completed in four prison establishments in the South West. These were: HMPs Channings Wood (55) and Gloucester (47), and HMP & YOI Guys Marsh (45), and the women's estate, HMP Eastwood Park (52).

12 'Dependent children' refers to all children aged 16 and under.

13 The prisons and the number of questionnaires administered are: HMP Dartmoor (41 domestic visitors; 22 prisoners), HMP Leyhill (50 and 16 respectively) and HMP The Weare (25 and 26 respectively).

References

Banks, C. and Fairhead, S. (1976) *The Petty Short Term Prisoner*. London: Howard League for Penal Reform.

Broadhead, J. (2002) 'Visitors welcome – or are they?', *New Law Journal*, 152: 7014–15.

Clancy, A., Hudson, K., Maguire, M., Peake, R., Raynor, P., Vanstone, M. and Kynch, J. (2006) *Getting Out and Staying Out: Results of the Prisoner Resettlement Pathfinders*. Bristol: Policy Press.

Corden, J., Kuipers, J. and Wilson, K. (1978) *After Prison: A Study of Post-release Experiences of Discharged Prisoners*. York: Department of Social Administration and Social Work, University of York.

Corden, J., Kuipers, J. and Wilson, K. (1979) 'Accommodation and homelessness on release from prison', *British Journal of Social Work*, 9: 75–86.

Ditchfield, J. (1994) *Family Ties and Recidivism: Main Findings of the Literature*, Home Office Research Bulletin 36. London: Home Office, pp. 3–9.

Fairhead, S. (1981) *Persistent Petty Offenders*, Home Office Research Study No. 66. London: HMSO.

Farrall, S. (2002) *Rethinking What Works with Offenders*. Cullompton: Willan.

Frude, N., Honess, T. and Maguire, M. (1994) *CRIME-PICS II Manual*. London: M & A.

Halliday, J. (2001) *Making Punishments Work: Report of a Review of the Sentencing Framework for England and Wales*. London: Home Office.

Her Majesty's Prison Service (1999) *The Prison Rules 1999*. London: Stationery Office.

Her Majesty's Prison Service (2002) *Performance Standards*, July 2002.

Home Office (1992) *National Prison Survey 1991*, Home Office Research Study No. 128. London: HMSO.

Home Office (2001) *Through the Prison Gate: A Joint Thematic Review by HM Inspectorates of Prisons and Probation*. London: Home Office.

Home Office (2003) *The South West Regional Resettlement Strategy*. Home Office: National Probation Directorate (www.probation.homeoffice.gov.uk/files/pdf/Resettlement%20finallowres.pdf, accessed 8 March 2007).

Home Office (2004) *Reducing Reoffending National Action Plan*. London: Home Office (www.homeoffice.gov.uk/docs3/5505reoffending.pdf, accessed 8 March 2007).

Home Office RDS NOMS (2005) *Offender Management Statistics 2004*, Home Office Statistical Bulletin 17/05. London: Home Office (www.homeoffice.gov.uk/rds/pdfs05/hosb1705.pdf, accessed 16 March 2007).

Hough, M., Allen, R. and Padel, U. (eds) (2006) *Reshaping Probation and Prisons: The New Offender Management Framework*, Researching Criminal Justice Series. Bristol: Policy Press.

Hudson, B. (2002) 'Punishment and control', in M. Maguire, R. Morgan and R. Reiner (eds), *The Oxford Handbook of Criminology*, 3rd edn. Oxford: Oxford University Press.

Hudson, K. (2006a) 'Capturing Data in the Female Estate'. Unpublished (SWing).

Hudson, K. (2006b) 'Maintaining Family Links: A Prisoner Questionnaire'. Unpublished (SWing).

Hudson, K. and Haines, A. (2005) 'Evaluation of the Going Straight Contract Pilot: Interim Report'. Unpublished (NOMS/SWing).

Hudson, K., Raynor, P. and Maguire, M. (2007) 'Offender management in late modernity: the birth of a seamless sentence', in Y. Jewkes (ed.), *Handbook on Prisons*. Cullompton: Willan.

Kemshall, H. (2003) *Understanding Risk in Criminal Justice*. Milton Keynes: Open University Press.

Lewis, S., Maguire, M., Raynor, P., Vanstone, M. and Vennard, J. (2007) 'What works in resettlement? Findings from seven Pathfinders for short-term prisoners in England and Wales', *Criminology and Criminal Justice*, 7 (1): 33–53.

Lewis, S., Vennard, J., Maguire, M., Raynor, P., Vanstone, M., Raybould, S. and Rix, A. (2003) *The Resettlement of Short-term Prisoners: An Evaluation of Seven Pathfinders*, RDS Occasional Paper No. 83. London: Home Office.

Maguire, M. (2004a) 'Resettlement of short-term prisoners: some new approaches', *Criminal Justice Matters*, 56: 22–3.

Maguire, M. (2004b) 'The Crime Reduction Programme in England and Wales: reflections on the vision and the reality', *Criminal Justice*, 4 (3): 213–37.

Maguire, M. and Raynor, P. (1997) 'The revival of throughcare: rhetoric and reality in automatic conditional release', *British Journal of Criminology*, 37: 1–14.

Maguire, M. and Raynor, P. (2006) 'How the resettlement of prisoners promotes desistance from crime: or does it?', *Criminology and Criminal Justice*, 6: 19–38.

Maruna, S. (2000) *Making Good*. Washington, DC: American Psychological Association.

Maruna, S. and Immarigeon, R. (eds) (2004) *After Crime and Punishment: Pathways to Offender Reintegration*. Cullompton: Willan.

Mills, A. (2005) *Settling into the Sentence: Life Sentence Prisoners and Family Ties*. Paper presented to European Society of Criminology Conference, Krakow, Poland, 31 August – 3 September 2005.

Mills, A. and Codd, H. (2007) 'Prisoners' families', in Y. Jewkes (ed.), *Handbook on Prisons*. Cullompton: Willan.

Murray, J. (2003) *Visits and Family Ties Amongst Men at HMP Camphill*. London: Action for Prisoners' Families.

NACRO (1993) *Opening the Doors. The Resettlement of Prisoners in the Community*. London: National Association for the Care and Resettlement of Offenders.

NACRO (2000) *The Forgotten Majority: The Resettlement of Short Term Prisoners*. London: National Association for the Care and Resettlement of Offenders.

Niven, S. and Stewart, D. (2005a) 'The role of family and friends in successful resettlement', *Prison Service Journal*, 159: 21–4.

Niven, S. and Stewart, D. (2005b) *Resettlement Outcomes on Release from Prison in 2003*, Home Office Research Findings 248. London: Home Office.

Noble, C. (1995) *Prisoners' Families: The Everyday Reality*. Ipswich: Ormiston Children and Families Trust.

NOMS (2005) *The NOMS Offender Management Model*. London: National Offender Management Service.

Paylor, I. and Smith, D. (1994) 'Who are prisoners' families?', *Journal of Social Welfare and Family Law*, 2: 131–44.

Social Exclusion Unit (SEU) (2002) *Reducing Re-offending by Ex-prisoners*. London: Office of the Deputy Prime Minister.

Visher, C. A. and Travis, J. (2003) 'Transitions from prison to community: understanding individual pathways', *Annual Review of Sociology*, 29: 89–113.

Chapter 6

PS Plus: a prison (lately) probation-based employment resettlement model

Andrew Cole, Ian Galbraith, Philippa Lyon and Heather Ross

Introduction

Unlike so many innovative projects developed in what are loosely regarded as 'partnerships' (Crawford 1998) between the Prison and Probation Services, PS Plus has emerged successful as a national prison-probation based employment programme which is part funded by the European Union. The project has evolved through a number of stages since it began as 'Head Start'. 'Head Start' was originally based at HMYOI Thorn Cross in the North West of England and focused on employment for young offenders upon release from prison. In 2000, 'Head Start' received funding from the European Social Fund (ESF) to expand into two additional prisons in the area. During this time, it forged strong links with community-based support services offering employment, training and educational placements for offenders. In 2002, a successful bid was made to ESF by the North West Prison Service area which resulted in the formation of PS Plus. The aim of PS Plus is outlined in its mission statement:

> PS Plus exists to enable offenders to become employable through identifying and removing barriers so they can lead law abiding lives in the community. (PS Plus Mission Statement 2006)

Currently, PS Plus provides services to around 50,000 offenders in 39 prisons and 15 probation areas. It aims to increase offenders' employability and assist them to find work and housing.

This chapter describes the three phases of development of PS Plus since 2002. It explores some of the challenges faced by the project, including its operation in a multi-agency environment and its application across a range of establishments. It focuses on four key aspects of the project: employment brokerage, motivational work, resettlement of women and 'through the gate' work which is supporting ex-prisoners post-imprisonment. Finally, it reflects upon the experiences of implementation and operation of the project in order to highlight best practice and lessons learnt, particularly focusing on how the PS Plus model works alongside and influences models of offender management evolving currently under the new National Offender Management Service (NOMS).

The project's evolution

A number of reports bear out PS Plus's emphasis on employment as a vehicle to reduce reoffending (CIPD 2004, 2006; HMIP 2001; SEU 2002; Webster *et al.* 2001). In response to these reports, the Prison Service produced a new resettlement policy which enhanced the role of the service in the resettlement of prisoners (HMPS 2001). It was within this context that PS Plus 1, a £28 million programme jointly funded by ESF and the Prison Service, was established primarily to tackle not only issues of employment, training and education (ETE) but also accommodation. It operated between 2002 and 2004 in 28 prisons and worked with 17,000 offenders.

During PS Plus 1 the problems of focusing on one element of service delivery, in this case employment, were recognised. It was soon accepted that no one factor contributed entirely to enabling offenders to gain employment. As research reviews (see McGuire 1995) have pointed out, success, in terms of reducing reoffending, requires a holistic pattern of interventions to support offenders. Therefore PS Plus expansion plans redefined its objective to concentrate not only on providing employment opportunities, but also on offering services which concentrated on improving the employability of offenders. In 2004, the National Offender Management Service (NOMS) made a further bid to the ESF which resulted in the formation of PS Plus 2. PS Plus 2 had a budget of £60 million and expanded its service provision to an additional eleven prisons and introduced a 'through the gate' service in partnership with the National Probation Service. This was an important development which enabled the introduction of the probation model in April 2006. Fifteen probation areas provided a wide range of employment and employability projects in the community. In 2007, PS Plus 3 replaced PS Plus 2 incorporating both the PS Plus prison and probation models. PS Plus 3 also changed the way in which employment services are delivered to prisoners. The brokerage of employment opportunities moved from individual case managers and specialist ETE brokers working inside prisons to a centralised 'brokerage team' working in the community.

PS Plus is primarily a series of projects delivering resettlement services to offenders. However, it continuingly seeks innovative and diverse ways of developing best practice which can be incorporated into mainstream provision. In the following sections, we elaborate on some of the key features of the project, highlight some of the challenges and draw some conclusions about how resettlement practice can be most effectively developed.

Employment, training and education

Building on recommendations contained in the Social Exclusion Unit's report (SEU 2002), ETE provision is delivered in all PS Plus prison establishments and probation areas. ETE has been the core business of the project since the beginning and all offenders taking part in PS Plus receive assistance with ETE to increase their employability. Improving employability of offenders is the main aim of PS Plus and it primarily works with prisoners nearing the end of their prison sentences and offenders in the community. The original aim of PS Plus was to find employment for prisoners but it became apparent that this was unrealistic for many offenders. The majority face multiple barriers to work, including poor work history, drug or alcohol addiction, a lack of basic skills and unsuitable or no accommodation (SEU 2002). Over half of all offenders have no qualifications (HMIP 2001) and ex-offenders are at least eight times more likely to be unemployed than anyone else in the community (ALI 2006). Together with accommodation, these factors have the greatest impact on reducing the likelihood of committing further offences (SEU 2002). This has been recognised by policymakers and outlined as follows:

> Ex-offenders are drawn disproportionately from the most socially excluded groups in society. By tackling the educational, housing and health inequalities they suffer from, we can help them to

re-establish themselves and contribute back to society. (Home Office 2005a: 5)

The PS Plus 2 model and all subsequent PS Plus projects aim to address all barriers to employment via a range of interventions, in order to increase the likelihood of obtaining work on release. PS Plus does not deliver all the interventions. Instead it works in partnership with other organisations, for example education courses are provided by OLASS (Offender Learning and Skills Service). By coordinating activity PS Plus staff ensure that offenders' chances of securing employment, training or education on release are maximised.

The PS Plus model incorporates an individual in-depth assessment with prisoners. Case managers oversee cases, coordinating interventions and making referrals to ETE brokers at appropriate points in offenders' sentences. They use all available information on offenders, including the Offender Assessment System (OASys), the PS Plus assessment and the Community Integration Plan (CIP). The CIP is a resettlement-focused action plan created individually for offenders which documents the priority employability actions and the referrals required to move towards agreed goals. The CIP is regularly reviewed by the case managers and summaries are provided to community agencies managing cases after release. These systems are used to determine appropriate ETE opportunities. Intervention work includes all aspects of ETE, from CV writing and mock interviews to brokering ETE interviews and securing placements.

Offenders work with ETE brokers to identify employment needs and plans for release. ETE brokers ensure that offenders' employment choices are realistic and attainable but discuss pertinent issues with them. For example, many offenders are unclear about how much information they are required to disclose to prospective employers. Consequently, they are provided with advice about disclosure and explanatory information on the Rehabilitation of Offenders Act 1974. Additionally, offenders are often unrealistic about the salaries they can expect or do not consider the risk implications of their offence on employment options. ETE brokers ensure that offenders are ready to enter the labour market via the use of motivational techniques or programmes, job clubs, preparation for work sessions and the provision of general advice and guidance, as well as by assisting offenders to prepare applications and secure job interviews.

An important element of PS Plus is the Beneficiary Access Fund (BAF). This is a dedicated budget used to improve the employability of PS Plus offenders by funding courses and providing appropriate equipment or other employment-related expenses. The aim is to ensure that offenders are not excluded from specific jobs because they lack suitable qualifications or equipment (particularly for self-employment). Examples of how the BAF has been used include the purchase of catering, hairdressing and construction based equipment, the funding of forklift truck training and subsequent licences and the purchase of site safety passports.

PS Plus strives to engage with employers, although this is difficult on a national basis as there is no central mechanism for making contact. Instead, ETE brokers work separately towards building a 'bank' of employers willing to employ ex-offenders. Additionally, employers are often approached individually to secure one job at a time. One of the aims of PS Plus 3 is to ensure a more effective approach to employers' engagement which will challenge recruitment policies and raise the awareness of employers about hiring offenders. This builds on available evidence that employers are often reluctant to employ offenders:

> Many recruiters have stereotypical attitudes about offenders which serve as a source of prejudice and as a barrier to their effective recruitment. Offenders are often deemed to be unreliable, untrustworthy and a serious threat to employees, customers and clients. (Fletcher *et al.* 2001: 40)

This development work during PS Plus 3 will consider the needs of employers and what they regard as suitable qualifications and work experience. It will also take account of local employment needs in order to ensure suitable jobs are found for offenders.

Overall, PS Plus has assisted offenders to gain employment and resettle in communities. Of the 17,000 offenders who participated in PS Plus 1, all increased their employability skills and over 2,400 offenders were in receipt of an ETE outcome on their release from prison. In addition, 165 new businesses were started by ex-prisoners who enrolled on the project. PS Plus 2 worked with over 31,000 offenders, with over 3,200 ETE outcomes secured. The total number of 'soft' outcomes[1] was over 28,400.

A number of further developments are planned during PS Plus 3. There is an increasing emphasis on the sustainability of outcomes which should assist in meeting the ongoing objective of reducing reoffending. A more proactive approach to engaging with potential employers will be developed by the centralised employment brokerage centre. It is also envisaged that offenders will be able to improve their 'workshop' skills by encouraging them to undertake work experience while still in custody or on licence. Further emphasis will be placed on supporting offenders' learning journeys through the transition from custody to community, providing continuity and increasing opportunities to complete qualifications.

Motivation plays a key role in ensuring that offenders continue to engage with the project and improve their employability. The work which PS Plus undertakes requires commitment and determination on the part of offenders, which cannot be provided by project staff. If offenders are motivated to change their circumstances, the chances of them engaging successfully to increase employability are greater. The next section outlines how the motivation of offenders is central to achieving the aims of PS Plus.

Motivation

A key challenge of PS Plus has been to explore ways of increasing offenders' motivation and engagement with resettlement provision. The PS Plus project includes a structured motivational approach, recognising that offenders' resettlement involves a complex interplay of personal and social risk factors in which offenders play active parts. Therefore, at the core of the project, is an emphasis on supporting offenders in their progress towards release and particularly on assisting the key transition from custody to community.

In order to facilitate change, PS Plus aims to link explanatory social factors with well documented cognitive behavioural factors underpinning many offending behaviour change programmes such as problem-solving skills, motivational and attitudinal change and goal-setting (HMPS 2004). It doing so, it combines work with both offenders' thinking and their social circumstances (Raynor and Maguire 2006). Furthermore, it considers motivation to change to be a dynamic rather than static concept dependent upon both internal and external factors (Prochaska and DiClemente 1982). In short, if the cognitive motivational foundations (i.e. desire and self-efficacy to change) are not present then practical resettlement support, for example job brokerage, is likely to be ineffective or unsustainable (HMPS 2004).

This section describes the range of motivational work piloted within the PS Plus model and the links between motivational work and other aspects of the model, in particular its ETE provision, and identifies elements which will be incorporated into future projects.

Developing a framework

Acknowledging the role of motivation in the change process, PS Plus adopted Prochaska and DiClemente's (1982) 'trans-theoretical model of change' as an appropriate framework for explaining the process of behavioural change. The model suggests that the process of change requires movement through a cyclical progression of six stages: 'pre-contemplation' (whereby change may have not even been considered as an option) via 'contemplation', 'decision' and 'action' through to the 'maintenance' of sustained behavioural change with less conscious effort. The final stage, 'lapse' recognises the reality that setbacks occur once maintenance has been achieved, and for some this will result in a shift back to an earlier stage in the cycle. Despite this integrative model's popular usage in the context of problem health behaviours such as smoking cessation and drug use (Prochaska *et al.* 1992), the basic concepts lend themselves well to wider examples of behavioural change including offenders' resettlement.

Using the 'Stages of Change' framework as a foundation, motivational work within PS Plus has encompassed two key strands: the development of motivational techniques for all PS Plus intervention staff and the delivery of two cognitive motivational programmes by dedicated facilitators. They are the Focus on Resettlement (FOR A Change) intervention and the shorter A–Z Programmes. Both interventions are designed to increase offenders' engagement with resettlement and are discussed in more detail later in this section.

Equipping project staff with the skills to support personal transition and change within the PS Plus model is pivotal. Case managers are allocated offenders initially. They in turn assign offenders to appropriate pathways within PS Plus after conducting a comprehensive assessment of their employability needs. The assessment is carried out on a one-to-one basis to accurately assess current levels of motivation and to begin prioritising needs and suitable intervention. Case managers are responsible for coordinating offenders' cases from assessment to release before handing over to probation-based link workers when offenders leave prison.

The 'Stages of Change' model and the motivational interviewing techniques developed by Miller and Rollnick (1991) were invaluable organisational development tools to PS Plus, with additional benefits for offenders. Adopting the framework provided project staff with meaningful and accessible understanding of the dynamics of personal change. It gave them the tools to deal with specific issues such as offenders' ambivalence. For example, many offenders say they would like a job but are ambivalent about actually getting one because of the perceived impact of their criminal records on employers or thinking they would be better off financially if they were unemployed. Project staff are equipped to challenge and work proactively with ambivalence. They use specific techniques to help offenders weigh up the advantages and perceived disadvantages of personal change and develop contingencies to reset goals and remain 'on track' after a setback. Equally, the approach means that referrals for specific ETE interventions are targeted at the appropriate point in sentences when offenders are ready and motivated to progress their goals and plans and move from decision-making to actual action (e.g. completing an application form).

Five PS Plus Development Managers became trainers in a 'Motivational Interviewing Toolkit' developed by the National Probation Service (Fuller and Taylor 2003) and they cascaded the training to all PS Plus intervention staff (case managers, employment, training and education and housing advice staff) at the 39 PS Plus 2 prison establishments. The training proved successful as evidenced by structured feedback and an internal evaluation (PS Plus 2005). The toolkit gave staff an underlying framework and an opportunity to develop and reflect on their own motivational style of working, despite many stating they already used such techniques. The evaluation report noted particularly that the training highlighted the complex nature of change processes within custodial environments and more realistic ways of dealing with events such as the refusal of Home Detention Curfew or planned accommodation for release falling through. A follow-up exercise six weeks after the training demonstrated that staff had become much more attuned to working in a motivational style (PS Plus 2005).

Understanding the significance of evaluation and monitoring, PS Plus collates a considerable amount of data and is keen to ensure that potential changes in recorded motivational levels are captured and evidenced. The Case Assessment and Tracking System (CATS) enables the project to do this.[2] The CATS was adapted to incorporate motivation data at the start of offenders' time on the project and to measure their employability journey. Offenders' motivational level is recorded by case managers following initial assessment and at each review by selecting the appropriate stage of change button on the database with supporting notes explaining why the level of change has been selected. The final update takes place prior to a pre-release case conference which occurs three weeks before prisoners are released. A positive change in motivational level, as indicated by movement through the stages, has been recorded for many offenders (PS Plus 2005).

Changes in motivation linked to PS Plus have also been found by Lowton (2006). She undertook interviews with a small sample of women who completed the FOR programme as part of PS Plus in North West England. Lowton (2006) found that the women had made positive changes to their lives since being on the programme. The women reported that problem-solving and goal-setting skills taught on FOR had helped to structure their resettlement plans and increased levels of confidence and feelings of control in their future. The results of this study also assisted in tailoring PS Plus interventions to the needs of female offenders discussed later in this chapter.

FOR A Change and A–Z programmes with PS Plus

Having introduced an overarching framework and model of personal change and motivation for both offenders and staff, PS Plus 2 included the delivery of two structured personal change interventions for offenders, namely the FOR A Change and A–Z Programmes, which were undertaken in partnership with the Offending Behaviour Programmes Unit (OBPU) of HM Prison Service. FOR is a 12-session groupwork programme with one-to-one elements designed to increase the motivation of offenders to become more proactive participants in realising their agenda for change. Targeted at those in the last three to four months of their sentences, it explores and develops offenders' thinking styles, problem-solving and goal setting towards resettlement.

Two resettlement 'pathfinder' evaluations (Lewis *et al.* 2003; Clancy *et al.* 2006) looked at the delivery and some interim outcomes from the FOR programme. These evaluations provided some encouraging evidence of the contribution this intervention makes to resettlement work. The more recent of the two studies focused on the post-release experience and the effect of FOR once offenders return to the community, including the impact on changes in employment status post-release compared with pre-imprisonment. It found positive changes as a result of participation in the programme (Clancy *et al.* 2006).

PS Plus delivery of the programme may also attest to some success of the FOR programme. Following the recruitment and training of a team of dedicated programme facilitators and treatment managers, the FOR programme was successfully delivered at three male prisons and one female prison between August 2005 and October

2006. A number of psychometric measures taken before and after the programme, including treatment motivation scores, attitudes to crime and stages of change data, are currently contributing to larger outcome studies being carried out by the Offending Behaviour Programmes Unit (OBPU) of HM Prison Service to assess the impact of the programme. These scientific psychometric measures complement more subjective ratings of motivational change made by the PS Plus case managers who regularly update the CATS database with evidence of perceived changes in offenders' motivational level. A visual comparison of the CATS data held on those undertaking the FOR programme revealed positive movement in motivational change while on the project, particularly if this was near to the end of sentences. Anecdotal evidence from programme participants and statements in their programme workbooks supported motivational change and the effect of FOR. However, in the absence of more rigorous experimental analysis, caution must be taken in attributing such a change solely to completion of the programme.

A key feature of the FOR programme which has provided valuable 'additionality' to the PS Plus model is the 'marketplace' session. This involves relevant agencies from the prison and community coming to hold a 'market' for their services in prisons. This enables FOR participants to discuss their resettlement release plans in more detail. The 'marketplace' demonstrates a clear example of best practice whereby effective programme components are clearly integrated with the PS Plus model. The 'marketplace' initiative provides offenders and ETE staff with a number of opportunities including being able to build upon the planning and contacts already made, consolidating the progress achieved so far through the face-to-face interaction and providing additional resettlement options in some cases. Feedback from those involved has been extremely positive. Offenders valued the opportunity to meet with a range of potential community support agencies while agencies welcomed the opportunity to contact offenders and prison resettlement staff and also the chance to network with each other.

The PS Plus experience of FOR has been positive and has demonstrated encouraging findings, particularly where early contact with the emerging NOMS system of community-based Offender Managers was established and the lessons learnt from FOR featured in the community supervision plan. A crucial element of FOR is its translation into the community and to this end work was undertaken to track participants once released on licence. Follow-up telephone interviews by the PS Plus FOR facilitators with community-based Offender Managers reported perceived increases in offenders' motivation following completion of the programme and positive changes to lifestyles following release attributable in part to participation in the programme. Furthermore, in the majority of cases, Offender Managers also reported that positive resettlement outcomes secured via PS Plus while in custody, for example employment and training, were successfully maintained in the community.

A–Z (denoting a journey) is targeted at those at the beginning of the motivational change cycle and is shorter and less structured than FOR. Its success within PS Plus has been demonstrated by changes in psychometrics and participants' personal accounts of change. Of specific note has been the positive effect of A–Z on shorter sentenced prisoners and those on remand where less time is available to undertake work. It has been particularly popular with female offenders who present with real challenges in terms of self-esteem and their ability to effect personal change (Lowton 2006).

Future initiatives

The use of the 'Stages of Change' framework and the various motivational techniques employed within PS Plus 2 remain an integral part of PS Plus 3. PS Plus key workers in prison establishments will continue to use motivational interviewing to ensure that motivational levels are appropriately assessed. Developments in the PS Plus 3 prison model will include the delivery of the 'Thinking Skills in the Workplace' programme developed and trialled by IMPACT, an ESF-funded employability action research project based in the North West. The five-session programme will introduce basic cognitive behavioural principles such as problem-solving but within the context of the workplace. A key feature of the intervention is motivational work delivered through either one-to-one motivational techniques or the WorkWise group programme as delivered within the probation Pathfinder areas.

The continuation of motivational work within the PS Plus model demonstrates the commitment of the project to approaching employability in the broader sense and to making an integrated contribution to offender management. Having incorporated a clear theoretical yet practical framework, the motivational and engagement work with offenders provides a firm and responsive basis on which to build the more focused interventions with employment, training and education. PS Plus 1 work specifically with women seems to have borne this out and is discussed in the next section.

PS Plus work with women

The evolution of PS Plus has also included innovation with motivational work with women offenders. Experiences in two women's prisons in PS Plus 1 ensured that the model would be delivered in six women's prisons during PS Plus 2. The target for employment outcomes were slightly lower in the female estate but the focus was necessarily on increasing employability and gaining employment as determined by the funding source. This threw up a potential problem as it was assumed that it was not possible to properly address employability issues with women prisoners because the range and complexity of personal issues resulted in employability coming far down their scales of priorities (Giordano *et al.* 2002; see Gelsthorpe and Sharpe, this volume, for further discussion).

In order to test this assumption and determine the most effective way to provide services to women a comprehensive literature review was undertaken of both published and unpublished research. This was complemented by internal data which were collected as part of mapping exercises and standards audits involving staff and prisoners. The structures used for this systematic review are comparable with those exposed by the EPPI-Centre (Gough and Elbourne 2002). Where possible the authors were contacted to confirm that valid interpretations had been made. Generally, the literature said very little about employability. Instead it tended to focus on general resettlement or process issues. Additionally, it involved very small samples. The key findings of the literature review were that: individual assessments should be carried out (Cruells and Igareda 2005); existing skills should be maintained (Scanlon and Thomas 2004); employment is a component of women prisoners' ideal self (Brookes and Leeming 2006); and employment should be addressed early in sentences (O'Keeffe 2003).

Internal data on women offenders' specific resettlement needs was gained through a mapping exercise at HMP Styal and a standards audit at HMP New Hall and HMP Morton Hall where the PS Plus prison model operated. The mapping exercise was part of a larger-scale data collection process to gather information to inform the development of a range of operational standards for the project and the audits were a review of practice against standards. Both exercises involved a number of in-depth interviews with PS Plus staff in the prisons. Additionally, the audit involved reading case records and interviews with prisoners. Thirteen staff and four women prisoners were interviewed. It was clear from the mapping and audit that housing need was a major barrier to resettlement and many prisoners had issues with alcohol, self-esteem, survival of sexual abuse, domestic violence, children being adopted or looked after and poor healthcare. Facilities to address these issues were limited or non-existent within the prisons. However, these issues were not seen as barriers to women prisoners wanting to or being able to improve their employability although it was likely that if appropriate facilities were in place to address them more effective resettlement would be achieved. Many of the women had no work experience. There were also significant numbers of older women who were first-time offenders with convictions for fraud. These prisoners tended to have relatively stable lives but required motivation, information, advice and guidance (Careers Advice) interventions. A high proportion of women were drug users but neither staff nor offenders saw this as a barrier to work.

A number of the staff had worked within both male and female prisons in PS Plus and the audit provided the opportunity to explore the differences encountered. They reported that the work in men's establishments was more focused but women had higher expectations of the help provided than men. The approach of men towards resettlement was described as modular so they would expect only employment assistance from employment workers and would limit information exchange with workers to employability-related information. By contrast, the approach of women was described as generic. They would regard any worker as capable of assisting with the entire range of issues they faced and would try and engage with them in a holistic way. This reinforced the key message from surveys and studies of women's multiple and complex resettlement needs (see Brookes and Leeming 2006; Corston 2007).

Efforts were also made to compare our review of information relating to women prisoners with the general literature available on working with women in the community. Again the information available was limited in that most research had looked at particular concepts such as 'glass ceilings' rather than issues which were relevant to the majority of released prisoners. The literature suggested that the interdependence of the issues facing women was crucial as Jenkins (2004: 165) commented:

Only through gaining an understanding of the local social and cultural interdependence which impacts on women's decision making processes will we be able to understand and take account of them.

Other researchers identified the higher importance of social factors and work/life balance issues for young women in making career choices (Eaton 1993; Giordano *et al.* 2002).

Two major conclusions were drawn from our review of current knowledge: namely that, women prisoners can be worked with effectively to increase their employability and employment on release; and the resettlement of women prisoners is best dealt with in a holistic way by generic workers. While the first conclusion was encouraging, the second presented problems as PS Plus 2 was locked into a structure which involved a number of specialist staff interacting with individual prisoners.[3] In order to address these structural difficulties, a training package was devised and delivered to all PS Plus staff and their managers working in women's prisons. It was based on delivering information on the review (summarised above) and then facilitating discussions of the implications for both establishment teams and for specialist workers (case management, employment, housing and management). This focused on how to take forward the learning from the review and use it to deliver employment work to women in the most effective way within the constraints that existed. The results were better than hoped.

In 2006, an analysis of the contribution of PS Plus to the overall achievement of employment outcomes in prison establishments was carried out. It revealed that the proportion of those who completed PS Plus and obtained work was slightly greater for women (27 per cent) than for men (22 per cent), although there were significant variations between establishments. The variations in the women's establishments appeared to be linked to the length of stay of prisoners: the lower the throughput, the higher the success rate in obtaining employment. No similar linkage was found in prisons for men. The analysis also demonstrated differences between male and female establishments in the contribution PS Plus made to employment outcomes. In women's establishments, PS Plus contributed 77 per cent of establishments' employment outcomes but only 24 per cent for men. This suggests that the employability of women can be improved by targeted interventions. Whether these successes can be achieved for other project innovations, including the 'through the gate' approach, is explored in the next section.

Through the gate and the NOMS era

The changes made in PS Plus 2 were structured by the lessons learnt in PS Plus 1. The PS Plus 2 prison-based model was expanded to incorporate probation staff and developed into an additional model of practice. This resulted in a number of challenges. Although PS Plus and seconded probation staff liaised with probation colleagues there remained an obvious gap in continuity in the level of dedicated provision for offenders in the community which had also been identified by the HM Inspectorate of Prisons and Probation (2001: 5). Its report stated:

> ... there needs to be much better liaison between prisons and probation area ... we do not believe that either service (prison or probation) makes best use of the resources that are available within the community or in partnership with non-governmental organisations.

To address this situation two challenges had to be overcome. The first stemmed from a lack of communication and information sharing. A process of information exchange was developed between the Prison Service, National Probation Service and PS Plus. Specific PS Plus assessments and plans, along with current risk of harm information which may influence employability, were shared. As the project grew the level of liaison and complexity of information exchange were refined to a high standard. However, the second challenge relating to dedicated resources provided by the Probation Service was less manoeuvrable. A key principle of PS Plus is the 'one-to-one' bespoke intervention which provides services to offenders and to the geographic areas they return to. It is widely recognised that there is a critical time frame when motivation and other external factors may adversely affect the potential of offenders to remain offence-free and follow up the employment or training opportunities arranged by PS Plus while in custody. However, despite acknowledging its importance, probation areas have been unable to provide services during the crucial time immediately after release due to resourcing issues. The situation is now changing. The creation of NOMS and the Offender Management Model (NOMS 2005) has increased the commitment of the Probation Service to work more closely with PS Plus. This has occurred partly as a result of the requirement to meet targets in respect of employment and partly as a result of the National Probation Directorate (NPD) 'Employment Pathfinder' programme. As the pathfinders ended probation areas already involved wanted to build on their experiences while other areas wanted to develop their ETE programmes for offenders. Contemporaneously, PS Plus 2 was developing its community model which allowed joint working to be established.

Two models converge

These developments also provided the opportunity to address the gap in the offenders' journey from custody to community and provided the space for PS Plus and the Probation Service to work together in closing the gap. In order to do this PS Plus established a pilot programme initially with three probation areas: Cambridgeshire, Cheshire and Greater Manchester. The purpose of the pilot was to test out the viability of a 'through the gate' community-based model in terms of both practice and process. Vital to the model was a direct commitment by PS Plus and the Probation Service to work with offenders throughout their sentence and on release in the community. The flow of information had to be both common and available to each organisation. To achieve a working model a range of information, research and alternative models were used to inform the development. The Offender Manager Model was a key input along with the use of a nationally recognised assessment tool, the Offender Assessment System (OASys).

A PS Plus prison-probation model of ETE delivery was established under ESF rules and in conjunction with the Prison Service, NPD and NOMS. Each probation area dedicated staff to working with prisoners on PS Plus programmes. The customised model gave an opportunity for community-based staff to meet offenders while in custody (travel and distance permitting), share in the development of the offenders' targets for release and, ultimately, work with offenders through the crucial time frame upon release.

The pilot proved to be an onerous piece of work involving two large organisations in the criminal justice field. It came at a time when both Prison and Probation Services were reforming under NOMS and their practices were being reshaped within a new general working model of the 'seamless sentence' (first enunciated in the Criminal Justice Act 1991). The main difficulties related to the implementation of the PS Plus prison-probation model were different IT systems and varying policies, priorities and budgets. Furthermore, probation areas were preoccupied with the implementation of the Offender Management Model which requires Offender Managers to assess offenders and determine the type and level of interventions for offenders. Each area developed working systems and procedures to ensure that PS Plus interventions were compatible with Offender

Managers' decisions. At the time of the pilot, probation areas agreed to work with prisoners serving less than 12 months in preparation for the arrival of 'Custody Plus'. But its subsequent suspension has simplified the PS Plus prison-probation model as it can concentrate on working with longer-term prisoners.

The pilot was successful in three main areas. Firstly, it provided for the four 'C's in the Offender Manager Model – consistency, continuity, consolidation, and commitment (NOMS 2005). Secondly, a joint model of assessment and electronic transfer of information was established and, thirdly, it was the only intervention which provided a 'seamless' move from custody to community, ensuring a much needed level of input by the Probation Service in the community which hitherto had been unavailable. In May 2006, 12 further probation areas began to work with PS Plus using the key principles of the pilot. All 15 areas have now tailored the model to fit their specific requirements in terms of their geographic and offender populations. Using the common assessment form and CATS case management system each area has developed its own bespoke model. The majority of areas have expanded it to work with offenders on licence, community orders and unpaid work. Many have developed new initiatives working with partner agencies.

Developments in the 15 probation areas mean that PS Plus has a greater scope of work with offenders. For probation areas the partnership with PS Plus has assisted their work under the Offender Employment Strategy by providing a framework of assessment and case management in conjunction with the National Probation Directorate's (NPD) 'Motivational Interviewing Tool Kit' (Fuller and Taylor 2003). Currently PS Plus provides a direct link to the introduction of employment targets by the NPD and NOMS while building on the 'What Works' approach. It also allows both the Prison and Probation Services to work together towards resettling offenders. The PS Plus project offers a practical model to assist probation areas in attaining their employment targets while equipping offenders with the long-term tools to gain sustained employment. For the Prison Service the community side of the model provides for more accurate and realistic resettlement outcomes. The model is also assisting the development of the roll-out of Offender Management Units in all prison establishments.

Concluding comments

The evolution of PS Plus as a very large-scale resettlement project engaging both prisons and probation areas working together in the first NOMS project has at times been tortuous. Nevertheless, it has provided large numbers of offenders with access to employment and training and has helped reduce offending. Four key elements contribute to its effectiveness.

First and foremost is the philosophy that any work with offenders, particularly with regard to resettlement, must be on an individual basis. All interventions offered by PS Plus are needs led, meaning that services are tailored to meet the needs of individuals rather than attempting to fit them into existing frameworks. In this way the project ensures that offenders receive the most appropriate assistance available and that the project is responsive to the diverse nature of the offenders it serves. There is a strong emphasis on education and upskilling to ensure that offenders are adequately qualified and prepared for employment. They also receive the advice, assistance and interventions required to make them job ready. By offering education, training and employment support along with supplying information, advice and guidance, PS Plus is also directly responding to the Government's recommendations set out in the Green Paper (Home Office 2005b: 12).

> The Government is committed to a strong programme to improve offenders' educational attainment, raise skill levels and secure better employment outcomes.

The second element is the central role motivation plays in underpinning all service activities or provision. PS Plus has demonstrated that support for offenders and training of staff is essential and also that offenders' motivational levels need to be recorded and tracked. The CATS database acts as an assessment tool and enables changes in motivational levels to be tracked in order to highlight when further work is required with individual offenders. In this way, assessments become part of service provision and not simply contributions to targets or an end in themselves.

The third and most successful aspect of PS Plus has been the approach to partnership working, both by creating good working relationships with other agencies internally and externally to the project and by working in partnership to deliver PS Plus. PS Plus interventions have always been delivered via voluntary sector providers, including SOVA[4] and Nacro[5] and in conjunction with other areas such as accommodation and risk management. This approach has allowed staff to sequence interventions appropriately. The fourth element of success is a useable IT system.

PS Plus has also faced a number of key challenges. One of the initial challenges was to integrate PS Plus into prisons, many of which already had existing resettlement provision for offenders. PS Plus was fortunate to have a large budget, governmental support and the genuine commitment of the major stakeholders. Few, if any projects, can realistically expect to have all these elements. In addition, a selling point for PS Plus was the holistic approach to resettlement services which most prisons were not able to offer. A European Social Fund (ESF) requirement is that all the services delivered must provide 'additionality' to existing services, thus enabling prison governors to increase provision within an establishment. In many establishments, the arrival of PS Plus allowed resettlement services to become more rounded and offer a wider range of interventions to prepare prisoners for release.

The main aim of PS Plus 1 was to get offenders into employment. Widened parameters in PS Plus 2 enabled staff to assist the harder to help offenders prepare for work after release, even if they were not job ready at the end of the project. In this way ETE provision could also focus on 'soft' outcomes. This was an important development for PS Plus, as all offenders on the project could show distance travelled even if employment was not secured immediately. PS Plus 2 prepared offenders for entry into the labour market and there was a focus on developing personal motivation to work. This also aligned effectively with one of the four key priorities of the National Employment Panel (NEP 2004). Yet some initiatives of the project were not successful. Mentoring by volunteers had been available in the first phase of PS Plus but did not continue thereafter because of operational difficulties. Staff reported that the mentoring had been highly valued and that it had been significant in gaining and sustaining employment on release. However, the processes involved in engaging prisoners with appropriate schemes were too time-consuming to be practical.

Having substantial funding to allow a project to go through such evolutionary phases has been a challenge in itself. However, its evolution and many internal audits have reaped many benefits to the structure of offenders' resettlement. The bringing together of Prison and Probation Services under NOMS to deliver services in a coordinated way is a significant challenge which PS Plus has met only because its evolution has enabled practice to develop throughout the phases of the project. Among other challenges has been engagement with employers which needs to be made more effective if it is to have a real impact on offenders' employment. Working strategically with major national employers and on an individual basis with small numbers of offenders both have limited impact. The development of a centralised brokerage team seeks to explore an alternative approach and supports the government's Offender Skills and Employment: What Next? agenda (DfES 2007).

An evolutionary project like PS Plus also provides a valuable evidence base of effective practice. It is currently being evaluated independently by the Institute of Criminal Policy Research (ICPR forthcoming 2007). The evaluation identifies the value of ETE and accommodation interventions in obtaining appropriate outcomes and a number of issues which need to be addressed in the development of further programmes of this nature. The ultimate challenge for PS Plus and for resettlement of offenders generally is to ensure that NOMS provides the necessary structure to enable effective resettlement practice to evolve.

Notes

1 Subjectively measured achievements such as increased confidence or self-esteem, but it also includes participation in activities to improve employability, e.g. job club.
2 This IT database provides a comprehensive assessment, case management, tracking and collation of statistical data service for the project. It also has a major advantage of immediate electronic transfer as beneficiaries move between establishments or through the gate. In this way the project is able to provide coordinated services across the prison estate and into the community in a way which was not previously possible and overcame two major hurdles facing many innovative programmes working with offenders in prison. The first is that good work can be lost if prisoners transfer to another establishment where the programme does not exist or have no accompanying records to state where they are in the programme's process. The other is the importance of continuity of service into the community (Maguire and Raynor, 1997; Clancy et al., 2006).
3 PS Plus 3 has since addressed this by having a single 'key worker' with direct contact with prisoners.
4 SOVA (works to strengthen communities by involving local volunteers in promoting social inclusion and reducing crime).
5 Nacro (National Association for the Care and Resettlement of Offenders) is an independent voluntary organisation working to prevent crime by

developing and implementing effective approaches to tackling crime and dealing constructively with offenders.

References

ALI (2006) *Recruitment with Conviction*. London: Ofsted. (See www.ofsted. gov.uk/assets/Internet_Content/Shared_Content/Migration/ali/ recruitmntconv_ali.pdf).

Brookes, L. and Leeming, J. (2006) *Reviewing the Barriers to Resettlement for Female Offenders Serving Short-term Sentences*. West Sussex: IMPACT.

Chartered Institute of Personnel Development (2004) *Employing Offenders: A Practical Guide*. London: CIPD.

Chartered Institute of Personnel Development (2006) *Employers and Offenders: Reducing Crime through Work and Rehabilitation*. London: CIPD.

Clancy, A., Hudson, K., Maguire, M., Peake, R., Raynor, P., Vanstone, M. and Kynch, J. (2006) *Improving Resettlement: The Second Phase Pathfinders*. Bristol: Policy Press.

Corston, J. (2007) *The Corston Report: A Report by Baroness Jean Corston of a Review of Women with Particular Vulnerabilities in the Criminal Justice System*. London: Home Office.

Crawford, A. (1998) *Crime Prevention and Community Safety: Politics, Policies and Practice*. Harlow: Longman.

Cruells, M. and Igareda, N. (eds) (2005) *Women, Integration and Prison*. Barcelona: Aurea Editores.

Department for Education and Skills (2007) *Offenders Learning and Skills*. Available at: www.dfes.gov.uk/offenderlearning/index.cfm?flash=1.

Eaton, M. (1993) 'Mitigating circumstances: familiar rhetoric', *International Journal of Sociology of Law*, 11: 385-400.

Fletcher, D.R., Taylor, A., Hughes, S. and Breeze, J. (2001) *Recruiting and Employing Ex-offenders*. York: York Publishing Services, in association with the Joseph Rowntree Foundation.

Fuller, S. and Taylor, C. (2003) *Toolkit of Motivational Skills: A Practice Handbook for using Motivational Skills in the Work of the Probation Service*. London: National Probation Service.

Giordano, P., Cernkovich, S. and Rudolph, J. (2002) 'Gender, crime and desistance: towards a theory of cognitive transformation', *American Journal of Sociology*, 107 (4): 990–1064.

Gough, D. and Elbourne, D. (2002) 'Systematic research synthesis to inform policy, practice and democratic debate', *Social Policy and Society*, 1 (3): 225–36.

Her Majesty's Inspectorates of Prisons and Probation (2001) *Through The Prison Gate – A Joint Thematic Review*. London: Home Office.

Her Majesty's Prison Service (HMPS) (2001) *Prison Service Order 2003 Resettlement*. London: Home Office.

Her Majesty's Prison Service (HMPS) (2004) *FOR Programme Theory Manual.* London: Home Office

Home Office (2005a) *The National Reducing Reoffending Delivery Plan.* London: Home Office.

Home Office (2005b) *Reducing Re-offending through Skills and Employment.* Green Paper, London: Home Office.

Institute for Criminal Policy Research (ICPR) (2007) *Coming Through: An Evaluation of the PS Plus 2 Programme.* London: ICPR

Jenkins, S. (2004) *Gender, Place and the Labour Market.* Aldershot: Ashgate.

Lewis, S., Vennard, J., Maguire, M., Raynor, P., Vanstone, M., Raybould, S. and Rix, A. (2003) *The Resettlement of Short-Term Prisoners: An Evaluation of Seven Pathfinder Programmes,* Home Office Occasional Paper No. 83. London: Home Office.

Lowton, J.E. (2006) 'A Qualitative Analysis of the Focus on Resettlement (F.O.R A Change) Programme: A Participants' Perspective'. Unpublished MSc thesis.

McGuire, J. (ed.) (1995) *What Works: Reducing Reoffending.* Chichester: Wiley.

Maguire, M. and Raynor, P. (1997) 'The revival of throughcare: rhetoric and reality in automatic conditional release', *British Journal of Criminology,* 37 (1): 1–14.

Miller, W.R. and Rollnick, S. (1991) *Motivational Interviewing – Preparing People to Change Addictive Behaviour.* New York: Guildford Press.

National Employment Panel (2004) *Leading Change, Changing Lives.* London: NEP.

NOMS (2005) *The NOMS Offender Management Model.* London: NOMS. (See: www.probation2000.com/documents/NOMS%20Offender%20Management%20Model.pdf).

O'Keeffe, C. (2003) *Moving Mountains: Identifying and Addressing Barriers to Employment, Training and Education from the Voices of Women (ex) Offenders.* Sheffield: Sheffield Hallam University.

Prochaska, J.O. and DiClemente, C.C. (1982) 'Transtheoretical therapy: towards a more integrated model of change', *Psychotherapy: Theory, Research and Practice,* 19: 276–88.

Prochaska, J.O., DiClemente, C.C. and Norcross, J.C. (1992) 'In search of how people change: applications to addictive behaviours', *American Psychologist,* 47 (9): 1102–14.

PS Plus (2005) 'Six Week Evaluation of Motivational Interview Training'. Unpublished report.

Raynor, P. and Maguire, M. (2006) 'End-to-end or end in tears? Prospects for the effectiveness of the National Offender Management Model', in M. Hough, R. Allen and U. Padel (eds), *Reshaping Probation and Prisons: The New Offender Management Framework.* Bristol: Policy Press.

Scanlon, J. and Thomas, R. (2004) 'Needs Analysis'. HMP Buckley Hall (unpublished).

Social Exclusion Unit (2002) *Reducing Re-offending by Ex-prisoners*. London: Office of the Deputy Prime Minister.

Webster, R., Hedderman, C., Turnball, P. and May, T. (2001) *Building Bridges to Employment for Prisoners*, Research Study No. 226. London: Home Office.

Chapter 7

Accommodation and related services for ex-prisoners

Mike Maguire and Jane Nolan

... it is absolutely clear that appropriate housing is the single most important factor in preventing re-offending. (Allender *et al.* 2005a: 20)

Introduction

Accommodation has always been one of the main problems associated with leaving prison and a central focus of resettlement work (Clancy *et al.* 2006; Lewis *et al.* 2003, 2007; Maguire *et al.* 2000; NACRO 2000a). Not only do many prisoners have a background of homelessness or 'sofa surfing' and hence have no prior home to return to, but a significant proportion of those who had some form of stable accommodation lose it – together with most of their possessions – while in custody. The Social Exclusion Unit's (2002) report *Reducing Re-offending by Ex-prisoners* concluded that only about two-thirds of those entering prison did so from what they (euphemistically) called 'permanent' housing, and that around one-third lost previous accommodation as a result of their incarceration. Indeed, Carlisle (1996) found that over 50 per cent of a sample of prisoners were unable to return to their previous address. Moreover, finding suitable new accommodation is a task often complicated by problems in communicating with providers, lack of income, poor job prospects and the stigma of having been in prison. Particular difficulties are faced by certain types of offenders, notably female offenders, black and minority ethnic (BME) offenders, young prisoners, high-risk offenders and those with substance misuse and/or mental health problems (Allender *et al.* 2005b; Calverley *et al.* 2004, 2006; Farrant 2006; Maguire *et al.* 2007; NACRO 2000a 2001, 2002). Despite apparent – though to some extent cosmetic – improvements in the last two or three years, one in eight prisoners still leave custody with the status of 'no fixed abode' and many more leave with only emergency accommodation arranged.[1]

The consequences of these problems are damaging not only for the ex-prisoners concerned, but for society as a whole. The reoffending rates of people who leave prison homeless have been found to be up to twenty percentage points higher than those who leave with stable accommodation (SEU 2002; see also Home Office 2004a, 2004b; NACRO 2000b; Seymour 2006). Such figures cannot of course be taken to imply that helping ex-prisoners to obtain accommodation will per se reduce levels of reoffending: both the homelessness and the offending may be symptoms of other problems. However, what is clear is that if offenders lack a suitable place to live it is more difficult for them to get and keep a job, or to engage effectively with any rehabilitative interventions. In other words, attention to accommodation problems is a fundamental building block for efforts to reduce reoffending: a *necessary*, if not a *sufficient*, condition for the reduction of reoffending.

In this chapter, we discuss these issues in the light of a study we conducted in 2006 in the South West region of England, in which the aim was to explore the nature and extent of the accommodation (and accommodation-related) needs of ex-prisoners in the region and the extent to which current policy and provision were able to meet these needs (Maguire *et al.* 2007). The chapter is structured as follows. First, we outline housing problems which typically face ex-prisoners and the main reasons behind them: some of these problems, it is noted, are faced by numerous other young people, vulnerable people and people of limited means who have not been involved in crime, but they are multiplied and exacerbated by a prison sentence. We then look at the different kinds of accommodation which may be available to ex-prisoners, and at specific issues surrounding each of them. This is followed by brief comments on specific problems faced by female, young and minority ethnic offenders and on difficulties in housing high-risk offenders. Finally, we discuss some current policy initiatives and ideas about how the situation might be improved.

Context

The nature and scale of the difficulties facing ex-prisoners can be properly understood only within the broader context of developments in housing policy and the housing market in England and Wales. These have created major problems for many groups beyond ex-prisoners, and it is unrealistic to think that offenders' needs can be met simply though more effective policy or practice on the part of the Home Office or correctional service agencies – important though this is. Significant amelioration of accommodation problems for ex-prisoners, as for other socially excluded or vulnerable groups, can be achieved only through a growth in the availability of affordable housing, combined with fair and effective housing allocation and support services.

Since the early 1980s, council house building has been minimal and Right to Buy schemes have enabled council tenants to buy their own homes at a discounted rate, with the result that the UK now has the highest rate of home ownership in Europe. At the same time, house prices have risen to levels which make it difficult for first-time buyers to enter the market at all. For those unable to contemplate buying their own home, or with insufficient funds to rent a decent property in the private sector, the situation can be grim. In some parts of the country, especially in the more affluent south, shortages of social housing are acute and waiting lists long. This impacts particularly heavily on the single homeless, who have grown considerably in number but for whom appropriate types of property tend to be in very short supply (Allender *et al.* 2005a; Cowan and Fionda 1994). These include many vulnerable people with high support needs, some of whom would in the past have been accommodated in the large mental hospitals which were closed during the 1980s, and others with major substance misuse problems. They also, of course, include many ex-prisoners, among whom such needs are common. Frequently, the only options left involve them in an insecure lifestyle drifting between sleeping rough, night shelters, 'sofa surfing' and rented rooms in poor quality multiple occupancy housing.

While many prisoners and ex-prisoners face all the same accommodation problems as poor and vulnerable people without a criminal record, the extra factor of spending time in custody adds further major obstacles. Prisoners earn little money, reducing their purchasing power still further. They have limited opportunities for communicating with outside agencies, making it difficult to conclude firm accommodation arrangements before they are released.

Importantly, too, the 'stigma' of having been in prison is a major factor casting a cloud over any effort they may make to improve their employment prospects or living conditions. Despite some government moves to combat it, there is little doubt that conscious or unconscious discrimination against ex-offenders is still to be found among providers of social housing, as well as private (Cowan and Fionda 1994; Dodd and Alakeson 2006; Hickey 2002; Metcalf *et al.* 2001; Reid-Howie Associates 2004a, 2004b; Rolfe 2001).

Housing options for prisoners on release

There is a range of possible accommodation options for people coming out of prison, though the suitability and feasibility of each depends heavily on the individual's history, family circumstances, financial means, employment prospects, need for support, and so on. In order to paint as comprehensive a picture as possible, brief comments will be made about each of the main routes that are adopted and the key issues associated with each. They can be summarised as follows: returning to prior accommodation; temporary accommodation, with family or friends; registering as homeless to apply for social housing (council or housing association); acceptance by a supported housing scheme; private rental; leaving with 'no fixed abode' or heading for a night shelter or bed and breakfast.

Returning to prior accommodation

Given the current state of the housing market, the most obvious starting point for any accommodation policy for prisoners is to assist as many as possible to retain any housing they had prior to coming into custody. This is not necessarily a desirable (or even allowable) solution in every case – for example, prisoners may have been living with criminal associates or drug dealers, or may have committed offences against a partner or children living there. There are also many cases in which offenders or those advising them believe that the chances of rehabilitation would be increased by their moving to another part of the country and avoiding 'old haunts'. However, in general the goal of keeping prior accommodation is considered the best one to aim for.

The difficulties of doing so can be daunting. First of all, although only a minority of prisoners own their own homes, any that do will normally face an immediate problem of inability to maintain mortgage repayments while inside – or, indeed, a longer-term problem caused by reduced earning power after release. Previous studies have shown that, among such prisoners, a high proportion end up losing their houses through sale or repossession (see, for example, Carlisle 1996; Reid-Howie Associates 2004a, 2004b). This is partly explained by owner-occupiers losing their employment on going to prison and struggling to find work when discharged (Carlisle 1996).

More common is the problem of retaining previously rented property (council, housing association or private). This is easier for prisoners who have a partner living in the property, but even in this case the loss of household income may make it difficult to keep up payments. Many relationships also fail to survive the separation caused by imprisonment, in which case the option of returning is lost anyway. For single prisoners who were renting a room or flat prior to conviction, a long-standing problem – and the source of many lost tenancies – derives from the rule that Housing Benefit will be paid only up to 13 weeks from when they enter custody. This means that many will either have to give up the tenancy or else mount up significant arrears while in prison. Until recently, this problem was often neglected by prison authorities (especially in the case of short-termers, who are not allocated an outside probation officer), but it is now quite widely recognised that early action is imperative and most establishments have policies to undertake preventive work starting during the reception process. What can be done is often limited, but in many cases resettlement workers are at least able to help prisoners close down tenancies so that no more debts accumulate, and in some cases creative solutions can be found through negotiation with landlords.

Temporary accommodation with friends or family

A sizeable proportion of prisoners leave custody with the intention of living on a temporary basis with friends or family members. For example, among a national stratified sample of 1,945 male, female and young male prisoners interviewed in 2003 during the last three weeks of their sentence, 17 per cent expected to be staying with friends or family members other than their parents or partners (Niven and Stewart 2005). This appears to be particularly common among young prisoners: a study by Farrant (2006) found that 30 per cent of a sample of young male offenders interviewed after release from custody were living with friends or family members other than their parents.

Those who take this route tend to be largely 'invisible' to policy-makers and practitioners concerned with prisoners' housing needs. Clearly, there are many other prisoners in more urgent need, and unless there are special reasons for doing so (such as sex offending or a high-risk assessment), resettlement staff will not normally explore accommodation issues with those who state that they already have somewhere to go: this is particularly true of prisoners serving under 12 months, who have no licence conditions to adhere to. Equally, such prisoners will not often appear in regional assessments of housing need nor in strategic plans to respond to it. However, this does not mean that they are ending up in suitable accommodation. Ex-prisoners' relationships with friends and family members can be tenuous and fragile, and may break down within a short period, leading to homelessness or 'sofa surfing'. Moreover, even if this does not happen, the need to rely on others for a 'roof over one's head' can in itself be damaging. This was a theme raised by Farrant (2006: 78), who summarises the feelings of the young men in her study as follows:

> Relying on others to take them in made them vulnerable to feeling that they 'owed' those who let them stay; it meant that they stayed in relationships that had become destructive and were damaging to both parties involved; it affected their opportunities for employment; and generally led to a more chaotic existence.

Again, in our own study in the South West, one offender we spoke to who was expecting to stay with his friend's mother on release, felt that this could lead to him being 'enticed back into offending', explaining:

> She gets all sorts of people coming round, accepts all sorts of prisoners … there's crack use there, it gets busted by the police a lot.

Social housing: local authorities and housing associations

The remainder of the discussion will focus on the kinds of prisoners with whom resettlement staff in prisons, and those responsible for resettlement strategies, concern themselves most: those at risk of leaving prison homeless (either because incarceration has lost them previous accommodation or because they were homeless on reception).

These include prisoners who are fully capable of sustaining a tenancy if they can acquire one, although particular attention will be paid to more vulnerable people with, for example, substance misuse or mental health problems who are likely to need various types and degrees of support in order to make progress towards more independent living. This section focuses on access to ordinary social housing. Subsequent sections cover supported housing and private rentals.

Until the 1980s, most 'social housing' – i.e. housing designated for people of limited means with demonstrable accommodation needs – was owned and controlled by local authorities, but in many areas large proportions of council stock have since been transferred to housing associations, which can be more flexible in their provision and can borrow money on the open market to improve or increase their properties. However, local authority housing departments still control housing strategy, operate the housing register (through which they have a strong say in which individuals are accepted as tenants by housing associations), run housing advice centres and assess homelessness applications.

The main mechanism for allocating social housing is through the housing register, which anyone with accommodation needs can apply to join.[2] Traditionally, those accepted have been added to a waiting list, their place determined by a points system based on needs and circumstances: on reaching the head of the list they are offered a council or housing association property which the housing officers consider suitable for their needs. This system is gradually being replaced by 'choice-based letting' (CBL) schemes, whereby all prospective tenants are categorised into 'bands' and all properties available at any particular time are advertised in one location: all those in a particular band can then 'bid' to rent any property for which they are eligible. Where several bid for the same property, decisions are made using criteria similar to those applied under the traditional system, time on the waiting list being a key factor.[3]

Generally speaking, few prisoners try to take this route of joining the general housing register. Waiting lists are long (several years in some areas), and many would not acquire enough points to have a chance of being offered a home in the foreseeable future. Some also have histories of rent arrears, anti-social behaviour or other negative factors which in some areas can exclude them from consideration (and they may be further disadvantaged by the new CBL system: Maguire *et al.* 2007). Rather, ex-prisoners' main hope of acquiring social housing lies in special provisions for *homelessness*, whereby local authorities have a statutory duty to house vulnerable people who have nowhere to live.

Part VII of the Housing Act 1996 (building on provisions in the 1977 and 1985 Acts) details the responsibilities of local authorities in regard to homelessness. Essentially, if individuals or families are deemed to be homeless and in 'priority need', local authorities have a duty to provide temporary accommodation immediately and to place them on a waiting list for more permanent housing. In deciding whether people are in priority need, they are required to consider whether they are 'vulnerable' as a result of circumstances including 'old age, mental illness or handicap or physical disability or other special reason' (s. 189(1c)). Government guidelines list some groups whose members should always be considered as potentially meeting the vulnerability criteria, such as homeless families with children, people with mental health needs, those fleeing domestic violence, and so on. Homeless prison leavers were not initially on this list, but were added following the Homelessness Act 2002, under which local authorities are required to consider whether an applicant is vulnerable as a result of having been in prison or remanded in custody.[4]

At first glance, one might therefore expect that ex-prisoners are now in a relatively favourable position for access to social housing. However, the opposite is often the case and, in practice, priority status is obtained by very small numbers. Indeed, one sizeable research project 'did not uncover a single ex-prisoner who had been housed by a local authority through the homelessness route' (Allender *et al.* 2005a: 20).

The reasons for this are complex but a number of factors are clear. First, the criteria for assessing vulnerability are vague and open to interpretation and local discretion. There is no strong central government pressure on local authorities to show that they are fulfilling their obligations in relation to ex-prisoners specifically – an area in which monitoring is anyway difficult, as housing statistics often do not separate out ex-prisoners as a separate group. Secondly, in order to be deemed to be in priority need, applicants must meet two other critical criteria: that they have not made themselves *intentionally homeless*, and they have a *local connection* in the local authority area.[5] Many local authorities have argued that ex-prisoners have disqualified themselves and become 'intentionally homeless' by offending and being sent to custody (Shelter 2005). This interpretation was discussed in some detail in the early 1990s by Cowan and Fionda (1994) who argued that it was fundamentally unjust in that ex-prisoners were essentially being punished twice. Their research also showed that 'the subjective views of the Housing Officer were important in determining intentionality in these cases' (p. 454). Although overt blanket exclusion of offenders on these grounds is no longer permitted, our own interviews echo the latter finding and indicate that the intentionality rule still creates a significant barrier for ex-prisoners in some areas (Maguire *et al.* 2007; see also Harding and Harding 2006).

The second criterion continues to prove an even greater obstacle. Establishing a 'local connection' can be problematic for ex-offenders whose custody career has broken links with the area in which they previously lived and, more importantly, it is often difficult to establish one in a new area through institutional residence. Being held in a particular prison does not establish a local connection to the area in which it is situated and, in some areas, even residing in a local supported housing project for a considerable period after release is not counted when it comes to applying for permanent housing. It can be argued that this rule is counterproductive in terms of reducing the likelihood of reoffending. It is often desirable for ex-prisoners to 'make a new start' in an area away from old criminal associates, drug cultures or threats of violence. Many of the prisoners that we spoke to feared that they would reoffend if they were to return to their previous home area (for similar findings, see Farrant 2006; Reid-Howie Associates 2004a, 2004b). For example, one said:

> All of my criminal ways are in [this area], my friends are all criminals and I'm trying to stay away from all that ... every time I get out of prison or even go out on the beer I see all my old friends who I used to get in trouble with – I don't want that for my children.

In short, despite its potential importance for efforts to reduce reoffending, social housing is beyond the reach of the vast majority of prisoners. There are acute pressures on council properties, and single-person accommodation – the type of unit most often sought by ex-prisoners – is in particularly short supply. Current government policy, backed up with performance targets, to reduce the use of 'bed and breakfast' premises to house homeless people, has further decreased the amount of temporary accommodation available.[6] In such circumstances, a natural response of housing authorities is to try to ease the pressure by interpreting the rules ungenerously, particularly in relation to unpopular (and in many people's eyes 'undeserving') groups such as ex-offenders. Hence, unless the current housing legislation for England is strengthened and/or the Government makes specific requirements in relation to prison leavers (as has been achieved in Wales) the amount of social housing available to them is likely to remain extremely limited.

Supported accommodation and 'floating support'

The term 'supported accommodation' covers a wide variety of provision, mostly entailing schemes run by voluntary agencies which offer support to people who have difficulties in living independently. While many such schemes are designed for the elderly or for people with physical disabilities, others are for people with types of problems commonly found among prisoners (such as substance abuse and mental health problems) and are consequently populated substantially by ex-offenders. Some, indeed, are aimed specifically at ex-prisoners: these include 'Approved Premises' run by the Probation Service, and a number of specialist hostels prepared to take on high-risk ex-prisoners run by organisations such as Stonham Housing Association. They range from large, generalist units based around communal living (sometimes referred to as 'traditional hostels') to shared houses or dispersed units, often specialising in clients with particular kinds of need. Until a few years ago, the support was .attached directly to the accommodation, in many cases provided by live-in staff. However, funding constraints have tightened, and fewer schemes now provide 24-hour on-site cover. Some have staff in residence during the day, but many have workers visiting daily together with an on-call system. Indeed, as will be discussed below, an even more significant development has been the uncoupling of funding for support from that for accommodation, which has encouraged a general shift towards the provision of 'floating support' whereby support workers are not attached to any particular building but visit vulnerable people wherever they live.

Supported accommodation is normally temporary in that there will be a limit on the time a client can stay (usually between 6 and 18 months). The aim is to prepare people for more independent living by giving them an opportunity to settle and acquire living skills and to address personal and social problems. Residents are formally referred by other agencies, including prisons, and are usually interviewed. They are expected to agree to the rules, demonstrate willingness to accept support and fit in with other residents. They can be evicted if they break the rules or fail to pay the rent (though this is usually covered by Housing Benefit). Most projects provide shared or individual cooking facilities, enabling residents to cater, plan and shop for themselves and thereby learn to budget and make progress towards independent living. The general trend is towards smaller and dispersed living units, and some larger units are being altered to allow more privacy and encourage independence, as well as to avoid problems such as close proximity of clients with different needs (for example housing drug users alongside those attempting to abstain from use, or high-risk with low-risk clients).

Our interviews with resettlement staff in prisons indicated that much of their work involved helping prisoners to gain places in such schemes, and that they are the preferred destination for many of the most vulnerable and isolated prisoners whose only realistic alternative option may be a night shelter (see below). Supported accommodation projects have major advantages over such alternatives as they provide an opportunity for residents to settle and to learn independent living skills. The privacy and the selection of residents reduces the likelihood of violence and allows a better quality of life. The support can also be more specialised. Many offenders we interviewed spoke very positively about supported housing generally.

However, supported accommodation also has some significant problems. There can be friction between residents, and some find it difficult to comply with rules. For example, while acknowledging that for some, 'supervised' support of this nature might be of help, one prisoner we interviewed felt that for him, 'the only difference [from prison] would be that there are no bars on the windows … it would just get on my nerves'. Importantly, too, the use of drugs and alcohol, which appears to be rife in emergency accommodation such as night shelters, can also be prominent within longer-term supported projects. Individuals with histories of long-term offending and substance abuse are housed together, and despite the best efforts of staff, this can easily produce an environment which is not conducive to desistance or resettlement. Those managing schemes have to steer a difficult path between a liberal approach, which can produce such an environment, and a stricter approach with rule enforcements that some residents cannot cope with. Many ex-prisoners do not manage to stay for the full period planned, either leaving of their own accord (some because they find the regime too restrictive, others for the opposite reason) or being evicted because of serious infractions of rules. This in turn creates new problems of homelessness, and unless some form of 'rescue' scheme is in operation (such as arrangements to rehouse people in a scheme more suited to their temperament and needs), those leaving can disappear from official view into an insecure life on the streets or in transient housing until they re-emerge through reoffending and a new prison sentence.

Perhaps most problematic of all, supported accommodation is very expensive. This is a continuing concern for Supporting People (SP), the agency which now provides most of the funding for housing support, as it greatly limits the numbers of people who can benefit. Supporting People authorities were set up across the country in 2003, with the task of commissioning housing support services for vulnerable people. Under the previous system, if a person was living in a hostel or supported accommodation scheme, their housing benefit included a sum to cover the support they received. However, with the decoupling of rent and support funds, the 'support' element of Housing Benefit, together with funds from other sources (including the Probation Service's 'PAGS' grant), was pooled into a pot of money to be distributed by SP commissioners on the basis of bids from housing support providers. This can be used to provide support to someone living in their own home or in the private rented sector, although the bulk of SP money still goes to residential schemes (sheltered housing for the elderly often accounting for the largest share).

SP funding levels are currently shrinking, and as commissioners seek ways of balancing budgets, there is a clear shift away from accommodation-based support towards the expansion of 'floating support'. This is not only cheaper than support attached to specific schemes (especially those supplying 24-hour live-in services), but is more flexible and reaches a larger number of clients: floating support workers can regularly visit vulnerable people in dispersed properties controlled by voluntary agencies, in social housing, in privately rented properties and even in theory (though rarely in practice) in properties where they are being put up temporarily by friends or family. On the other hand, those running supported accommodation schemes often argued to us that, while floating support may be beneficial for clients with low or medium support needs, many ex-prisoners in particular require much more support – and in some cases monitoring and surveillance – than floating support workers, many of whom have little training or experience in working with offenders, are able to provide on short visits. In their view, the movement of funding away from accommodation schemes with support staff on the premises is short-sighted and is creating shortages of places for ex-prisoners at high risk of reoffending, including those with major substance abuse and mental health problems and, indeed, high-risk sexual and violent offenders who may spend a few months after release in Probation

Service Approved Premises but thereafter have few appropriate housing options.

Finally, those living in supported accommodation, like those in temporary housing of any kind, ultimately face the problem of 'moving on' – where to go when their stay comes to an end. As already discussed, demand for social housing far outstrips supply and providers – especially housing associations – quite often appear to find reasons for avoiding more 'difficult' kinds of tenants such as ex-prisoners. Although one of the aims of supported housing is to teach residents skills that will make them suitable tenants, we were told by project managers that their 'graduates' were often treated no differently than offenders coming directly out of prison, and faced similar problems in terms of disqualification from priority need status, particularly on the grounds of lacking a 'local connection'. For the great majority, the only move on option remains private sector rental.

Private rental

Because of the acute shortages of social housing, policymakers and practitioners in the housing field – not least local authorities – are increasingly looking to the private sector to absorb current and future demand. This has recently been seen in the encouragement by the Department of Communities and Local Government (DCLG) of policies centred around the concept of 'housing options'. Although not officially articulated as such, this appears to entail a recognition by government that, as the social housing stock continues to shrink, the traditional goals of providing council or housing association accommodation to all those in need are becoming increasingly unrealistic and, more specifically, 'priority need' applications under the homelessness legislation are causing severe problems for many local authorities. In-depth interviews are held with clients considering making such applications in order to give them a 'realistic' understanding of their 'full housing options' – often with an emphasis on ways of accessing the private rented sector. At the same time, voluntary and statutory support providers are also now turning to the private sector to house people they are supporting, an option made more feasible by the growth of floating support.

Despite the current enthusiasm for the private sector, some major difficulties from the point of view of ex-prisoners should be noted. To gain a new private rented tenancy often requires a deposit or bond as well as four weeks rent in advance. Not only is this difficult to arrange from prison, but most prisoners have insufficient savings – not boosted by the meagre prison wages – to fund a deposit. In addition, Housing Benefit does not cover the whole rent, as it does in council or housing association properties. The tenant must pay the shortfall out of his/her other benefits or income. This is particularly problematic for people under 25, as the level of Housing Benefit is set for a single room with shared facilities – a rule that Harvey and Houston (2005) argue has contributed significantly to youth homelessness. Furthermore, the problems faced by many prison leavers in finding employment mean that they are likely to depend on benefits for some time after leaving custody, with the result that they will be unable to sustain a tenancy in private rented housing except in the most deprived areas and dilapidated properties. A manager in a supported housing project we visited said that, despite the prospect of increased independence, many of their tenants were loth to move out from good quality project accommodation into 'the pits'. Finally, while council and housing association flats/houses are permanent housing (once a probationary period is passed), tenancies in the private rented sector are less secure. Most tenancies are short-hold (six months) and eviction is possible at the end of this time. In fact, the most common cause of homelessness in some housing districts is eviction from short-hold private tenancies.

'Crisis' facilities: night shelters, day centres and outreach

As noted above, a significant minority of offenders still leave prison without an address to go to even on the first night, while others have merely been helped by the prison authorities to book into a bed and breakfast and will be effectively homeless within a few days. For those who leave with little money and nowhere to live, night shelters (sometimes called 'direct access hostels') often constitute the first port of call or, looked at another way, the last resort. They will provide an immediate roof and a meal for (nearly) all adult male callers, and are often the only accommodation available for long-term rough sleepers and for those evicted from elsewhere. Importantly, too, they take people 'moving through' as well as those intending to settle in the area. The accommodation offered is normally a single room with shared bathroom and toilet facilities. An evening meal and breakfast is provided. Usually, rooms are booked for the night and vacated after breakfast; in some, a room can be booked for longer, but 28 days will normally be the maximum stay. Most are staffed 24 hours, with two waking staff at night for larger night shelters. Rules are likely to include no violence, and drugs and alcohol are not allowed on the premises, though this is often difficult to enforce.

The immediacy of shelter and support offered to men (though not generally to women or younger people) who are otherwise reluctant to engage with welfare services gives night shelters a particularly important role for homeless ex-prisoners. Part of their value lies simply in acting as a safety net: a person can return several, or even many times, to a night shelter, a vital resource especially for those with drug or alcohol problems who may relapse many times, or may be evicted from other forms of accommodation, before (hopefully) they succeed in stabilising their lives enough to make other options feasible. Importantly, too, they provide opportunities for staff or volunteers to make regular contact with, and gain the trust of, seriously excluded people (who tend to be wary of anyone they associate with 'authority'), with a view to persuading them to accept help in addressing their needs. A similar function is performed by outreach workers in day centres, which are often linked to night shelters and provide somewhere for the homeless (both men and women) to use as a base during the day.

Unfortunately, night shelters and direct access hostels are associated in many people's minds (including those who stay in them) with substance misuse, drug dealing and violence. In our study, 20 per cent of prisoners interviewed (13 of 64) referred to this problem. For example, discussing his previous release to a direct access hostel, one stated that 'there were drug addicts, prostitutes [going] back and forth ... the place was rundown' and described being attacked for his discharge and crisis grant. Another said that 'a lot of people in hostels take drugs, and that impacts on me taking drugs', and a third that 'they are full of drug addicts ... which made the addiction worse ... it was hard to get away from it'. One even went so far as to say that he 'would sleep on the street first', arguing that he would 'be back to square one – all those druggies and shit like that, I could slip back'. In a nutshell, as one put it, for most offenders night shelters and large hostels are 'pretty demoralising places to go to ... everyone's using, you're all living in one room.'

Clearly then, although such images may be exaggerated, these kinds of accommodation are generally not to be recommended as an environment for those who are trying to 'stay clean' and avoid reoffending. The lack of privacy, the lack of opportunity for clients to acquire independent living skills and the stigma attached to having a hostel address have all been clearly illustrated in research (Hutson 1999; Rosengard 2002). Nevertheless, for all their problems, night shelters are perhaps best described, in the words of an experienced prison resettlement worker we spoke to, as 'a necessary evil'.

Diversity and groups with special needs

While prisoners of all kinds are likely to face the obstacles we have outlined, some groups have greater than average needs or are more likely to encounter particular problems. Diversity issues can all too easily be forgotten among all the difficulties involved in assisting prisoners with accommodation, but it is important to recognise that special arrangements may be needed to ensure that some groups are not unwittingly excluded or disadvantaged. We comment briefly in turn on female, young, and black and minority ethnic prisoners, as well as noting particular problems raised in housing high-risk offenders (and especially sex offenders). More detailed coverage of these topics can be found in other chapters in this volume.

Female prisoners

Women's prisons in England are widely dispersed (there are no female prison establishments in Wales at all) and many women are held at long distances from their home locality. This increases the risk of broken relationships and of losing existing accommodation: for example, Niven and Stewart (2005) found in their resettlement survey that, among prisoners who had been living with a partner prior to custody, women (36 per cent) were less likely then men (63 per cent) to be returning to live with them on release.[7] It also makes it more difficult to find a new place to live. Prison resettlement staff in our study cited good working relationships with local housing providers as crucial to the successful rehousing of prisoners, but the wide range of areas to which women hope to return means that in many cases staff have no such links and little knowledge about the availability and suitability of accommodation. Again, female prisoners in the Niven and Stewart survey were less likely to have accommodation arranged on release (62 per cent) than both adult male (69 per cent) and young prisoners (90 per cent).[8]

There is also little housing provision for vulnerable women, and even less specifically for female ex-offenders, despite the fact that they tend to have greater and more complex needs than their male counterparts (Barrow Cadbury Trust 2005; Borrill et al. 2003a, 2003b; Department of Health 2002; HMIP 1997; Maden et al. 1994; O'Brien *et al.* 2001; Prison Reform Trust 2000; Singleton *et al.* 1998). Where it does exist, female-specific hostel provision often struggles to maintain high occupancy rates. At the same time, accommodation which caters for both men and women would be inappropriate for many female ex-offenders, due to their prior experience of male violence or sexual abuse. The overall position is summed up well in a report by the Scottish Executive (2001: 1):

> The small numbers of women offenders and the multiple issues they present make accommodation provision hard to plan and supply. Female-specific accommodation projects are in short supply, undesirable for most authorities due to a woman's need to maintain family and other personal ties in her immediate local community and unpopular among women offenders. There are significant concerns about the suitability of housing women in mixed hostels, and women themselves express a strong preference for self-contained accommodation.

Finally, accommodation issues for many women prisoners are closely tied up with those of maintaining custody of their children. Two-thirds of female prisoners are mothers of children under the age of 16, and in many cases they are the primary or sole carer. Imprisonment not only has massive negative effects on the relationship between mother and child (children frequently develop emotional and behavioural problems as a result of separation from their mother) but a lack of stable accommodation on release often means that women are unable to regain custody of children who have been taken into care (Caddle and Crisp 1996, 1997; HMCIP 1997). The 'Catch 22' here is that, without having custody of their children, these women are unlikely to be considered 'in priority need' by local authorities and thus to be offered suitable accommodation (Carlisle 1996; Reid-Howie Associates 2004a, 2004b).

Young prisoners

Young offenders, too, have wide-ranging needs and are a particularly vulnerable subgroup of prisoners who tend to have experienced high levels of social exclusion and whose histories abound with mental health problems, substance abuse and disrupted family backgrounds. Indeed, Barrow Cadbury Trust (2005) found that a massive 49 per cent of young prisoners (aged 18–21) had previously been in local authority residential care. The need for accommodation with appropriate levels of support is extremely important for this group, but the appropriateness of 'hostel'-like accommodation is questionable, as a key aim is to help them leave behind their institutional backgrounds and make progress towards adulthood and independent living (Scottish Executive 2001: 13).

Farrant (2006: 78) describes the young prisoners in her study as being 'beset with housing problems. They had left home at an early age; lived in unstable, and often unsafe, conditions; some had housing difficulties prior to their time in prison, whilst significantly more saw their housing situation worsened by imprisonment.' One in five reported that they had either been homeless at the point of imprisonment or had been made homeless as a result of being sent to prison. Despite this, many described the housing advice they had received in custody as 'inadequate', 'unavailable' or 'useless'.

Most young ex-prisoners have poor educational qualifications and little earning power, and are even more likely than older offenders to experience accommodation problems because of inability to afford rental tenancies – a problem exacerbated by Housing Benefit rules introduced in 1996 whereby people under 25 receive lower benefits than those over 25.[9] In addition, the minimum wage is lower for people under 21, and the Job Seekers Allowance is lower for those under 25 (Renshaw 2000). All these issues further compound the poor financial status of many young offenders and make it extremely difficult for them to secure and maintain accommodation. For example, research by Harvey and Houston (2005) found that nearly 87 per cent of a sample of disadvantaged males under 25 experienced a shortfall in paying the rent, compared to 56 per cent of those aged 25 and over (see also Barrow Cadbury Trust 2005; Farrant 2006; Howard League 2005).

On the plus side, the Homelessness Act 2002 identifies homeless people under 18 as a vulnerable group that should be deemed in 'priority need' for accommodation by local authorities. In addition, the Youth Justice Board has stated that it is 'committed to preventing homelessness among young offenders' and has a 100 per cent target for young people to be released from custody into 'suitable accommodation' (Patel 2004: 5). However, worthy as these aims are on paper, they do not reflect the reality that many young people are unaware of (or are easily defected away from claiming) their entitlements, or simply do not take up poor quality accommodation they are offered.

Black and minority ethnic prisoners

While a fair amount is known about their resettlement needs generally, there is very little available statistical data specifically on the housing needs of offenders from black and minority ethnic (BME) backgrounds. Previous research suggests that these are likely to be greater than those of white prisoners, due to some extent to discrimination in the housing service field as in many other areas of practice (Calverley *et al.* 2004). Respondents in our own research (Maguire *et al.* 2007) suggested that partnerships involving prisons, probation, community organisations and smaller, specialist agencies may be most effective in addressing the housing needs of BME offenders, as they are more likely than large organisations to have a full understanding of the specific problems involved. However, it was also rightly pointed out that if significant progress is to be made, a necessary urgent step is to ensure that there is more BME representation on strategic bodies and management groups concerned with housing policy and service delivery, and that BME-sensitive targets are set for services (thereby encouraging the collection of better data about both needs and outcomes). It should also be emphasised that 'BME' is a crude catch-all term, and that offenders from different ethnic and cultural backgrounds may have different needs.

High-risk and 'priority and prolific' offenders

Finally, housing ex-prisoners who are assessed as posing a high risk of harm – especially sex offenders – presents daunting challenges. Here, concerns about the welfare of offenders often take second place to concerns about risks to community safety, although the two are generally compatible. Those who fall under the statutory Multi-Agency Public Protection Arrangements (MAPPA) are often first housed in Approved Premises (i.e. probation hostels) when they leave prison, so the real problems begin when the time comes to move on from there. Not only are many housing providers reluctant to accept high-risk offenders as tenants, but there are dangers in sudden transition from a highly structured and controlled environment to one in which there is little surveillance of their activities. Moreover, in many neighbourhoods any hint that a new resident is a sex offender can lead to protests and vigilante action, so extra care has to be taken around confidentiality.

Not dissimilar problems arise in the case of 'priority and prolific' offenders (PPOs), many of whom have serious drug problems, engage in anti-social behaviour with neighbours and have poor records of keeping up rent payments. A recent Home Office study based on OASys data (Dawson 2007) found that PPOs were: less likely than other offenders to be in suitable accommodation, less likely to be in permanent accommodation and less likely to be in accommodation that is in a suitable location. Moreover, 'their accommodation needs were judged by OASys assessors to be more strongly linked to their offending behaviour than was the case for other offenders' (Dawson 2007: 6).

Improving the situation

Although much of the above gives a bleak picture of the accommodation situation facing ex-prisoners, it is important to acknowledge that recent years have seen much more serious government attempts to address it than in the past. Cooperative working between practitioners from different agencies has also increased markedly. While these developments have yet to bear much fruit, they have the potential of bringing about real change in the future, provided that momentum is sustained.

Strategic developments

A key driver for change has been recognition by central government of the importance of effective resettlement work – including accommodation and related support services – to its high priority goal of reducing reoffending. This has helped to shape sweeping organisational reforms, including the establishment of the National Offender Management Service (NOMS) and the introduction of the NOMS Offender Management Model to promote standardised assessment and sentence planning processes and the 'end-to-end' management of offenders, including 'through the gate' (NOMS 2005; Raynor and Maguire 2006). Most important for the accommodation of ex-prisoners has been the development of national and regional Reducing Re-Offending Action Plans and Strategies, and their seven associated 'Pathways' (Home Office 2004b). The key policy thrust has been to persuade non-criminal justice agencies to play a more committed and proactive role in reintegrating offenders into the community. Mechanisms to encourage this have included the establishment of high-level regional multi-agency partnership boards with a remit to deliver services to reduce reoffending, performance targets aimed at elevating work with ex-offenders in agencies' priorities, pooling of funding streams, joint commissioning of services and the publication of national strategic frameworks to guide these processes (NOMS 2006). Regarding accommodation, NOMS has begun to work more closely with the DCLG and is seeking to influence national and regional housing bodies to take more account of ex-offenders in their strategic plans. Probation services have also begun to take part in joint commissioning of accommodation services with Supporting People, whereby they can highlight the needs of ex-prisoners. Other recent developments include the funding by NOMS of experimental 'Gateways', which act as a single channel in a particular area for referring offenders to housing providers (Maguire *et al.* 2007).[10]

Organisational and practical improvements

From our discussions with numerous stakeholders in the South West region, it was clear that awareness of ex-prisoners' accommodation problems, and of their relevance to reoffending, was increasing and that, though patchy, cooperation between probation or prison staff and housing-related practitioners was growing. However, while this first stage of awareness-raising and attitude change is essential to further progress, much greater change is required if any serious dent is to be made in the deep-seated problems outlined in this chapter. We end with a series of suggestions regarding the best 'way forward', based on a broad consensus of views put forward by our interviewees. As there is little space for further discussion, these are listed in the form of headings with a few explanatory comments.

1 Action should be taken at the earliest opportunity to help prisoners retain any form of stable accommodation that they had prior to imprisonment
This is an issue receiving significantly more attention within prisons than in the past, but implementation is still patchy (Reid-Howie Associates 2004a, 2004b). What can be done is often limited, but at a minimum the tenancy can be closed down so that no more debts accumulate. In some cases, too, creative solutions can be found through negotiation.

2 More should be done to systematise and simplify referral and access to housing and related services, whether in the public, private or voluntary sectors
This can involve a wide range of actions, including:

- resources and training to improve accommodation advice in prisons;
- earlier starts to referral processes;
- encouragement of visits to prisons by housing providers;
- greater engagement with accommodation issues by probation, including joint commissioning (with Supporting People) of supported accommodation;
- development of 'one-stop shops', provider forums or 'Gateways';
- development of standard assessment and referral forms;
- development of advocacy services to challenge unfair decisions;
- more proactive and assertive outreach (e.g. through day centres and street homelessness workers) to those missed by formal systems;
- more rent deposit schemes;
- incentives to landlords to take on ex-prisoners as tenants, such as guaranteed payment of rent through void periods and support packages to assist them in dealing with problems such as anti-social behaviour.

3 More attention should be paid to 'throughflow', 'rescue' and 'move on'
This means better systems for assisting ex-offenders to 'move on' from temporary accommodation into more permanent and independent housing, or to a different type of supported accommodation as they reach the stage where this is desirable; it also includes systems for 'rescuing' those who are evicted. These may include:

- effective action by large providers who control a variety of accommodation and support, and can move offenders as progress is made or if they 'relapse' (e.g. back from a dry house to a wet house);
- collaboration between smaller providers to provide a similar system;
- investment in more medium-risk supported accommodation for those leaving Approved Premises or other high support facilities;
- protocols between supported housing providers and local authorities, such as one in the South West whereby a number of

district councils have agreed to house at least one 'move on' case
per year;

- offers of continuing floating support to those who are moving into
independent accommodation.

4 Practical services should be provided within a framework of relational continuity and motivational support

A key message from resettlement studies (see, for example, Clancy *et al.*
2006; Lewis *et al.* 2003; Maguire and Raynor 2006) is that interventions
are more likely to be successful if ex-prisoners are motivated to stop
offending and if both practical advice and psychological support
are provided by someone they know and trust – ideally based on
a relationship forged before release. The process of desistance from
crime is often characterised by lapses and setbacks, and offenders
easily lose motivation or are defeated by practical obstacles (Farrall
2002; Farrall and Calverley 2005; Maruna 2000). Prisoners sentenced
to over 12 months at least have a probation officer (now called an
offender manager) to relate to after release, but for many vulnerable
short-termers released without any supervision there is a strong
unmet need for support and advice, not only immediately after
leaving prison, but for some months afterwards. Many of the
stakeholders and the prisoners we interviewed were strongly in
favour of mentoring schemes for this group. The value of 'floating
support' workers in helping clients manage their accommodation
(for example, in a rented flat) was also widely recognised. However,
relatively few ex-prisoners at present receive either form of support,
increasing the chances that they will fail to overcome crises and will
reoffend and/or lose their accommodation.

5 Greater attention is needed to diversity issues, groups with special needs and the housing of high-risk offenders

An urgent first step here is to improve the quality of relevant data
to gain a better picture of housing needs and supply in relation
especially to women, BME and young ex-prisoners. Where women
are concerned, there is a need for more small supported housing
projects and improved cross-authority information systems to ensure
that their occupancy rates are maintained. To improve services to
BME offenders, more ethnic monitoring of referrals and decisions
about housing allocation is desirable. For young offenders, many
problems revolve around finances and schemes involving help with
rents and deposits are widely advocated. Education programmes on

living skills and tenancy sustainability are another important piece of the jigsaw.

Finally, regarding the housing of high-risk offenders, a promising development has been the signing of protocols under the MAPPA umbrella between criminal justice agencies and groups of local authorities, whereby high priority can be given to such cases and suitable locations found (for example, away from schools or families with children). One such protocol in the South West is signed up to by ten district councils: this not only identifies MAPPA cases as meriting priority attention for assessment and allocation of social housing, but stipulates that the exclusionary criterion of lacking a 'local connection' will be disregarded by the housing authorities, making movement between districts much easier.

Concluding comments

The accommodation of ex-prisoners remains one of the most important, yet most intractable, problems in the whole resettlement and reducing reoffending agenda. On the one hand, it has been made more difficult in recent years by rising house prices and declining social housing. On the other, there has been an increase in awareness of the problems and in the desire to tackle them. Solutions are complex and progress is slow, but a number of core principles – which apply to all forms of resettlement practice – are becoming more widely accepted as essential if reoffending is to be reduced. These include effectively coordinated partnerships across different agencies and areas, high-quality assessment and planning of interventions and the development of trusting relationships and motivational support. All of this, of course, takes time, and a continuing concern is that patience and enthusiasm may wane (not least on the part of politicians), resources shrink and the current 'window of opportunity' closes again.

Finally, it is important to mention the potential contribution that could be made by 'Custody Plus', a sentence created under the 2003 Criminal Justice Act but as yet not implemented.[11] If and when it finally comes into operation, it will consist of a short period in custody followed by a longer period of community supervision. Its importance where resettlement is concerned lies in the plan, for the first time, to extend statutory post-release supervision to short-term prisoners – the group with both the greatest welfare needs and the highest risk of reoffending. This would give such prisoners access to probation advice, connections and resources, from which they are currently largely excluded, and ensure that their accommodation needs were assessed and taken into account in sentence planning 'through the gate'. In its absence, there is a serious risk that the long-term neglect of the resettlement needs of this group will continue, most attention and resources being directed at offenders for whom NOMS has statutory responsibility (i.e. those sentenced to one year or above).[12]

Notes

1 A recent halving of the proportion of prisoners leaving with 'no fixed abode' seems to be largely due to a combination of the removal of a previous financial incentive (in the form of a higher discharge grant) for prisoners to say that they were NFA, and the introduction of a Prison Service performance indicator aimed at increasing the proportion of prisoners with an address to go to for their first night of freedom. However, in many cases, the latter has been simply a bed and breakfast establishment or other very temporary accommodation, and a more rigorous performance indicator is to be introduced.

2 Certain groups such as asylum seekers are excluded, and those who already own a home will only be considered in exceptional circumstances.

3 See, for example: www.jrf.org.uk/knowledge/findings/housing/123.asp.

4 Homelessness (Priority Need for Accommodation) (England) Order 2002 (section 5.3). In Wales, as part of wider National Assembly policy to improve services to ex-offenders, secondary legislation was used to include homeless ex-prisoners among those deemed *automatically* to be in priority need. Therefore in Wales, homeless prison leavers do not need to demonstrate that they are 'vulnerable', but can be deemed to be in priority need either as a result of their status as a homeless prison leaver, or their vulnerability (see, for example: www.wales.gov.uk/cms/2/Social JusticeAndRegenerationCommittee?month=200503).

5 Under s. 191.1 of the Housing Act 1996: 'A person becomes homeless intentionally if he deliberately does or fails to do anything in consequence of which he ceases to occupy accommodation which is available for his occupation and which it would have been reasonable for him to continue to occupy'. Under s. 199.1, a person has a local connection to an area (a) because he is, or in the past was, normally resident there, and that residence is or was of his own choice, (b) because he is employed there, (c) because of family associations, or (d) because of special circumstances.

6 The laudable aim of this is to encourage local authorities to raise

standards and increase the stock of decent affordable housing, by making more effective use of housing association properties and through more effective partnerships with private landlords. This, however, is not easy to achieve, and in many areas the overall pressure on accommodation has increased.

7 This may be partly related to the greater distances between home and prison and partly to women's decisions to escape abusive relationships, although on the latter point Eaton (1993) found that many women return to an abusive relationship owing to a lack of alternatives.

8 A Prisons Inspectorate report (HMCIP 1997) likewise found that only 11 per cent of women received help in prison with their housing needs, and fewer than one in six even knew that help was available (compared to one in four men).

9 The official justification for this is that it is deemed appropriate for this group of individuals (provided that they are childless) to live in single-room accommodation with a shared kitchen and toilet, and entitlements are based on this expectation.

10 See also: http://noms.homeoffice.gov.uk/noms-regions/south-west/swag/.

11 It was scheduled to be introduced in November 2006, but in the summer of that year it was suddenly announced that its introduction had been 'deferred': indeed, many observers believe that it has been in effect abandoned due to insufficient resources.

12 It should be noted that, while the Regional Offender Managers' major focus is on offenders under sentence or on statutory licence, their remit to contribute to the reduction of reoffending gives them a responsibility to promote more effective services for other ex-offenders – notably short-term prisoners after release.

References

Allender, P., Brown, G., Bailey, N., Colombo, T., Poole, H. and Saldana, A. (2005a) *Prisoner Resettlement and Housing Provision: A Good Practice Ideas Guide.* Coventry: Coventry University.

Allender, P., Brown, G., Bailey, N., Colombo, T., Poole, H. and Saldana, A. (2005b) *Report on Prisoner Resettlement and Housing Provision Research Project.* Coventry: Coventry University.

Barrow Cadbury Trust (2005) *Lost in Transition: A Report of the Barrow Cadbury Commission on Young Adults and the Criminal Justice System.* London: Barrow Cadbury Trust.

Borrill, J., Maden, A., Martin, A., Weaver, T., Stimson, G., Farrell, M., Barnes, T., Burnett, R., Miller, S. and Briggs, D. (2003a) *Differential Substance Misuse Treatment Needs of Women, Ethnic Minorities and Young Offenders in Prison: Prevalence of Substance Misuse and Treatment Needs.* Home Office

Online Report 33/03, London: Home Office. (See: www.homeoffice.gov.uk/rds/pdfs2/rdsolr3303.pdf).

Borrill, J., Maden, A., Martin, A., Weaver, T., Stimson, G., Farrell, M., Barnes, T., Burnett, R., Miller, S. and Briggs, D. (2003b) 'Substance misuse among white and black/mixed race female prisoners', in M. Ramsay (ed.), *Prisoners' Drug Use and Treatment: Seven Research Studies*, Home Office Research Study 267. London: Home Office.

Caddle, D. and Crisp, D. (1996) *Imprisoned Women and Mothers*, Home Office Research Study 162. London: Home Office.

Caddle, D. and Crisp, D. (1997) *Mothers in Prison*, Home Office Research Findings No. 38. London: Home Office.

Calverley, A., Cole, B., Kaur, G., Lewis, S., Raynor, P., Sadeghi, S., Smith, D., Vanstone, M. and Wardak, A. (2004) *Black and Asian Offenders on Probation*, Home Office Research Study No. 277. London: Home Office.

Calverley, A., Cole, B., Kaur, G., Lewis, S., Raynor, P., Sadeghi, S., Smith, D., Vanstone, M. and Wardak, A. (2006) 'Black and Asian probationers: Implications of the Home Office study', *Probation Journal*, 53 (1): 24–37.

Carlisle, J. (1996) *The Housing Needs of Ex-Prisoners*. York: Centre for Housing Policy.

Clancy, A., Hudson, K., Maguire, M., Peake, R., Raynor, P., Vanstone, M. and Kynch, J. (2006) *Getting Out and Staying Out: Results of the Prisoner Resettlement Pathfinders*. Bristol: Policy Press.

Cowan, D.S. and Fionda, J. (1994) 'Meeting the need: the response of local authorities' housing departments to the housing of ex-offenders', *British Journal of Criminology*, 34 (4): 444–58.

Dawson, P. (2007) *The National PPO Evaluation – Research to Inform and Guide Practice*, Home Office Online Report 09/07. London: Home Office. (See: www.homeoffice.gov.uk/rds/pdfs07/rdsolr0907.pdf).

Department of Health (2002) *Women's Mental Health: Into the Mainstream*. London: Department of Health.

Dodd, M. and Alakeson, V. (2006) *Private Sector Provision of Employment Services for Young Adults at Risk: A Social Market Foundation Report for the Barrow Cadbury Trust*. Accessed via: www.bctrust.org.uk/snapshots/employment-services-young-adults/employment-services-young-adults.pdf.

Eaton, M. (1993) *Women After Prison*. Buckingham: Open University Press.

Farrall, S. (2002) *Rethinking What Works with Offenders*. Cullompton: Willan.

Farrall, S. and Calverley, A. (2005) *Understanding Desistance from Crime*. Maidenhead: Open University Press.

Farrant, N. (2006) *Out for Good: The Resettlement Needs of Young Men in Prison*. London: Howard League for Penal Reform.

Harding, A. and Harding, J. (2006) 'Inclusion and exclusion in the re-housing of former prisoners', *Probation Journal*, 53 (2): 137–53.

Harvey, J. and Houston, D. (2005) *Research into the Single Room Rent Regulations*, Research Report 243. Leeds: Department for Work and Pensions.

Her Majesty's Chief Inspector of Prisons (HMCIP) (1997) *Women in Prison: A Thematic Review*. London: Home Office.

Hickey, C. (2002) *Crime and Homelessness*. Dublin: Focus Ireland & PACE.

Home Office (2004a) *Reducing Crime – Changing Lives. The Government's Plans for Transforming the Management of Offenders*. London: Home Office. (See: www.noms.homeoffice.gov.uk/background-to-noms/.)

Home Office (2004b) *Reducing Re-offending National Action Plan*. London: Home Office. (See: www.probation.homeoffice.gov.uk/files/pdf/NOMS%20National%20Action%20Plan.pdf.)

Howard League (2005) *The Key to the Future? The Housing Needs of Young Adults in Prison*, Housing Briefing December 2005. Howard League. (See: howardleague.org/fileadmin/howard_league/user/pdf/housing_final_01.pdf.)

Hutson, S. (1999) 'Young homeless people and supported housing', in S. Hutson and D. Clapham (eds), *Homelessness: Public Policies and Private Troubles*. London: Cassell.

Lewis, S., Maguire, M., Raynor, P., Vanstone, M. and Vennard, J. (2007) 'What works in resettlement? Findings from seven Pathfinders for short-term prisoners in England and Wales', *Criminology and Criminal Justice*, 7 (1): 33–53.

Lewis, S., Vennard, J., Maguire, M., Raynor, P., Vanstone, M., Raybould, S. and Rix, A. (2003) *The Resettlement of Short-term Prisoners: An Evaluation of Seven Pathfinders*, RDS Occasional Paper No. 83. London: Home Office.

Maden, A., Swinton, S. and Gunn, J. (1994) 'A criminological and psychiatric survey of women serving a prison sentence', *British Journal of Criminology*, 34: 2.

Maguire, M. and Raynor, P. (2006) 'How the resettlement of prisoners promotes desistance from crime: or does it?', *Criminology and Criminal Justice*, 6 (1): 19–38.

Maguire, M., Hutson, S. and Nolan, J. (2007) *Accommodation for Ex-Prisoners in the South West Region: Final Report*. University of Glamorgan.

Maguire, M., Raynor, P., Vanstone, M. and Kynch, J. (2000) 'Voluntary after-care and the Probation Service: a case of diminishing responsibility', *Howard Journal*, 39: 234–48.

Maruna, S. (2000) *Making Good*. Washington, DC: American Psychological Association.

Metcalf, H., Anderson, T. and Rolfe, H. (2001) *Barriers to Employment for Offenders and Ex-Offenders: Part 1 – Barriers to Employment for Offenders and Ex-Offenders*, Research Report No.155. Leeds: Department for Work and Pensions. (See: www.dwp.gov.uk/asd/asd5/rport155/Main1.pdf.)

NACRO (2000a) *The Forgotten Majority: The Resettlement of Short-Term Prisoners*. London: National Association for the Care and Resettlement of Offenders.

NACRO (2000b) *Good Resettlement the Key to Reduced Re-offending Among Released Prisoners*. Press release, 4 September.

NACRO (2001) *Women Behind Bars: A Positive Agenda for Women Prisoners' Resettlement*. London: National Association for the Care and Resettlement of Offenders.

NACRO (2002) *Resettling Prisoners from Black and Minority Ethnic Groups*. London: National Association for the Care and Resettlement of Offenders.

National Offender Management Service (NOMS) (2005) *The NOMS Offender Management Model*. London: NOMS. (See: www.probation2000.com/documents/NOMS%20Offender%20Management%20Model.pdf.)

National Offender Management Service (NOMS) (2006) *Reducing Reoffending Housing and Housing Support Framework*. London: National Offender Management Service.

Niven, S. and Stewart, D. (2005) *Resettlement Outcomes on Release from Prison, 2003*, Findings 178. London: Home Office.

O'Brien, M., Mortimer, L., Singleton, N. and Meltzer, H. (2001) *Psychiatric Morbidity among Women Prisoners in England and Wales*. London: National Statistics.

Patel, N. (2004) *Accommodation Needs of Young Offenders*. London: Youth Justice Board for England and Wales.

Prison Reform Trust (2000) *Justice for Women: The Need for Reform*, The Wedderburn Report. London: Prison Reform Trust.

Raynor, P. and Maguire, M. (2006) 'End-to-end or end in tears? Prospects for the effectiveness of the National Offender Management Model', in M. Hough, R. Allen and U. Padel (eds), *Reshaping Probation and Prisons: The New Offender Management Framework*. Bristol: Policy Press.

Reid-Howie Associates Ltd (2004a) *The Provision of Housing Advice to Prisoners in Scotland: An Evaluation of the Projects Funded by the Rough Sleepers Initiative*. Edinburgh: Scottish Executive Social Research Development Department. (See: www.scotland.gov.uk/Resource/Doc/25725/0023527.pdf.)

Reid-Howie Associates Ltd (2004b) *The Provision of Housing Advice to Prisoners in Scotland: An Evaluation of the Projects Funded by the Rough Sleepers Initiative*, Research Findings 181/2004. Edinburgh: Development Department Research Programme, Scottish Executive. (See: www.scotland.gov.uk/Resource/Doc/25725/0029568.pdf.)

Renshaw, J. (2000) *Advice on Accommodation*. London: Youth Justice Board. (See: www.yjb.gov.uk/Publications/Resources/Downloads/AccomVulnerYP.pdf (accessed 21 January 2007).

Rolfe, H. (2001) *Barriers to Employment for Offenders and Ex-Offenders: Part 2 – A Literature Review*, Research Report No. 155. Leeds: Department for Work and Pensions. (See: www.dwp.gov.uk/asd/asd5/rport155/Main2.pdf.)

Rosengard, A. (2002) *The Future of Hostels for Homeless People*, Research Findings No. 122. Edinburgh: Scottish Executive Central Research Unit.

Scottish Executive (2001) *Criminal Justice: Accommodation Services: A Review and Consultation Paper*. Edinburgh: Scottish Executive Justice Department.

Seymour, M. (2006) 'Recurring cycles: pathways of homelessness, crime and imprisonment', *Prison Service Journal*, 166.

Shelter (2005) *Homeless? Read This: The Rules on How and When the Council Has to Help You*. London: Shelter. (See: england.shelter.org.uk/files/seealsodocs/328/HomelessReadthis%2Epdf.)

Singleton, N., Meltzer, H., Gatward, R., Coid, J. and Deasy, D. (1998) *Psychiatric Morbidity among Prisoners in England and Wales*. London: Stationery Office.

Social Exclusion Unit (SEU) (2002) *Reducing Re-offending by Ex-prisoners*. London: Office of the Deputy Prime Minister.

Chapter 8

The voluntary sector and prisoners' resettlement

Anthea Hucklesby and Jackie Worrall

Introduction

The voluntary sector has been involved in criminal justice for a considerable period of time (Carey and Walker 2002). It has a strong tradition of working with prisoners both inside prison and in the community. Historically, it has provided additional services rather than contributing to the Prison Service's core functions. However, recent developments have increased the focus on the voluntary sector as a potential provider of core criminal justice services. The rising prison population means that there are more prisoners leaving custody than ever before. Contemporaneously, the Probation Service, the traditional provider of aftercare, is overstretched and is required to focus on higher-risk and/or longer-term prisoners. Consequently, many low-risk and short-term prisoners leave custody without support despite having high reconviction rates (HMIP 2001; SEU 2002). The government has signalled its intention to reduce reoffending through the National Reducing Re-offending Action Plan (Home Office 2004). Central to this is the provision of services in the seven pathways to resettlement. Many of the pathways relate to areas in which the voluntary sector has traditionally provided services. Indeed, the voluntary sector has been a 'trailblazer' for the provision of resettlement services both in prisons and in the community without which the statutory services would be starting from a much lower base and with far less knowledge and experience. For these reasons the voluntary sector is seen as an appropriate vehicle to provide resettlement services and to plug gaps in provision which the statutory sector is unable to offer. The concept of contestability takes this forward whereby voluntary sector organisations as well as the statutory sector and private companies will be able to bid for government funding to provide services. Moves to use the voluntary sector further in resettlement fits squarely into the broader government agenda to increase 'community' involvement in the provision of services more generally.

The voluntary and community sector is already heavily involved in the provision of services in prison. The true extent of involvement is unknown (Martin 2002) but the most recent figures available estimate that at least 550 voluntary organisations are occupied in providing services for prisoners or ex-prisoners and their families and around 12,000 individuals are working for voluntary and community sector organisations inside establishments (HM Prison Service 2002b)

This chapter draws on our experiences of providing and evaluating resettlement projects operated by the voluntary sector at the beginning of the twenty-first century. It discusses the policy context and the drive to increase voluntary sector provision of resettlement services before going on to explore some of the challenges and barriers which exist currently. The chapter ends by analysing examples of voluntary sector resettlement projects. Before doing this, what we mean by the voluntary sector is defined.

Definitions

Recent debates about the role of the voluntary sector in the criminal justice process tend to treat it as a homogenous whole. However, the sector is diverse comprising a few national organisations such as Nacro, some regional organisations and many local organisations, a lot of which are very small and have turnovers of less than £100,000 (Etherington and Passey 2002; Gill and Mawby 1990; HM Prison Service 2001; Padel 2002). This diversity makes defining the voluntary sector problematic (Etherington and Passey 2002; Gill and Mawby 1990; Padel 2002). Nevertheless, voluntary sector organisations have a number of common features (Etherington and Passey 2002; HM Prison Service 2001). All voluntary sector organisations are non-profit-making and most are charities. Consequently, their activities are confined by their charitable aims and the requirement to comply with charities law. A third feature of voluntary sector organisations is that they have management committees made up of volunteers who are responsible for the management and financial affairs of the organisation (Department of Education and Skills 2004).

Recently, various terms have been used in official discourse about voluntary sector involvement in criminal justice. It has been described as the voluntary and community sector (VCS) and the third sector, presumably to distinguish it from the statutory and private sectors. This chapter will use the term voluntary and community sector (VCS). Nevertheless, the word 'voluntary' is itself problematic as it suggests that organisations provide services freely or cheaply using an unpaid 'workforce' when the reality is that they have employees, infrastructures and overheads like many other organisations and some may not use 'volunteers', i.e. unpaid helpers, at all. This definition also includes a range of agencies dealing with social policy issues such as housing, employment and health. Some of these will be in the statutory sector yet, as the Prison Service itself recognises, they have a lot in common with voluntary sector organisations in terms of their relationship with the Prison Service (HM Prison Service 2001).

The work of VCS organisations involved in criminal justice can be split into two main areas, namely reform of the criminal justice process, i.e. campaigning groups, and service providers (Bryans *et al.* 2002; Padel 2002). The focus of this chapter is on the second of these groups which provides services to prisoners in prison and when they return to the community. Normally, organisations focus on either campaigning or service provision. For example, the Prison Reform Trust is largely a penal reform organisation whereas the Inside Out Trust is a service provider. Nevertheless, some organisations such as Nacro and Women in Prison do both although, in the case of Nacro, its two operations are technically split. Even without organisations which have dual functions, the distinction between campaigners and service providers is often blurred and can change over time. For outsiders, this may be confusing and mean that the nature and purpose of organisations is misunderstood. One important consequence of this is that many VCS organisations are perceived to be working on behalf of offenders and prisoners. CLINKS (Department of Education and Skills 2004) sees this as an advantage suggesting that this means that VCS organisations are more supportive of prisoners than statutory agencies. However, this has the potential to make it appear that they are opposed to the work of the Prison Service and can engender concern about their motives and objectives in being involved in service provision for prisoners. In this way it may contribute to animosity between VSC workers and prison staff because staff perceive VSC workers as 'being on the side of the prisoners'. There is some anecdotal evidence that there may be some truth in this. Prison Service managers have recently suggested that VCS organisations, such as Citizens Advice Bureaux and the Samaritans, which are perceived as independent and not prisoner-focused, are more readily accepted and seen as more credible than other VCS organisations which are more directly engaged with prisoners' issues. This suggests that the Prison Service may be more comfortable working with organisations which have a reputation for providing a high-quality service to the general public in the community. Such organisations also have the benefit of assisting offenders to connect with mainstream society.

The involvement of the VCS in the criminal justice process has a range of benefits and provides additionality to statutory services in a number of respects (Bryans *et al.* 2002; Gill and Mawby 1990). Most notably, they are able to apply for funding from a range of sources not available to statutory agencies alone including charitable trusts (HM Prison Service 2001). This has been one of the driving forces behind Prison Service attempts to work more closely with the VCS. The diversity of the VCS means that the organisations have many different strengths and expertise working with a wide range of offenders/prisoners. Consequently, the sector is well placed to provide services which will address the varied needs of different groups of offenders and in so doing assist the Prison Service with its diversity agenda. Furthermore, there is some anecdotal evidence that prisoners from minority ethnic groups are more willing to approach and work with VCS organisations (see Williams *et al.*, this volume). The VCS are less constrained by bureaucracy and targets than the statutory sector and have the potential to be more flexible, innovative and risk taking (Bryans *et al.* 2002; Gill and Mawby 1990). The VCS are grounded in local communities and bridge the transition from prison to the community primarily because they are likely to have extensive local networks. VCS staff and volunteers are committed and enthusiastic and bring a wide range of skills and experience to their work, which may differ from those available in the statutory sector (CLINKS 2004). This provides an opportunity for the organisations to learn from each other and to develop best practice (Nutley and Rimmer 2002). While contributing to institutional targets they can also add value by broadening out the services provided to prisoners and offer services, which would otherwise be unavailable (Bryans *et al.* 2002; CLINKS 2004; Gill and Mawby 1990). More specifically, they can offer services to prisoners who do not want to engage with the statutory agencies.

Many of the benefits which accrue because the VCS are working in prisons are intangible and unmeasureable. One of these is the challenge it provides to prison culture (Nutley and Rimmer 2002).

Often VCS organisation involvement requires prisons to question their practices. For example, VCS organisations have had a role in challenging prisons to see prisoners in a different light through the provision of Listeners schemes, which have made the Prison Service aware that prisoners are able to help themselves (Nutley and Rimmer 2002). They also bring in different practices which may influence how the prison operates (Nutley and Rimmer 2002). Furthermore, they may bring about improvements to the quality of the services provided as statutory staff are 'infected' with VCS staff enthusiasm and commitment (Gill and Mawby 1990).

Government policy for VCS involvement in resettlement

The government sees the VCS as playing a vital role in society. Accordingly, it is seen as a 'cornerstone of a healthy society and a partner in delivering world-class services' (Home Office 2005). To this end, the government is promoting and enhancing the role of VCS organisations and has introduced a range of initiatives 'Compact Plus', 'Futurebuilders' and 'ChangeUp' to facilitate this (Home Office 2005). This followed the publication of the 'Compact on the Relations between the Government and the VCS' in 1998 (Home Office 1998). The Compact resulted from an extensive inquiry into the future of the voluntary sector (Commission on the Future of the Voluntary Sector – the Deakin Commission 1996). It signalled a 'step-change' in government and voluntary sector relations acknowledging the contribution made by the voluntary sector (Etherington and Passey 2002). The Compact included a framework for a new approach to partnership and set out a shared vision for voluntary sector involvement in public services. Principles were established in terms of issues such as funding, accountability, policy developments and consultation and good practice as well as procedures for dealing with problems and conflicts and codes of practice were to follow (Home Office 1998). This enthusiasm for VCS involvement filtered down to the Prison Service and National Offender Management Service which published a number of documents. These signalled their intentions to increase voluntary sector participation in the provision of services to prisoners generally and specifically to the resettlement agenda.

In 2001 the Prison Service published a strategy for working with the VCS (HM Prison Service 2001). It recognised the importance of the VCS to the Prison Service, particularly as a provider of services in key areas such as drug treatment, suicide prevention, basic skills, family ties, health care and resettlement and in providing a bridge between prison and community. Further, the Prison Service recognised that partnership with the VCS would enable it to tap into additional funding sources from Europe and charitable trusts. The strategy, therefore, recommended greater involvement of the VCS in the work of the Prison Service and recognised that it could make a contribution to meeting its aims, particularly in terms of maintaining and strengthening prisoners' community ties and reducing reoffending. While recognising that problems existed, the strategy aimed to develop and strengthen the partnership between the Prison Service and the VCS. This required effective management to ensure that the VCS contributed to Prison Service objectives and priorities and needed effective communication and planning, consultation and involvement in decision-making, adequate and long-term funding and monitoring and evaluation of outputs and outcomes. It was intended that the strategy would promote genuine and effective partnership between the Prison Service and voluntary sector and ensure that voluntary sector activities were fully integrated into prisons. It also aimed to introduce fair and open competition among service providers.

At the time of publication of the strategy, the Prison Service had already established a national voluntary sector coordinator but the strategy recommended that each Prison Service area should also have coordinators. Additionally, it suggested that establishments should have either full- or part-time coordinators at senior management level, whose role would be to manage services and support provided by the VCS. No resources were made available for these posts but they were created by a Prison Service Order (No. 4190), which also set out a strategy for working with VCS groups in prisons (HM Prison Service 2002a). Contemporaneously, the Prison Service published guidelines for voluntary and community sector staff and volunteers (HM Prison Service 2002b). These recognised the value of the work being undertaken but also highlighted the need for work to be appropriate and effective. The document provided information about the prison estate and offered practical guidance about how to access prisons and work safely in them.

The creation of NOMS means that the role of the VCS in the provision of services to offenders is going to expand. NOMS engaged with the voluntary sector early on, launching a draft strategy and consultation on its role (NOMS 2005a). This process culminated in the publication of an Action Plan for an effective partnership between NOMS and the VCS (NOMS 2005b). NOMS also has a VCS Team (formerly the Voluntary Sector Unit) which publishes a regular newsletter. These developments clearly signal the intention of NOMS to develop the role of the VCS in the provision of criminal justice services.

The VCS sees the creation of NOMS as an opportunity for greater involvement in service provision to offenders. The introduction of a market for the provision of services for offenders under 'contestability' should mean that there will be increased opportunities for the VCS to deliver services to offenders and to undertake activities traditionally carried out by the statutory sector. It will provide opportunities for VCS groups to work in partnership and develop consortia with each other as well as with the public and private sectors. In theory, this will enable all parties to play to strengths and share resources and expertise. However, the VCS has concerns about how contestability will operate in practice. These include how the bidding process will operate and the resources involved, the involvement of the private sector, the length of contracts, the funding of monitoring and evaluation, and the independent status of the VCS. The fear of many VCS organisations is that there will be too many barriers for many VCS organisations to compete to provide services. A particular concern is lack of capacity especially when many organisations are small and lack the resources to bid and/or provide services even at a regional level. It is difficult to envisage, also, Regional Offender Managers commissioning services from a myriad of small and diverse VCS organisations as the logistics of coordinating these is likely to be prohibitive. The government has recognised the potential for the lack of capacity to stymie its plans for greater involvement of the VCS and has put measures in place to expand it (Home Office 2005).

In order to contribute to offender management the VCS will have to adapt. It will be a competitive, contract-driven culture in which service providers will have to be fully accountable and meet targets. The climate has already started to change in preparation for the introduction of contestability with VCS organisations jostling for position in prisons and working towards Prison Service key performance targets. In many ways this environment runs counter to the ethos of VCS organisations and they will have a stark choice about whether to compromise or opt out of contestability and continue to rely on other sources of funding and support, although it is far from clear what will happen to these alternatives in the future or indeed whether unfunded VCS organisations will be welcome in prisons (Sampson 2002). Some VCS organisations will face ideological issues, particularly in relation to receiving government funding, working with the private sector and involvement in enforcement and breach proceedings. In essence, VCS organisations will have to choose between staying true to their ideals and becoming more commercial organisations (Sampson 2002). Contestability also has the potential to reduce the independence of VCS organisations and the advantages which go with it, and turn them into quasi-governmental agencies. Arguably, one of the motives of the government in introducing contestability may be to stifle opposition to its crime policies by making VCS organisations dependent on statutory funding thus making it impossible for them to criticise policies for fear of losing their financial security (Gill and Mawby 1990; Kendall and Knapp 1996; Ryan 1996; Taylor 1996; Walker 2006). Indeed, there is a recent example of this threat when Nacro was placed in considerable financial difficulties when Home Office funding for its service provision all but dried up during Michael Howard's tenure as Home Secretary (Walker 2006; Wilson 2001). As Sampson (2002) points out, the temptation to chase the funding can be almost overwhelming so it is important for organisations to have a clear strategy in terms of how far they are willing to compromise their ideals in pursuit of access to prisons and funding.

Several recent developments have the potential to limit the involvement of the VCS and particularly to exclude smaller-scale, localised projects which are not explicitly focused on reducing reoffending from providing resettlement services (Padel 2002; Sampson 2002). Firstly, the increasing importance of accredited programmes creates potential dangers for the VCS. The advantage of these programmes is that they represent a more systematic and standardised approach to the provision of services to offenders. However, the nature of accredited programmes and the criteria and processes required to achieve recognition means that some, if not all, VCS organisations are unlikely to be able to provide them (Padel 2002). The growth in importance of accredited programmes also diminishes the scope for diversity and new ideas to develop which is perceived to be a particular strength of the VCS (Padel 2002). Secondly, statutory services are under increasing pressure to demonstrate the effectiveness of services particularly in terms of reoffending. Yet a lot of the work undertaken by VSC organisations indirectly, rather than directly, influences key performance indicators (Padel 2002). The challenge to the VCS and especially the smaller organisations, is very real as the experience of the contracting out of drug services in prisons has demonstrated (Sampson 2002).

Despite the enthusiasm for the VCS to be involved in resettlement activities there is little evidence of their effectiveness, particularly in terms of reducing offending. There has been very little monitoring and evaluation of resettlement work undertaken by the VCS. There are several reasons for this. Firstly, under current arrangements funding for monitoring and evaluation is limited if it exists at all. Consequently, any evaluation which is undertaken is often inadequate and methodologically flawed. Secondly, independent evaluation is against the ethos of many VCS organisations and there can be a general reluctance on the part of an organisation to subject its work to independent scrutiny (Sampson 2002). This may be because of the high importance given to confidentiality and anonymity. Thirdly, workers and volunteers often perceive paperwork and other activities associated with monitoring and evaluation as worthless and keeping them away from their 'proper' work with offenders. As a result, it is a low priority and is often the first activity to stop when workloads increase. Consequently, records are incomplete or missing altogether. Fourthly, many organisations are unable to identify clear objectives or measurable outcomes for their work to be monitored or evaluated (Sampson 2002; see also Wincup and Hucklesby, this volume).

The evidence which does exist suggests that schemes run by the VCS are less effective than those run by statutory agencies (Clancy *et al.* 2006; Lewis *et al.* 2003). Clancy *et al.* (2006) explain this disparity in terms of the involvement of probation officers inside prisons who provide a professional input and focus on motivation and thinking skills. This suggests that differences in the effectiveness of services provided by the statutory agencies and the VCS may be explained by variations in the focus of their work. The 'What Works' movement has ensured that the work undertaken by the statutory sector concentrates on dealing with offending-related behaviour and with motivating offenders to change as well as immediate practical issues such as finding accommodation. By contrast, many VSC organisations tend to focus on dealing with practical problems such as housing, benefits and so on. While this may result in meeting short-term targets and measures of success such as ensuring that prisoners do not leave prison without somewhere to sleep and an appointment at the Benefits Agency, its long-term effectiveness is less clear. Consequently, the resettlement activities of VCS organisations may be 'successful' in terms of outputs, i.e. finding accommodation or employment, but their 'effectiveness' in terms of outcomes relating to longer-term goals such as reducing reoffending is unknown (issues about measuring the effectiveness of resettlement services are discussed in more depth in Wincup and Hucklesby, this volume). Increasingly, however, short-term output measures are being used as proxy measures for determining the VCS contribution to reducing offending. Nevertheless, requirements to measure adequately the contribution of the VCS to resettlement involves making sure that the distinction is made between 'doing good' and 'doing well' (Tonkiss and Passey 1999).

VCS provision of resettlement services

It has been recognised for some time that the VCS can help to fill gaps in resettlement provision, especially for prisoners serving sentences of less than 12 months who are not currently required to have statutory supervision. The nature of the work undertaken varies but includes working with offenders in custody to help them cope with or plan for their release and providing drop-in centres and mentoring support after release. However, at the start of the twenty-first century the work was identified as being uncoordinated, untargeted and haphazard (HM Prison Service 2001). There was little awareness of what was provided in particular prisons and often governors were not aware of which organisations were working in their prisons and why (HM Prison Service 2001). There was no central record of which organisations were working in which prisons and no routine monitoring of the quality of the services provided (HM Prison Service 2001). Work was also concentrated in particular prisons largely because they were easily accessible geographically, local funding sources existed or the governor was amenable. This particular issue still presents challenges to the VCS and Prison Service as it is much easier to provide services in or close to large urban areas than on 'greenfield sites' where no significant local populations exist.

In 1999, CLINKS published a report of a study of the work of the VCS in four prisons (CLINKS 1999). The report found that the work of the VCS in prisons lacked a philosophical and practical framework (Martin 2002). It found no evidence of a strategic view of the role of community-based organisations nor was there an accurate record of the agencies working in the prison. There was also no clarity about how the organisations had started working in the prisons and what work they were doing (Martin 2002). Prisons had no way of establishing the credibility of VCS organisations and where good practice existed it tended to rely on the goodwill of individual staff. There did not appear to be any central coordination of the contribution made by the VCS and no process for reviewing or evaluating its input. Nevertheless, the report also found a great deal of goodwill and the Prison Service demonstrated a high degree of commitment and enthusiasm for the work of the VCS, showing interest in ways to implement work rather than limit or exclude it. The report recommended that there should be clear policy statements and strategic guidelines with management structures and coordination of the work of outside agencies. As we have seen, since publication of the report, significant improvements have been made in the coordination and management of VCS work in prisons.

Additionally, the CLINKS report (1999) highlighted issues with the lack of focus of services on prisoners' needs and on factors related to reoffending. This issue has also been raised more recently because of concerns that some VCS organisations are providing services to prisoners in their specialist areas without regard to whether this is required and/or appropriate. In other words, they provide the service they want rather than what is necessarily needed. In some cases, this has resulted in organisations being denied access to prisons, which could be avoided if consultation had taken place earlier. The importance of the VCS providing services which prisons need and want is important. There are costs and resource implications for prisons of accommodating VCS organisations and prisons need to be able to see tangible benefits, particularly in relation to contributing to their KPTs. Prisons, therefore, cannot be expected to simply open their doors to all VCS organisations who wish to work prisons even if this is funded. VCS organisations in conjunction with the Prison Service need to think carefully about what services are required. This will also avoid overlap and gaps in service provision in particular prisons. CLINKS (1999) also raised issues about the validity of some services, the lack of integration into the prison regime and the quality of the services provided.

Another consequence of the lack of oversight of services provided by the VCS particularly in prisons is that the quality of the service is not monitored routinely. Consequently, 'maverick' services could be offered and workers and volunteers were able to act inappropriately (CLINKS 1999). Instances of inappropriate behaviour of staff and volunteers still occur and this is more likely when lone workers are in establishments. In conjunction with high levels of staff sickness in some organisations, this indicates that some VCS organisations need to review recruitment and selection procedures, and ensure that adequate staff training and supervision takes place, including full induction to the Prison Service and the particular establishments being worked in. In order to gain the trust and respect of prison staff, VCS organisations need to demonstrate that they and their staff are accountable and that they deal with any issues swiftly and decisively. Service level agreements between the VCS and the Prison Service ensure that responsibilities and procedures are clear for both parties.

The main issue facing the provision of resettlement services by the VCS is lack of funding. Funding for services comes from statutory sources, charitable trusts and sometimes from European Union sources such as the European Social Fund. Most funding is time limited and often for relatively short periods of three to five years. In reality, this means that projects become fully operational for only a short period because they spend the first year or so dealing with implementation issues and spend the final year trying to obtain future funding whilst staff leave because of the insecurity of their jobs. The time-limited nature of most projects also results in valuable expertise and experience being lost. So far most of the funding has been for relatively small-scale 'pilot' projects which operate in no more than three or four prisons/areas. Consequently, they provide little indication of how they will work on a bigger scale or the potential issues which may be faced when pilot projects are scaled up. Funding issues have also limited the services which can be provided in each prison. After an initial period, workloads increase and invariably demand outstrips supply. Workers become overstretched and, with no additional resources, either work with only a proportion of the prisoners who seek help or provide a more superficial service than is required. Both solutions mean that gaps in provision continue and that some prisoners' expectations are raised but ultimately remain unmet.

The VCS faces barriers to working in prisons. It is recognised that the climate in which VCS work has changed recently but problems still remain although they may be less entrenched and/ or less frequently encountered. While governor grades often accept that VCS organisations have a valuable role to play in the provision of services in prisons, rank-and-file officers sometimes do not. A strong stereotypical view of the VCS as 'do-gooders' who did not understand prisoners or prisons remains (Bryans *et al.* 2002). This is sometimes translated into obstructive behaviour whereby prison officers 'forget' to bring prisoners for meetings or groupwork. Other problems arise because the activities of the VCS are not prioritised so that officers are moved away to other duties, rooms are unavailable and so on. This means that workers sometimes find it difficult to operate services effectively. Crucial to dealing with such issues is a dedicated member of prison staff who can champion their cause.

However, reliance on one individual rather than clear procedures and systems might endanger the project when that individual moves on, which frequently occurs in the Prison Service. Integration into prisons and effective partnership working can assist in overcoming such barriers.

The Prison Service and VCS organisations have very different cultures. While the Prison Service is regimented, hierarchical and bureaucratic, VCS organisations tend to have a much looser flatter structure. This is always going to present challenges to partnership working. These can be particularly stark for VCS organisations as they are working within the culture of the Prison Service and this can make it difficult for employees or volunteers from the VCS. Prisons tend to be male-dominated and the occupational culture of prison staff appears to share many of the characteristics of police culture (Reiner 2000). Recently, official reports have highlighted the extent of racism in the Prison Service (CRE 2003; House of Commons 2006) and there have been allegations of physical abuse in some establishments (for example, see Howard League 2002). Many VCS workers struggle with these attitudes and behaviour as it is contrary to the culture and ethos of many VCS organisations. Challenging it, however, might have repercussions making it difficult, if not impossible, to continue to work in the prison. Organisations trying to confront behaviour on behalf of their staff are often concerned that they will be denied access to prisons in future. Prisons are difficult and sometimes hostile environments in which to work and many VCS workers report feeling isolated and stressed, sometimes resulting in periods of sick leave or workers leaving altogether. These problems are exacerbated by the fact that VCS workers often work alone or in small teams. However, it should be acknowledged that many VCS organisations and workers also have stereotypical views of prison staff and regard them as unsympathetic and uncaring in their treatment of prisoners (Padel 2002). Differences in the cultures of the Prison Service and the VCS are always going to present challenges to partnership working. In other areas of criminal justice these are starting to be overcome but the unique working environment of custodial institutions clearly presents additional issues.

VCS organisations have also come up against other more tangible problems. Space is at a premium in prisons and VCS organisations often have to work in inadequate and limited space sometimes well away from the prisoners they are trying to work with. There have also been considerable difficulties with the bureaucracy of working in prisons. Activities such as getting the telephone or ISDN lines installed, using IT equipment and having access to the internet is problematic and time-consuming. All staff require security clearance and this can take a considerable amount of time and cause delays in starting projects as well as gaps in provision while replacement workers are cleared.

The degree of integration of resettlement services provided by the VCS varies. There are examples of services which are fully integrated into prison systems. These often access prisoners through induction and receive referrals from other services. By contrast, some services are less well integrated relying on prisoners self-referring or with ad hoc referrals to and from other services within the prison. Levels of integration are often linked to the degree of partnership between the Prison Service and the VCS organisation. One area where integration appears to be minimal and inconsistent is information exchange. Many VCS organisations do not have access routinely to LIDS (the IT scheme detailing prisoners held in prisons) or prison files, making their work more difficult. Often this relates to a lack of trust on the part of the Prison Service that such information is its property and that VCS workers may use it inappropriately. There are also issues about the information collected by VCS organisations. While some prisons allow information about prisoners to be taken out of the prison others do not. This is not only inconsistent but it makes providing a service through the prison gate difficult because community workers are not able to access information on the work which has been undertaken in prison. Furthermore, any risks associated with particular individuals will not be available to community workers or volunteers. These issues can also cause problems for the evaluation of VCS services. Recently, several prisons have refused to allow one project and/or its evaluators to access the Police National Computer (PNC) numbers of prisoners they have worked with meaning that reconvictions studies cannot be undertaken.

An advantage often cited in official documents of resettlement services provided by VCS organisations is the continuity of service they can provide through the prison gate. On the one hand this is obvious as it is usually impractical for Prison Service staff to work in the community. On the other hand, there is no evidence to suggest that VCS organisations are effectively doing this. Evidence of the resettlement pathfinders suggests that statutory agencies, i.e. the Probation Service, are more successful in keeping in contact with prisoners in the community (Clancy et al. 2006; Lewis et al. 2003). In addition, some VCS organisations have concentrated their efforts on providing services in prisons and not in the community for a number of reasons including the need to carve out and maintain a role within the prisons, particularly in light of the opportunities provided by contestability and high workload in prisons which have militated against community work.

Nacro: a case study

Nacro is one organisation involved in the provision of services to prisoners and to offenders in the community. Since it was established in 1966 it has delivered employment and training to offenders in the community, provided housing for offenders, trained prison staff and supported offenders and ex-prisoners by providing practical help, information and guidance to facilitate resettlement in the community. In this section, we describe three resettlement initiatives it has been involved with.

Resettlement Pathfinder

In 1999 the Home Office funded a number of pilot projects to test effective models of resettlement for prisoners serving shorter sentences (Clancy *et al.* 2006; Lewis *et al.* 2003). Nacro was one of the voluntary and community sector organisations involved in the delivery of the pilots. The funding available allowed for support only in Birmingham prison but Nacro was able to obtain some charitable funding which made it possible to provide some post-release support. This meant that an assessment of risk and need could be made inside the prison and, where necessary, a referral could be made to the community-based worker who provided support for as long as was necessary. The post-release work began at the gate and facilitated community links. The project planned to offer weekly contact but in fact the majority of participants failed to keep in contact (Lewis *et al.* 2003). This highlights one of the problems for VCS organisations providing resettlement services. There may be great value for offenders in a relationship which is voluntary on both sides but once offenders are in the community there is no compulsion for them to remain in contact. This impacts upon long-term work with offenders as well as making the monitoring of long-term targets difficult.

The model made it possible for prisoners to access the support they needed after release but there were a number of problems inherent in providing a service in the prison. This was primarily due to the transfer of prisoners between prisons as a result of overcrowding in the system (Lewis *et al.* 2003). Throughout the project, prisoners were moved out at short notice, even if they had engaged with the project and work had been done with them. The project lost over one-third of its participants while they were still in prison. Despite the difficulties, which meant that successful outcomes were limited, the project did help to establish the need for working with prisoners prior to release to develop a resettlement plan which identified the nature and level of support needed, and for ensuring that continuing support was available for those assessed as having difficulty in coping alone.

A good practice guide developed from the evaluation aimed at addressing the needs of short-term prisoners identified key components for developing the necessary support (Vanstone and Lewis 2002). This included bringing in representatives from different agencies, involvement of the relevant community organisations and provision for meeting diverse needs. After release the guide recommended consistent contact arrangements and providing transport from prison, and commented on the need for a sustainable support network in the community. The evaluation confirmed that short-term prisoners' resettlement needs were typically a combination of difficulties in accessing opportunities and resources and pointed to the need for a holistic and integrated approach which ensured continuity of contact pre- and post-release, involving a high level of contact addressing not only practical problems but also lifestyle, attitudes and motivation to change. However, by the time that the evaluation report was published, the funding for the projects had ended and the pilot projects had finished. In common with many pilots, the Birmingham Pathfinder was not replaced or offered further funding from any of the prisons.

HMYOI Portland

In 1999, Nacro approached the Monument Trust, one of the Sainsbury Family Charitable Trusts, to ask for help in developing a pre- and post-release support service for the most vulnerable of the juveniles then held in HMYOI Portland. The involvement of charitable trusts has been of great importance in the development of the VCS projects. Many of the trusts have supported new and innovative ideas, creating opportunities to test models of service delivery.

At the time the project was set up, there was little constructive activity for young people, there was no resettlement planning and there had been allegations of cruelty and abuse on the part of officers.

With funding from the Trust, Nacro set up the On Side Project. This comprised a small team of key workers who were based inside the prison. They identified the most vulnerable prisoners and began to work with them some three months prior to release. The key worker would spend time with the young man in the period leading up to release, identifying risks and problems and agreeing a resettlement action plan. The same worker remained in contact after release and provided whatever support was necessary, including finding accommodation, getting a job or liaising with parents. It was also likely to involve meeting the young person at the gate and taking them to their first appointments. Building on the evaluation of the Pathfinder Projects, the service also helped the young men to rethink their own behaviour and to take responsibility for their actions. One of the criteria for involvement in the project was that the young person was assessed as being motivated to change. The project was evaluated internally and the results showed an identifiable reduction in offending among participants (Nacro 2006). Clearly it is always difficult for one project or intervention to claim credit for desistance from offending because there will always be a number of variables which might impact on changing behaviour. However, feedback from individual participants demonstrated how important they had found the relationship with an adult who provided a positive role model and who offered both practical and emotional support.

When the juveniles were removed from the prison, the project, with further funding from the Monument Trust, began to work with the young offender population. The context for this phase of the work was very different. The prison had established a resettlement team, both the governor and the resettlement manager sat on the project steering group and the prison contributed funding to the project, which resulted in it becoming much more integrated with the prison regime. Although the climate was more promising it was soon apparent that working with these young men was more challenging. Their behaviour was more entrenched, the majority had drug and alcohol issues, many came from abusive backgrounds and a significant number had mental health issues. An internal evaluation of the project suggested that there was a reduction in the seriousness and frequency of offending when prisoners were involved with the project but there remained a high risk of further offending of some sort (Nacro 2006). The project also demonstrated the extent of the barriers facing project participants as they returned to the community. Finding somewhere to live proved to be almost impossible. There was little accommodation available to offenders and, in many cases, the young men had already failed in the accommodation which did exist. The numbers who needed intensive and prolonged support far outstripped the staffing resources available. This meant that, although it was unquestionably a valuable project, there had to be additional resources if the service was going to offer the degree of support needed for more than a handful of prisoners. Another difficulty was the increasing number of young men who resided in London and Kent, which made the provision of after-release support problematic. This was resolved, at least in part, by a partnership arrangement with the Depaul Trust which provided support for young men returning to London.

Pyramid Project

The Northern Rock Foundation was looking to fund resettlement projects which aimed to reduce offending in the North East. They approached Nacro, who proposed a project involving an integrated resettlement service which would provide a holistic approach to resettlement and which embodied all the lessons learned from previous projects. It drew heavily on the experience in Portland. The Northern Rock Foundation made a similar approach to the Depaul Trust and the outcome is a partnership project providing both pre- and post-release support for prisoners returning to Tyneside and the Tees Valley. The project was called the Pyramid Project. Nacro established a resettlement team in HMP Holme House (a male local prison) and a single worker in HMP Low Newton (female establishment) while the Depaul Trust worked in Deerbolt (Young Offenders Institution). Workers were to make the initial contact with prisoners and, when necessary, refer them on to a community-based team who would offer longer-term support. Prisoners could also be worked with exclusively in the community. Both VCS organisations and the staff employed had run resettlement projects in the prisons previously. While advantageous in many respects, this posed challenges in terms of convincing prison staff and prisoners that the 'new' service had a different focus.

An important part of this project was to find and cement relationships with organisations which could offer services to prisoners in the community. These included housing providers, local employers and training providers. The sustainability of resettlement projects relies on the availability of these services to provide placements and opportunities for prisoners leaving custody. However, finding and maintaining these contacts is time-consuming and workers found it difficult to do this alongside other commitments. Developmental work is often another victim of high workloads within the prisons.

The project included the development of a volunteer mentor service in recognition of the need for this more prolonged support. Mentors are able to act as advocates, providing practical help and offering emotional support. The lessons have already been translated across to Portland, where the latest phase of work, the Milestones Project, is providing a mentoring service to young men returning to communities in the South West. Volunteer mentoring builds upon the idea that a relationship with a responsible adult can help offenders to desist from offending. While there is a cost in involving volunteers it is substantially less than the cost of a fully paid member of staff so that more mentors can be available to offer support without incurring additional cost. It provides an opportunity for people from a range of backgrounds to work with offenders and to begin to understand why they may have offended and how offenders themselves have often been victims. However, as discussed in Hucklesby and Wincup (this volume), there is little evidence of their effectiveness. It has also raised issues about the problems of retaining volunteers. Offenders are a difficult group of people to work with and providing mentoring can be challenging. It can be demoralising, particularly when offenders routinely fail to keep in touch or miss meetings.

Conclusion

The VCS already makes a significant contribution to the delivery of resettlement services and their involvement is likely to increase further in the future. However, the context in which they provide services is changing and this is likely to have an extensive impact on VCS involvement in resettlement. The introduction of contestability will have the greatest impact. Potentially, it will result in VCS involvement in the provision of core criminal justice functions and in particular providing services which link with the resettlement pathways and assist in meeting the targets which accompany them. However, many questions remain unanswered, most notably whether the VCS will decide to compete for contracts, what services will be put out to tender, whether the private sector will decide to become involved in the provision of resettlement services and when commissioning is going to begin.

The work the VCS undertakes currently provides valuable additional services which contribute to meeting the resettlement needs of offenders, particularly through its ability to bring in additional resources, its capacity to be creative and innovative and its enthusiastic and committed staff. However, effective involvement requires more than enthusiasm and the VCS will need to change if it is to be involved in the provision of statutory services. Equally, there will have to be changes to the procurement and commissioning processes if the VCS is to have a genuine opportunity to participate. The signing of the compact between government and the VCS has failed to deliver a balanced relationship between the VCS and potential statutory funders. Despite the recent appointment of the Compact Commissioner concerns remain about short-term contracts, full cost recovery, lack of time for bid preparation, over-prescriptive contracts and a sense that there remains a perception that the VCS should be providing services that are cheap or free.

If the VCS is to have equal status in new partnerships with the statutory and private sectors, organisations will have to be accountable, establish their credibility as service providers, ensure that they understand the implications of full cost recovery and deliver services within agreed budgets and targets. There will be a requirement to be involved in enforcement, which may impact on credibility with service users. All of these factors will need to be considered when VCS organisations decide whether they wish to bid to provide statutory services. The VCS must also face the fact that there is little evidence of its effectiveness in providing services. This is not to suggest that it is not effective but rather that this remains largely unproven. This is essentially because a lack of resources has generally inhibited any robust evaluation of activities and outcomes. For the future, contracts must include the costs of evaluation or there must be a commitment from commissioners to evaluate services. Some practicalities also need to be addressed. On the one hand, VCS staff must be fully committed to recording and monitoring outcomes. On the other hand, the statutory sector must be prepared to allow the VCS access to information that will make evaluation and longer- term follow-up possible.

In the years since the compact was signed there have been significant improvements in the working relationships between the VCS and the Prison Service. The ad hoc and uncoordinated contributions highlighted in the CLINKS report (CLINKS 1999) have been largely replaced by service level agreements and partnership working is being increasingly translated into multidisciplinary teams working towards shared performance targets. However, there still remain practical and cultural difficulties which can inhibit effective working. There is still a long way to go.

The development of offender management is seen as an opportunity to improve services to offenders, to reduce offending and, thereby, to protect the public as well as increase the contribution of the VCS. Where ideology and practicalities permit this is a welcome way forward. There is, however, an alternative. Some organisations will continue to refuse to accept government money, and will rely on charitable trusts and fund-raising activities to finance their work so that they do not compromise their freedom both to comment on government policy and to deliver services with outcomes which they believe to be important and appropriate for their service users. It is a measure of the size and diversity of the VCS that there is scope for some organisations to move into a contract-driven commissioning culture while others retain a more traditional VCS status.

References

Bryans, S., Martin, C. and Walker, R. (eds) (2002) *Prisons and the Voluntary Sector*. Winchester: Waterside Press.

Carey, M. and Walker, R. (2002) 'The penal voluntary sector', in S. Bryans, C. Martin and R. Walker (eds), *Prisons and the Voluntary Sector*. Winchester: Waterside Press.

Clancy, A., Hudson, K., Maguire, M., Peake, R., Raynor, P., Vanstone, M. and Kynch, J. (2006) *Getting Out and Staying Out: Results from the Resettlement Pathfinders*. Bristol: Policy Press.

CLINKS (1999) *Community Based Organisations and Four Prisons in England*. York: Prisons-Community Links.

CLINKS (2004) *Reviewing Voluntary Sector Activities in Prison*. York: CLINKS.

Commission for Racial Equality (2003) *Towards Racial Equality: An Evaluation of the Public Duty to Promote Race Equality and Good Race Relations in England and Wales*. London: CRE.

Commission on the Future of the Voluntary Sector (1996) *Meeting the Challenge of Change. Voluntary action into the 21st Century*. London: Commission Secretariat/NCVO.

Department for Education and Skills (2004) *Reviewing Voluntary Sector Activities in Prisons*. London: Department of Education and Skills.

Etherington, S. and Passey, A. (2002) 'The UK voluntary sector', in S. Bryans, C. Martin and R. Walker (eds), *Prisons and the Voluntary Sector*. Winchester: Waterside Press.

Gill, M. and Mawby, R.I. (1990) *Volunteers in the Criminal Justice System: A Comparative Study of Probation, Police, and Victim Support*. Milton Keynes: Open University Press.

Her Majesty's Inspectorates of Prisons and Probation (HMIP) (2001) *Through the Prison Gate: A Joint Thematic Review by HM Inspectorates of Prisons and Probation*. London: Home Office.

Her Majesty's Prison Service (2001) *Working with the Voluntary and Community Sector: Getting it Right Together*. London: HM Prison Service.

Her Majesty's Prison Service (2002a) *Strategy for Working with the Voluntary and Community Sector*, Prison Service Order 4190. London: Home Office.

Her Majesty's Prison Service (2002b) *An Introduction to Working with the Prison Service: Guidelines for Voluntary and Community Sector Staff and Volunteers*. London: HM Prison Service.

Home Office (1998) *Compact: Getting It Right Together. Compact on the Relations between Government and the Voluntary and Community Sector in England*, Cmnd 4100. London: Home Office.

Home Office (2004) *Reducing Re-offending National Action Plan*. London: Home Office.

Home Office (2005) *A Bright Future for the Voluntary and Community Sector*, press release, 22 March. London: Home Office.

House of Commons (2006) *Report of the Zahid Mubarek Inquiry*, H-C 1082-1. London: Stationery Office.

Howard League (2002) *Prison Watch*, June. London: Howard League for Penal Reform.

Kendall, J. and Knapp, M. (1996) *The UK Voluntary Sector*. Manchester: Manchester University Press.

Lewis, L., Vennard, J., Maguire, M,. Rayner, P., Vanstone, M., Raybold, S. and Rix, A. (2003) *The Resettlement of Short term Prisoners: An Evaluation of Seven Pathfinders*, RDS Occasional Paper No. 83. London: Home Office.

Martin, C. (2002) 'Recent progress in community-based voluntary sector work with the Prison Service', in S. Bryans, C. Martin and R. Walker (eds), *Prisons and the Voluntary Sector*. Winchester: Waterside Press.

Nacro (2006) *On Side – On Side 2 – Milestones: Nacro's Resettlement Programme for Young People Leaving Portland Young Offender Institution*. London: Nacro.

National Offender Management Service (NOMS) (2005a) *The Role of the Voluntary and Community Sector in NOMS: report of the Consultation on the Draft Strategy*. Home Office: NOMS.

National Offender Management Service (NOMS) (2005b) *Action Plan for the Development of Effective Partnership with the Voluntary and Community Sector*. London: Home Office.

Nutley, K. and Rimmer, S. (2002) 'A governor's perspective', in S. Bryans, C. Martin and R. Walker (eds), *Prisons and the Voluntary Sector*. Winchester: Waterside Press.

Padel, U. (2002) 'Voluntary sector provision in the penal system', in S. Bryans, C. Martin and R. Walker (eds), *Prisons and the Voluntary Sector*. Winchester: Waterside Press.

Reiner, R. (2000) *The Politics of the Police*, 3rd edn. Oxford: Oxford University Press.

Ryan, M. (1996) *Lobbying from Below: INQUEST in Defence of Civil Liberties*. London: UCL Press.

Sampson, A. (2002) 'Principles and pragmatism: surviving working with the Prison Service', in S. Bryans, C. Martin and R. Walker (eds), *Prisons and the Voluntary Sector*. Winchester: Waterside Press.

Social Exclusion Unit (2002) *Reducing Re-offending by Ex-prisoners*. London: Office of the Deputy Prime Minister.

Taylor, M. (1996) 'Influences on voluntary agencies', in D. Billis and M. Harries (eds), *Voluntary Agencies: Challenges of Organisation and Management*. London: Macmillan Press.

Tonkiss, F. and Passey, A. (1999) 'Trust, confidence and voluntary sector organisations: between values and institutions', *Sociology*, 33 (2): 257–74.

Vanstone, M. and Lewis, S. with Raynor, P. (2002) 'Draft Good Practice Guide for the Resettlement of Short-term Prisoners'. Unpublished report to the Home Office.

Walker, R. (2006) 'The Influence of Penal Reform Pressure Groups on Penal Policy and Practice 1980–2000'. Unpublished PhD thesis, University of Hull.

Wilson, C. (2001) 'Networking and the lobby for penal reform: conflict and consensus', in M. Ryan, S. Savage and D. Wall (eds), *Policy Networks in Criminal Justice*. Basingstoke: Palgrave.

Part 3

The resettlement of specific groups of prisoners

Chapter 9

Women and resettlement

Loraine Gelsthorpe and Gilly Sharpe

Introduction

Research studies consistently show that reoffending rates are high
following imprisonment; if there is any good work with offenders
within prisons it is sometimes quickly undone once offenders are
released back into the community and face the prospect of finding
somewhere to live and enough money to survive on (Social Exclusion
Unit 2002). Thus it is widely recognised that offenders need more
support in the post-release period than policy currently allows
for. Indeed, awareness of the need for better integrated and more
effective services for offenders has arguably underpinned the birth
of the National Offender Management Service (NOMS) following
the Correctional Services Review led by Lord Carter (2003) at the
invitation of the government. One aim of this new coordinated service
(linking prisons and probation) is to prevent offenders from falling
in between the cracks, especially short-term prisoners (where women
are highly represented) who may have benefited very little from
prison-based pre-release schemes and aftercare initiatives which are
both demand and resource led. As a consequence of this, women's
needs are not always given the attention that they deserve.

Around 70 per cent of women receive sentences of less than one
year (Home Office 2007). Until the Criminal Justice Act 2003, prison
release policy meant that the majority of women leaving prison
did so free of licence conditions and assistance, voluntary aftercare
within the Probation Service having virtually disappeared because of
financial constraints and the fact that statutory duties have had to

take precedence (Maguire *et al.* 1998, 2000). It was intended in the Act to replace sentences of imprisonment of under 12 months (i.e. short sentences) with a new sentence called 'Custody Plus' (partly to be served in custody and partly on licence in the community, with the possibility of conditions being attached to the licence either by the court or by the prison governor, and with the possibility of recall to prison following any breach of conditions). From the resettlement perspective this was important since it meant that short-term prisoners would for the first time be subject to supervision. Sceptics did not believe that this would necessarily mean practical support to effect a smooth transition from prison to life in the community, but it was generally felt to be a move in the right direction as long as there could be resources to meet demand from this 'needy' group and as long as there could be specific provision for women. However, in May 2006, Lord Bassam, junior government minister, announced a delay in the implementation of Custody Plus, and this has become an indefinite postponement.

Research evidence and women's stories relating to their release from prison highlight accommodation and housing problems in particular, which often include poor practice on the part of local authority Homeless Persons' Units (Women in Prison 2006). There is evidence of other needs too in terms of training and employment. Moreover, research on women's barriers to resettlement upon leaving prison has identified substance misuse problems, inappropriateness of social networks and lack of emotional support as being most prevalent alongside accommodation problems (Brookes and Leeming 2006).

The key message from surveys and studies of women's multiple and complex resettlement needs, supported by a recent Home Office review of vulnerable women in the criminal justice system (Corston 2007), appears to be that a coordinated multi-agency response is required, with provision in the community which is capable of being sustained over a long period if necessary (Gelsthorpe *et al.* 2007). Moreover, general provision needs to be 'gender-informed' or 'gender-sensitive'. That is, it needs to take into account distinctive features of women's lives and needs in order to facilitate effectiveness. This is especially so in light of the Equality Act 2006. Following the introduction of a public sector race equality duty in 2001 after the Stephen Lawrence Inquiry findings, and the introduction of a disability equality duty,[1] there is now a duty on public bodies to promote equality between men and women.[2] This is important new legislation since it encourages moves to end institutional sexism.

The consequences for criminal justice agencies are clear. They must endeavour to promote equality in the treatment of men and women. This does not mean that they should be treated in exactly the same way; rather, it means that they should be treated appropriately, according to need.

This chapter reviews women's resettlement needs by drawing on available research and evidence, firstly in relation to women's 'criminogenic needs' and secondly in relation to desistance. Thirdly we turn to what is known more directly about women's resettlement needs. Fourthly, we look at some recent initiatives addressing women's resettlement needs.

Women's criminogenic needs

The research literature suggests that most women involved in the criminal justice system are young and criminally unsophisticated (in terms of previous convictions), and a high proportion are lone mothers. Many have lived on state benefits, few have been in paid employment, many have large debts, about one in ten will have experienced homelessness and around two in five will have experienced foster or other state care prior to imprisonment (Carlen 2002; Fawcett Society 2004; McIvor 2004). Evidence relating to women prisoners in particular reveals that the majority of these women come from a background of severe social exclusion. They typically have a history of unmet educational, health, housing and economic needs (Carlen 2002; Fawcett Society 2004; McIvor 2004) and complicated resettlement needs – with possible overlap between their criminogenic and resettlement needs (Clarke 2004; Gelsthorpe 2004; Morris et al. 1995). The majority of women offenders have drug and mental health problems that may only worsen in prison (e.g. Wedderburn Committee 2000). A significant number of women in prison will have self-harmed or attempted suicide or experienced other kinds of psychological stresses and illnesses (Loucks 2004). Dynamic risk factors such as financial difficulties, disproportionate childcare responsibilities, drug misuse, lack of formal qualifications and criminal records are all known to act as barriers to achieving financial independence and severely restrict how successful women may be in avoiding further offending (Hedderman 2004; HMCIP 1997; Wedderburn Committee 2000). A high proportion of women offenders have also experienced sexual and/or physical abuse either in their childhood or in their present adult lives (Fawcett

Society 2004; HMCIP 1997; Hollin and Palmer 2006a; Morris *et al.* 1995).

Recent analysis of O-DEAT data[3] drawn from OASys, the national offender assessment tool, suggests that a key characteristic of women offenders is the likely presence of *multiple* presenting problems. Of a sample of 158,161 female offenders assessed in 2005:

- 39 per cent had been victims of domestic violence;
- 33 per cent had accommodation needs;
- 32 per cent had misused drugs;
- 29 per cent had education and training needs;
- 28 per cent had financial needs;
- 24 per cent had misused alcohol;
- 16 per cent had particular needs in relation to employment; and
- 10 per cent were assessed as posing a medium, high or very high risk of harm to children (NOMS/NPS 2006).

In sum, although women's offending tends to be under-explored and less well understood than offending by men, it is now recognised that they are likely to have different 'criminogenic needs' (Hedderman 2004) because their routes into offending and reasons for offending are often different from those of men (Jamieson *et al.* 1999). New theoretical perspectives have been developed which locate women's offending within paternalistic power relations, poverty and distress (e.g. Baskin and Sommers 1998; Chesney-Lind 1997; Gelsthorpe 2004). And, as Judith Rumgay (2004a) has suggested, victimisation may combine with a lack of resources to become a pathway into crime. This is not to suggest that victimisation *causes* offending behaviour, rather that victimisation, combined with poverty and little or no support, may impact on women's psychological well-being in a way that may lead to increased drug and alcohol problems (Green *et al.* 1999).

One recurring question is how far women's and men's needs differ. Roberts (2002: 111) argues that within the criminal justice system, women's needs are identified 'by comparison with those of men'. This is worrying, particularly in light of evidence that key elements of women's criminogenic needs may be different from those of men. From a snapshot of OASys data in February 2005, for example, 56 per cent of women offenders (compared with 35 per cent of men) had needs in the area of relationships, and 59 per cent of women (compared with 37 per cent of men) had needs in relation to well-being (NOMS/NPS 2006). But even where it is argued that there is a degree of similarity in criminogenic needs for men and women (for example, in relation to criminal history, unemployment, substance misuse), it is still not clear how needs evolve and how they interact; there may be differences here which relate to gender. This is a point which Hollin and Palmer emphasise in their critique of the literature in this area. As they put it: 'A common need does not imply that aetiology or level of importance of that need is the same for men and women' (2006b: 179).

It is also important to recognise that perceptions and assessments of needs may be shaped by political and economic factors. Kelly Hannah-Moffat (2005), for instance, has argued that definitions of need in contemporary criminal justice practice are narrowly defined and fused with risk, and that the needs of offenders have been either reframed as 'criminogenic' needs, or rather dynamic risk factors, or else ignored altogether where they are not amenable to change through criminal justice intervention – for instance poverty or structural discrimination. She suggests that risk assessment, while apparently a morally neutral and 'scientific' activity, is in fact imbued with professional subjectivity, for example though the use of ratings scales in actuarial tools such as OGRS[4] (Hannah-Moffat 2005). This process potentially disadvantages women, since their needs (in relation to past experience of victimisation, for example) may only be targeted if they are statistically linked to recidivism, as well as amenable to intervention.

Women and desistance

It is also relevant to look at work on desistance to see what might be relevant to women's resettlement needs. Leaving aside definitional problems,[5] Hirschi and Gottfredson (1983), among others, concluded that desistance is first and foremost an age-related phenomenon (a maturational issue), but other factors have been identified in the process of 'going straight' too. These factors include leaving home, family formation, shame, stable employment and disassociation from a delinquent peer group (Farrall and Bowling 1999; Sampson and Laub 1993). Maruna (1999), however, has been critical of explanations of desistance which focus exclusively on external social forces and changes, and instead argues that narrative theories (whereby ex-offenders develop a coherent pro-social identity for themselves) provide a more adequate explanation of the processes of desistance. Whatever the differences in perspective here, most contemporary researchers agree that desistance is a *process*, as opposed to an *event* (Bottoms *et al.* 2004; Laub and Sampson 2001, 2003; Maruna 2001).

However, a further issue with the study of desistance is that, as in other fields of criminological research, women's experiences have been ignored (Uggen and Kruttschnitt 1998).[6] Graham and Bowling (1995) have revealed clear gender differences in the processes of desistance, with girls and women having shorter criminal careers overall and desisting sooner than men (see also Jamieson *et al.* 1999). Graham and Bowling also found that for females, social transitions such as leaving home, forming emotional and social relationships, and having children are highly correlated with desistance from crime (see also McNeill 2003).

Mary Eaton (1993) laid the foundations that the notion of desistance cannot be adequately addressed from a single perspective (that is, questions about the impact of marriage, getting a job or having children, for example, will not on their own explain the nature of desistence and what will facilitate it). Having interviewed 34 female ex-prisoners who had managed to transform their lives, Eaton surmised that female offenders can only change their lives when they have access to the multiple structural pre-conditions of social justice, particularly housing, employment and health facilities. Structural factors alone, however, are insufficient. Instead, she argued, women offenders need to feel that they are people of worth who have something to contribute, and the key to recognition is reciprocal relationships, or mutuality (Eaton 1993).

Similarly, we learn from an American study that neither marital attachment specifically, nor job status, factors frequently associated with male desistance from crime, may be strongly related to desistance on their own (Giordano *et al.* 2002). It is arguable that individuals need a minimum level of resources[7] to draw on in order to begin cognitive and social transformation processes (Farrall 2005; Giordano *et al.* 2002). Giordano *et al.* (2002) suggest that women are more likely than men to describe religious transformations or to focus on their children as catalysts for any changes they make in their behaviour. Men more often attribute prominence to prison or treatment, or focus on family more generally. Many of the women in Giordano and colleagues' study who were more successful as desisters crafted highly traditional 'replacement selves' (e.g. child of God, good wife, involved mother) that they associated with their pathways out of crime, but work was not a key factor. This may be explained by a shift in the market economy and the fact that women are frequently marginalised in unstable service sector jobs.

Analysis by Judith Rumgay (2004b) rehearses the themes of reciprocal relationships and mutuality, highlighting ways in which work with women offenders can contribute to their ability to sustain a commitment to establishing a crime-free lifestyle. Based on an evaluation of the Asha Centre in Worcester (which we describe in more detail later in this chapter), she argues that the support of the group at the Centre was the most frequently mentioned factor in sustaining the women's commitment, as contact with other group members provided support, gave insight into the women's circumstances, and reduced feelings of social isolation. Elsewhere, in a searching analysis of a wide range of research findings on desistance, Rumgay (2004c) develops these themes to suggest that women's desistance from crime may reflect a mixture of things: opportunity, 'identity scripts', self-efficacy and resilience. Successful desistance from crime may also be rooted in recognition of an opportunity to craft an alternative, desired and socially approved personal identity. In this regard, Rumgay argues, common identities that may present themselves (e.g. mother) may also provide a 'script' by which women can enact a conventional pro-social role. Women's perceptions as to how accessible such a new script may be will determine their confidence in their ability to enact it successfully, thus altering the women's sense of agency and efficacy. Studies of resilience and coping further illuminate the skills and strategies that may be utilised to protect and sustain a newly created self-identity (Blanchette and Brown 2006). All of this adds support to the idea that desistance from crime should be viewed as a *process* (Bottoms, *et al*. 2004; Laub and Sampson 2001, 2003; Maruna 2001) in which skills and advantages accumulate over time, mutually reinforcing each other and gradually enhancing the woman's capacity to avoid recidivism.[8] In other words, there is a need not only to focus on 'fixing' individual shortcomings (as Rumgay 2004c, puts it), but also to help women offenders develop 'social capital' (Bourdieu 1986; Field 2004) – systems of social and economic support – as well as individual skills, to increase perceived self-efficacy in avoiding further offending by empowering women to participate in broader infrastructural developments.

Women and resettlement

Research shows that reoffending rates are high following imprisonment (Cunliffe and Shepherd 2007); work with offenders within prisons may be undone once offenders are released back into the community.

But what will help *women* in terms of resettlement in the community? The Criminal Justice Act 2003 proposed the introduction of supervision for offenders serving short sentences, but supervision does not necessarily amount to support for resettlement (or 're-entry' as it is sometimes known). Women often say that the key problem facing them upon release is lack of money (Hamlyn and Lewis 2000; Wilkinson 2004). Many return to live on benefits, many report delays in obtaining these, and there are confusions about entitlements and discharge grants and geographical differences in the way in which loans and grants are paid out. Women have also stressed the need for more opportunities to improve literacy and numeracy in community-based programmes, not just in prison, so that they can increase their employment potential (Hamlyn and Lewis 2000; Morris *et al.* 1995). Women's relationships do not always survive their imprisonment. Where this is unexpected it compounds the difficulties in developing independent living and often leads to depression. Moreover, some women face huge difficulties in re-establishing relationships with their children after release from prison, especially where children have been taken into care or where the separation has been long-term. Women are often located in prisons far from their home communities, which exacerbates the difficulties of release and reintegration. Put simply, it is no exaggeration to say that for many women the trials begin once they are released from prison.

Research evidence and women's stories relating to their release from prison highlight accommodation and housing problems in particular (MacRae *et al.* 2006; Malin 2004). It is difficult to obtain accurate estimates of the accommodation needs of women offenders, partly because they may become involved in the provision of sexual services or may tolerate abusive relationships to prevent themselves from becoming homeless. But for financial reasons women may have had to relinquish their existing tenancies, or they may be reluctant to return to where they lived prior to their imprisonment, hence post-prison accommodation may fall through. In addition to small numbers of female offenders who are officially recognised to be in need of accommodation, supported accommodation for women, particularly in hostels, is scant. Her Majesty's Inspectorate of Probation (1996) has repeatedly raised the issue of the small number of hostels for women (there are five women-only approved premises in England and Wales at present), but the added difficulty here is that these premises sometimes struggle to maintain high occupancy rates. This is at least partly because the provision has the disadvantage of being located at a considerable distance from women's normal places of residence, making it more difficult to maintain personal ties. Other reasons relate to the criteria for admission which revolve around high-risk factors – although they can be lowered to reflect women's patterns of offending behaviour (Malin 2004). Such accommodation difficulties may of course be compounded by women's experiences of mental health difficulties or by issues relating to ethnicity (Todd 1996; Vaughn and Badger 1995; see also Gelsthorpe 2006, on ethnic minority women offenders as 'the "other other"', whose needs are doubly neglected). Wincup (1996), among others, has argued that single-sex hostels are better placed to develop links with agencies which may be of help to women and are more likely to operate regimes aimed at increasing women's self-esteem.

Many of these difficulties are rehearsed by the Social Exclusion Unit's report on reducing reoffending (2002) which, inter alia, looked at the housing needs of ex-prisoners. As well as noting that around one in three prisoners are not in permanent accommodation prior to imprisonment with many sleeping rough, and that as many as a third of prisoners lose their housing on imprisonment, the report also notes special difficulties for women. The high proportion of single women among prisoners means that there are fewer partners to maintain housing in their absence, and fewer prisons means greater distance from 'home' which makes it difficult to contact and negotiate with potential housing providers. Many women with children are caught in the double-bind that they are unable to receive their children from care without suitable accommodation, and unable to obtain suitable family accommodation without first regaining custody of their children.

It is fitting to add the trenchant criticism of Pat Carlen when commenting on the development of prison programmes designed to 'make women see their problems in a new (law-abiding) light'. Carlen (2003) draws attention to the fact that many women continue to leave prison with no safe place to live. She cites a prison officer alert to the problems: '"resettlement" without a home is just so much hot air. If they haven't a home (and, in the case of mothers, a home suitable for their children to be with them), what do we resettle them to?' (cited in Carlen 2003: 34).

Further resettlement problems for women relate to education and training. Research evidence suggests that only around a fifth (Morris *et al.* 1995) to a third (Hamlyn and Lewis 2000) of women reported having found work at post-release interviews (see also Home Office 2003). A study of the educational and employment needs of 100 women in HMP Brockhill concluded that there was high motivation to both improve education skills and employment prospects (McMahon and Seemungal 2003). But importantly, the women's own concerns upon leaving prison revolved around finding accommodation and resolving child custody issues, combined with the shadow of a potential relapse into drug use. Furthermore there was a gap between the kinds of assistance women anticipated they would need upon release and the kinds of assistance they believed they would actually receive. They drew particular attention to their need for stable accommodation, help with remaining drug-free, assistance with education and job advice and general support. However, few women believed they would receive such support, and many did not expect to receive any help at all (McMahon and Seemungal 2003).

A review of women's views of barriers to resettlement on leaving prison in the North West of England has identified 'overcoming substance misuse problems', 'lack of suitable accommodation', 'inappropriateness of social network' and 'lack of emotional support' as being most prevalent. Difficulties accessing training and employment were also seen as common obstacles by prisoners, although, very importantly, the majority stressed that they did not feel ready for either education or training in the foreseeable future (Brookes and Leeming 2006; see also Deedes 2007).

What works with women offenders?

The evidence suggests that although there is some overlap in needs, criminal justice provision designed for men does not necessarily meet the needs of women (Worrall 2002).[9] Moreover, most women offenders have multiple problems so an effective response is likely to require the involvement of a range of voluntary and public sector organisations. Effective work is thought to be empowering, emphasising positive pathways out of offending, rather than focusing exclusively on the list of 'criminogenic needs' derived from evaluations of offending programmes designed for men (Blanchette and Brown 2006; Roberts 2002; Zaplin 1998). This work also accommodates women's learning styles (Zaplin 1998). Lofland's (1969) concept of 'normal-smiths' who are prepared to convey to offending women that they are capable of achieving their aspirations of pro-social, conventional roles reminds us of the importance of connecting women to agency support networks *beyond* the criminal justice system. Women themselves appear to value services that are holistic, accessible and practical, and whose staff listen to them, demonstrate empathy, have a sense of humour and believe that the women can change (Roberts 2002; Trotter *et al.* 2006).

Recent policy and practice initiatives

The key message appears to be that what is required is a coordinated multi-agency response to women, available within the community, across the crucial transitions between community and custody where women have been incarcerated and capable of being sustained over a long period if necessary. This message was underlined recently in Baroness Corston's review of women in the criminal justice system (Corston 2007), and it fits with key findings from an evaluation of the prisoner resettlement Pathfinder projects (Clancy *et al.* 2006; Lewis *et al.* 2003).

Recent policy developments and reforms show that this message is beginning to be taken on board. For example, the Women's Offending Reduction Programme (WORP) was launched by the government in 2004 to help coordinate departments and sensitise them to women's needs. The intention is to draw together the various services in the community which provide support for issues such as mental health problems, drug misuse, domestic violence, childcare, education, employment and housing. Moreover, drawing on evidence from Glasgow's 'one-stop shop' Centre 218 for women offenders who have experienced custody (Loucks *et al.* 2006), the then Home Secretary announced in March 2005 that there would be provision of £9.15 million for the Together Women Programme (TWP) for two demonstration projects for women offenders, ex-offenders and those at risk of offending. The TWP framework proposed a combination of one-stop shop type provision with linked 'Women's Offending Action Teams'. The action teams should provide a 'floating service' from point of arrest to release from prison, helping to locate resources in the community that support diversion from the criminal justice process or from custody, or support resettlement. The idea is that the one-stop shops provide a focal point for the delivery of services to women. The responsibility for delivering these projects was allocated to the newly formed National Offender Management Service (NOMS).

TWP thus promises an integrated approach to service delivery '... building on existing services ... [and will] demonstrate how a coordinated multi-agency approach, tailored to meet women's complex and interrelated needs, can be effective in achieving the stated objectives' (Yorkshire and Humberside NOMS 2006). However, while TWP energies are focused on the two demonstration projects – Yorkshire and Humberside and the North West[10] – there is clear need to explore what might be available *beyond* these demonstration projects and in other geographical areas. Moreover, as Clive Coleman has observed in the *Guardian*, demonstration projects are often 'fabulous' for the reason that they are given the resources to show that something can work; a roll-out of similar projects is often funded at a lower level (Coleman 2007).

Initiatives also include the Reducing Re-offending National Action Plan – cross-government work on resettlement and rehabilitation. The strategies identified in the plan for addressing offenders' needs revolve around seven pathways: accommodation; education, training and employment; mental and physical health; drug and alcohol misuse; finance, benefits and debt; children and families; and attitudes, thinking and behaviour. All are intended to take account of women's needs, although evidence that they have done so has been found wanting (Corston 2007). We comment on two particular developments below – accommodation and health – since they are arguably pivotal in terms of addressing *women's* resettlement needs.

Accommodation

The role of housing in resettlement cannot be overstated. The Supporting People initiative – a UK government programme developed in 2003 – brings major changes to the planning, funding and delivery of housing-related support for over one million people, including ex-offenders as a particularly needy group. The programme brings together at local authority level the main partners of housing, health, social services and probation to plan strategically and commission services which are cost-effective, reliable, transparent and needs-led. However, as Malin (2004) among others has pointed out, there are concerns about the ambitious nature of the initiative and its budget allocation. Nevertheless, there is evidence of action on this front. Charged with responsibility for inspecting all Administering Local Authority areas (ALAs), the Audit Commission has reported that some local authorities have initiated joint working with other agencies (e.g. the NHS) and put into practice the aims and principles of Supporting People but, disappointingly, the findings suggest considerable geographical variation (Audit Commission 2006).

It is important to note that the National Probation Service is phasing out its mixed-sex accommodation in order to create women-only provision in every region. Innovative practice includes the New

Bridge Project in Liverpool, the use of women prisoners as housing advisers (at HMP Low Newton) with training and support from Nacro and prison and probation staff, St Mungo's supported housing and short-stay hostel initiative, and Time for Youth located in London and Harlow and surrounding communities. This project involves case work with young people aged 16–24 at risk of offending and in need of housing support and there is specific Home Office funding for work with young women (Malin 2004). Rothera Women's Project situated in Bradford, West Yorkshire, offers single-bed spaces in four houses for women aged 18 and above, accommodating women offenders and those at risk of offending, and the Dorcas Project in Staffordshire advises women on release from prison and helps with payment of deposits, for example. The Kent Resettlement Project run by the Langley House Trust offers dispersed supported housing for women ex-offenders aged 18 and above. There is also some small-scale provision for women with special needs (e.g. Hebron House in Norwich which caters for women 18–45 who are drug or alcohol dependent, Yasmin House in Bournemouth which offers drug treatment programmes for vulnerable women, and the Missing Link Association in Bristol which serves women with particular mental health needs). In addition, the YWCA, Eaves4Women, Equinox Women's Service, Penrose Housing Association and Centrepoint all provide hostel/foyer accommodation for women ex-offenders. However, much of this provision is based in London and there are areas of the country which have very little accommodation for women offenders (see Gelsthorpe et al. 2007). In any case, the general perception is that demand for supported accommodation far exceeds supply.

Health

The initiative concerned with Supporting Women Into The Mainstream is also important (Department of Health 2006). Prompted by awareness of women's needs, women at risk (i.e. those in contact with the criminal justice system), the health effects of domestic and sexual violence and abuse, and the new gender duty, the Department of Health has recognised the need to give direct attention to mental health care for women in the criminal justice system. Thus the Care Services Improvement Partnership (CSIP) has been charged with the task of ensuring not only gender equality in the delivery of services, but gender specificity in the shaping of services (Department of Health 2006). This means more women-only provision in medium secure services and low secure units, but crucially also mainstreaming 'gender-sensitive' approaches elsewhere in the system too, although it is not yet clear whether theory on how things are meant to work and practice on the ground match up.

Also, a recent report by the National Institute for Mental Health in England anticipated the transfer of formal responsibility for health in prisons from the Prison Service to Primary Care Trusts in April 2006 (Butler and Kousoulou 2006). The report highlights the importance of good liaison and collaboration between criminal justice and health professionals not only in custodial settings, but also in recommending diversion for offenders with mental health problems – both from the criminal justice system into the health system and from custody into community criminal justice provision. Of particular significance for women is the interface between forensic and mainstream services for offenders with mental health problems, which is likely to be hindered greatly if data-sharing protocols between the health and penal systems are not in place. Where mental health problems combine with chaotic substance misuse, access to specialist substance misuse services can be hampered by stigma, including women's fear of child protection proceedings, lack of childcare and transport, and a lack of gender- and ethnically-sensitive provision (Butler and Kousoulou 2006).

Potential and reality: what else is to be done?

From these policy developments we can see that the potential for change and the delivery of effective resettlement services for women is considerable. However, the reality may be very different. The capacity of agencies to attend to gender-specific needs is under question; the quality of inter-agency cooperation is variable; and the position of the voluntary sector in a supportive role may be stronger in some geographical areas than in others. There is also a need to examine whether or not the pathways identified under the Reducing Re-offending National Action Plan adequately take account of women's needs. Indeed, the Corston review recommends that two further pathways be made mandatory in every regional resettlement plan for women: support for women who have been abused, raped or have experienced domestic violence, and support for women who have been involved in prostitution (Corston 2007: 46). The two demonstration projects for women set up under the Women's Offending Reduction Programme (WORP) will be important, but they are limited in scope (Home Office 2004).

Malin draws attention to imaginative ideas relating to the emergence of a 'community chaplaincy national network', with church-based communities working to support ex-offenders and assist in their resettlement. Soleillet in France also serves to inspire (Malin 2004). This specialist project accommodates women, children and, exceptionally, couples with children; it takes in women who have been released definitively, but also those on conditional release or who are on home leave. What is thought to be distinctive about the approach is the aim to reinsert the ex-offender into civic life.

However, there are other models of practice in England and Wales which perhaps already promote the reintegration of women in this way and which move away from what Raynor (2004) has described as the 'offender responsibility' model of resettlement (reflecting the idea that offenders themselves should be held responsible for their own actions and not treated as victims of social or personal problems). As will be clear from other chapters in this book, this model of reintegration largely revolves around 'offending behaviour programmes' of a cognitive behavioural variety. But this model of practice is limited in relation to women (Gelsthorpe et al. 2007) and the evidence thus far suggests that 'scripts for survival' (Rumgay 2004c) should include integration into mainstream services. In this sense, the work of the Asha Centre in West Mercia is widely perceived to exemplify good practice. Unlike Centre 218 (Loucks et al. 2006), it does not include residential support, but it clearly helps women address multiple problems and works towards their integration into mainstream services. Critically, the ethos of the Centre, described in more detail below, involves continued support for women and it does not differentiate between offenders, ex-prisoners and other disadvantaged women.

Towards women's resettlement: an example of good practice

The Asha Women's Centre[11] owes its existence to women-centred work by the local Probation Service, developed over nine years from 1992 to 2001. The Service had developed a group programme (in effect an empowerment programme) based centrally in women-only premises. The programme did not receive Home Office Accreditation[12] and it was subsequently recognised that it would more appropriately be delivered and developed from an independent, voluntary sector setting. The Asha Centre thus opened in April 2002 with a grant from the regional crime prevention directorate; it is a registered charity that now derives its funding from a mixture of charitable and statutory sources, including the Probation Service and the Home Office.

The aim of the Asha Centre is to link women isolated by disadvantage to resources that will help them to improve their social and economic potential. All staff, volunteers and centre users are women, and no men are allowed in the building during operational hours. This is a key factor in enabling the centre to work with women who do not access mainstream services because of histories of sexual and physical abuse by men and the mental health problems that frequently follow. Centre users are referred by other agencies, except for direct access to English language courses for women with limited English (mainly Pakistani Muslims).

Women referred to the Centre are offered an initial assessment and planning interview, the purpose of which is to help them identify the issues that are preventing them from fulfilling their potential and the resources that can be mobilised to help them overcome those obstacles. An important element of the Centre ethos is that women determine their own goals and progress; this is partly necessitated by the fact that only limited personal support can be routinely provided by staff. On the other hand, most of their experience of the Centre will be in small groups, and the mutual support, advice and influence of other Centre users has proved invaluable in motivating women. This also has a 'normalising' effect on women ex-offenders and can help reduce stigma following imprisonment.

The Centre attracts a wide range of women, and their capacity to progress varies considerably. Nevertheless, a focus is maintained upon progression, albeit gently for those whose confidence or mental health is damaged. In recent years a marked emphasis on the acquisition of educational qualifications and credits (however basic) has proved valuable in encouraging women to set long-term goals. There are no age limits for referrals, and in practice these range from 17-year-olds to women over 65.[13] Other distinctive features of provision include an information, advice and guidance (IAG) advisor on site to help women to plan progression to employment, training and voluntary work; transport for users who could not otherwise access the Centre; facilities for Probation Service work with women offenders (groupwork programmes and individual reporting); and English language courses (ESOL).

The Centre has a staff of about 17 (mostly part-time) and a volunteer group of around 20 people who carry out a range of tasks including support for users. The Centre costs around £200,000 p.a. to operate, and it is likely that at least 100 women are using its facilities very actively at any one time. The cost per capita is therefore less than £1,000 per annum. There are links with an extensive range of statutory and voluntary sector referrers. In the latter case a pattern of cross-referrals (e.g. with HomeStart, Citizens' Advice Bureaux, advocacy, counselling and housing benefit charities) quickly built up as the Centre became more established.

About half of all referrals come from health professionals (community mental health teams, health visitors, GPs, etc.). Probation officers and social workers are the other principal statutory referrers, with a few referrals coming from employment services. Over the past five years, the Asha Centre has also developed uplinks with other women-centred organisations in the county. A county-wide consortium of women-centred provision, inviting other relevant organisations such as the Soroptomists and Women's Institutes to link to the centres, is planned.

A range of outcomes can be identified as demonstrating the effectiveness of the Asha Centre: participation by women who have not accessed other relevant services, including take-up of courses, advice sessions and signposting; self-reported improvements in functioning, measured at intervals through 'How do I feel?', a self-assessment scale; acquisition of qualifications and skills; and progression to mainstream further education, higher education, employment and voluntary work (Roberts 2000).

Two further evaluations of Asha's provision are relevant in this context. One concerns the Programme for Women Offenders that was the starting point of the development of the Asha Centre and which is still offered to women under the new title 'Exploring Women's Lives'. It has proved a valuable element in provision, empowering women who are ready to progress to mainstream provision (Roberts 2000). The analysis showed that while the differences were not statistically significant, women completing the programme had fewer reconvictions over a two-year period than any other of the groups examined (custody, probation order and community service order). A qualitative evaluation of the same programme analysed and reported outcomes for participants and views of partner organisations on the work of the centre, which were, on the whole, very positive (Rumgay 2004c). Currently, there is ongoing evaluation of a European Social Fund-supported project aimed at overcoming obstacles to progression to education, employment and voluntary work for disadvantaged women.

Like other similar organisations, the Asha Centre experiences the advantages and disadvantages of being a voluntary sector provider.

On the one hand, it has the freedom to innovate and pursue promising features of practice. A current example is the apparent effectiveness of training courses leading to qualifications and progression to mainstream training. The evident commitment shown by many centre users for these courses supports Rumgay's (2004c) notion that women need the opportunity and support to craft a new identity. On the other hand, funding constraints severely limit developments. Indeed, a substantial proportion of management time is devoted to fundraising, and the Centre typically carries a sufficient reserve for only six months' operation. Such funding uncertainty can lead to the risk that organisers have to respond (chameleon-like) to the interests of potential funders. It has proved extremely difficult to secure long-term guarantees of financial support, even from those services referring many women. Assured levels of funding from health, probation and the local authority (especially children's services) would assist the Centre to maintain stability and further develop its activities.

Needless to say, this is not the only model of provision available to facilitate resettlement, but it serves to suggest what might be achieved through the voluntary sector. There are other types of community provision for women (Gelsthorpe *et al.* 2007), most notably a network of women's resources centres; not all have experience of working with women offenders or, in this context, ex-prisoners, but many do have experience of working with disadvantaged women with multiple problems and this is key to the resettlement of women prisoners. Again, there is geographical unevenness in provision, and many voluntary sector organisations report uncertain funding, frustration with statutory agencies (especially health and housing) in terms of their taking responsibility for women's needs, and anxiety that closer involvement with the statutory sector might compromise their independence and creativity, or lead to a diminution of the supportive ethos which they try to foster. Despite these reservations, however, the network of women's resources centres and other mainstream voluntary sector provision for women carries huge potential for women's resettlement. Voluntary sector expertise in supporting women in a safe environment and the model of links with other mainstream agencies which many have developed combined with a funding stream from the statutory sector (without constraining strings) could be fruitful in ensuring better attention to women's resettlement needs.

Conclusion: community intelligence

A decade or so ago the situation with regard to women and resettlement was exceedingly bleak. It is encouraging that the government is giving attention to longer-term provision, but how far the push for gender awareness in provision will be sustained is unclear. The new 'gender duty' enshrined in the Equality Act 2006 will serve as a reminder of women's particular needs, but it will not necessarily release resources to ensure that policy becomes practice within the statutory sector. While voluntary sector provision is patchy, there is evidence of innovative, gender-sensitive and effective work with disadvantaged women. Notwithstanding concerns that voluntary agencies may lose their distinctive voice in working with women if they engage more closely with the statutory sector, there is potential for this work to be developed.

Corston (2007) recommends a national Commission for Women in the criminal justice system with a commissioner at director level to act as a 'champion' for women offenders and women at risk of offending. The commission should (ultimately) sit within the Department of Communities and Local Government (DCLG). But we should note that the formation of the Youth Justice Board has had no effect on custody rates for young people (Youth Justice Board 2006), and we can perhaps expect no different of a Commission for Women, at least not by itself. Indeed, in spite of this recommendation for a national lead on women offenders and greater provision for women offenders in the community (messages which have been given in other national reports – see the Wedderburn Committee 2000, for example), our recent study of both existing and potential provision in the community among voluntary sector agencies in particular suggests a lack of communication within and between agencies (Gelsthorpe *et al.* 2007). A number of projects report low levels of referrals from statutory criminal justice agencies. It may well also be the case that this type of provision is not being referred to in pre-sentence reports, which may contribute to women's likelihood of receiving a custodial sentence rather than a community penalty. Hence there is an urgent need to educate Probation Officers/Offender Managers and Regional Offender Managers (who may well become responsible for commissioning services within the new 'contestability' framework for Probation which involves 'buying in' services for offenders or 'contracting out' to agencies and organisations)[14] so that they use existing community provision for women. 'Intelligence-led policing' has become almost de rigueur within policing circles.[15] We think that there is some merit in adopting the notion of 'intelligence-led community provision' so as to promote the use of networks of resources for women in the community. But this provision should not be cast exclusively as resettlement provision, for that might make custody seem perfectly palatable to sentencers (to sweeten the bitter pill). Rather, such provision should be rooted in community resources, serving women offenders alongside non-offenders, thus promoting inclusion and normalisation, and reducing stigma, for, ultimately, the task of resettlement is one of connecting women to agency support networks *beyond* the criminal justice system.

Notes

1 The disability equality duty came into force in December 2006.
2 The gender equality duty came into force in April 2007. (See Fawcett Society (2006) and www.fawcettsociety.org.uk.)
3 OASys Data Evaluation and Analysis Team.
4 Offender Group Reconviction Scale.
5 For example, how do we know when someone has stopped offending? What does 'desistance' mean – slowing down, or committing different, less serious or less frequent offences? How long should the follow-up period be to really test whether or not someone has changed his or her patterns of offending behaviour?
6 A special issue on desistance in the *Journal of Contemporary Criminal Justice* (Kazemian and Farrington 2007) provides a useful overview of factors relevant to desistance (in terms of definitions, dynamic factors, cognitive predispositions, social bonds, offender typologies in terms of persisters or desisters, and so on) but gender-related factors are mentioned in only two of the articles. Most of the empirical research upon which the articles are based revolve around samples of males.
7 Including, for example, an adequate income and stable accommodation.
8 Further support for this idea may be found in US-based studies such as Horney *et al.* (1995) and Giordano *et al.* (2002).
9 Most 'treatment' provision is focused on the needs of male offenders because men's offending and reoffending tends to be more frequent and serious.
10 In Yorkshire and Humberside the Foundation Housing Consortium has been commissioned to deliver the TWP in Doncaster, Leeds and Bradford. The delivery of TWP began in Doncaster Women's Centre at the beginning of 2007 and in Leeds and Bradford in spring 2007. In the North West TWP is to be delivered via Lighthouse in Liverpool and the Salford Foundation in Greater Manchester.

11 We are grateful to Jenny Roberts for her kind permission to draw on the Asha Centre section of a report prepared for the Fawcett Society which she initially drafted (Gelsthorpe *et al.* 2007).

12 The Correctional Services Accreditation Panel was set up in 1999 as part of the government's Crime Reduction Programme. It is a non-departmental public body which serves to check offender treatment programmes against a set of so-called 'what works' principles for prison and probation services to use in reducing reoffending. If a programme meets the relevant criteria is becomes an 'accredited programme'.

13 It has in practice proved necessary to exclude a very small number of women whose aggressive behaviour was discouraging other users. No referral is refused except where a woman has committed an offence against children (because of the crèche).

14 Much depends on the final passage of the Offender Management Bill 2006 through Parliament. The opposition to the Bill has been much greater than anticipated, especially in the House of Lords.

15 Intelligence-led policing is a collaborative enterprise based on improved intelligence operations and community-oriented policing and problem-solving, which the field has considered beneficial for many years. The aim is to incorporate 'intelligence' into the planning process to reflect community problems and issues. This involves information sharing across agencies and quality analysis of data as well as special training.

References

Audit Commission (2006) *Review of the Supporting People Initiative*. London: Audit Commission.

Baskin, D. and Sommers, I. (1998) *Casualties of Community Disorder: Women's Careers in Violent Crime*. Boulder, CO: Westview Press.

Blanchette, K. and Brown, S. L. (2006) *The Assessment and Treatment of Women Offenders: An Integrative Perspective*. Chichester: Wiley.

Bottoms, A., Shapland, J., Costello, A., Holmes, D. and Muir, G. (2004) 'Towards desistance: theoretical underpinnings for an empirical study', *Howard Journal of Criminal Justice*, 43 (4): 368–89.

Bourdieu, P. (1986) 'The forms of capital', in J.G. Richardson (ed.), *Handbook of Theory and Research in the Sociology of Education*. New York: Greenwald Press.

Brookes, L. and Leeming, J. (2006) *'Getting off the Merry-go-round': Reviewing the Barriers to Resettlement for Female Offenders Serving Short-term Sentences*. Liverpool: Hope University.

Butler, P. and Kousoulou, D. (2006) *Women at Risk: The Mental Health of Women in Contact with the Judicial System*, Care Services Improvement Partnership, Health and Social Care in Criminal Justice.

Carlen, P. (ed.) (2002) *Women and Punishment. The Struggle for Justice.* Cullompton: Willan.

Carlen, P. (2003) 'A strategy for women offenders? Lock them up, programme them ... and then send them out homeless', *Criminal Justice Matters*, 53, Autumn.

Carter, P. (2003) *Managing Offenders, Reducing Crime: A New Approach.* London: Prime Minister's Strategy Unit.

Chesney-Lind, M. (1997) *The Female Offender: Girls, Women and Crime.* London: Sage.

Clancy, A., Hudson, K., Maguire, M., Peake, R., Raynor, P., Vanstone, M. and Kynch, J. (2006) *Getting Out and Staying Out: Results of the Prisoner Resettlement Pathfinders.* Bristol: Policy Press.

Clarke, R. (2004) *'What Works?' for Women Who Offend: A Service User's Perspective. Exploring the Synthesis Between What Women Want and What Women Get*, A Report for the Griffins Society Visiting Programme. (See: www.thegriffinssociety.org.)

Coleman, C. (2007) 'Courting controversy', *Guardian*, 14 February.

Corston, J. (2007) *The Corston Report: A Report by Baroness Jean Corston of a Review of Women with Particular Vulnerabilities in the Criminal Justice System.* London: Home Office.

Cunliffe, J. and Shepherd, A. (2007) *Re-offending of Adults: Results from the 2004 Cohort*, Home Office Statistical Bulletin 06/07. London: Reconviction Analysis Team, RDS-NOMS.

Deedes, R. (2007) *Women Going Home from Prison: Does Experience Match Expectations?* Unpublished MSt dissertation, Institute of Criminology, University of Cambridge.

Department of Health (2006) *Supporting Women into the Mainstream. Commissioning Women-Only Community Day Services.* London: Department of Health.

Eaton, M. (1993) *Women After Prison.* Milton Keynes: Open University Press.

Farrall, S. (2005) 'On the existential aspects of desistance from crime', *Symbolic Interaction*, 28 (3): 367–86.

Farrall, S. and Bowling, B. (1999) 'Structuration, human development and desistance from crime', *British Journal of Criminology*, 39 (2): 252–67.

Fawcett Society (2004) *A Report of the Fawcett Society's Commission on Women and the Criminal Justice System.* London: Fawcett Society.

Fawcett Society (2006) *Understanding Your Duty. Report on the Gender Equality Duty and Criminal Justice System.* (See: www.fawcettsociety.org.uk.)

Field, J. (2004) *Social Capital.* London and New York: Routledge.

Gelsthorpe, L. (2004) 'Female offending. A theoretical overview', in G. McIvor (ed.), *Women Who Offend.* London: Jessica Kingsley.

Gelsthorpe, L. (2006) 'The experiences of female minority ethnic offenders: the "other other"', in S. Lewis, P. Raynor, D. Smith and A. Wardak (eds), *Race and Probation.* Cullompton: Willan.

Gelsthorpe, L., Sharpe, G. and Roberts, J. (2007 forthcoming) *Provision for Women Offenders in the Community*, Final Report. London: Fawcett Society.

Giordano, P., Cernkovich, S. and Rudolph, J. (2002) 'Gender, crime and desistance: toward a theory of cognitive transformation', *American Journal of Sociology*, 107 (4): 990–1064.

Graham, J. and Bowling, B. (1995) *Young People and Crime*, Home Office Research Study No. 145. London: Home Office.

Green, C., Flowe-Valencia, H., Rosenblum, L. and Tait, A. (1999) 'Do physical and sexual abuse differentially affect chronic pain states in women?', *Journal of Pain and Symptom Management*, 18 (6): 420–26.

Hamlyn, B. and Lewis, D. (2000) *Women Prisoners: A Survey of their Work and Training Experiences in Custody and on Release*, Home Office Research Study No. 208. London: Home Office.

Hannah-Moffat, K. (2005) 'Criminogenic needs and the transformative risk subject', *Punishment and Society*, 7 (1): 29–51.

Hedderman, C. (2004) 'The "criminogenic" needs of women offenders', in G. McIvor (ed.), *Women Who Offend*. London: Jessica Kingsley.

Her Majesty's Chief Inspectorate of Prisons (HMCIP) (1997) *Women in Prison: A Thematic Review*. London: HMSO.

Her Majesty's Inspectorate of Probation (1996) *Women Offenders and Probation Service Provision. Report of a Thematic Inspection*. London: HM Inspectorate of Probation.

Hirschi, T. and Gottfredson, M. (1983) 'Age and the explanation of crime', *American Journal of Sociology*, 89: 552–84.

Hollin, C. and Palmer, E. J. (2006a) 'Offending behaviour programmes: controversies and resolutions', in C. Hollin and E.J. Palmer (eds), *Offending Behaviour Programmes. Development, Application, and Controversies*. Chichester: Wiley.

Hollin, C. and Palmer, E.J. (2006b) 'Criminogenic need and women offenders: A critique of the literature', *Legal and Criminological Psychology*, 11: 179–95.

Home Office (2003) *Statistics on Women and the Criminal Justice System*, a Home Office publication under Section 95 of the Criminal Justice Act 1991. London: Home Office.

Home Office (2004) *Women's Offending Reduction Programme. Action Plan*. London: Home Office.

Home Office (2007) *Sentencing Statistics 2005, England and Wales*, Home Office Statistical Bulletin 03/07. London: Home Office.

Horney, J., Osgood, D. and Marshall, I. (1995) 'Criminal careers in the short-term: intra-individual variability in crime and its relation to local life circumstances', *American Sociological Review*, 60: 655–73.

Jamieson, J., McIvor, G. and Murray, C. (1999) *Understanding Offending Among Young People*. Edinburgh: HMSO.

Kazemian, L. and Farrington, D. (2007) 'Preface', *Journal of Contemporary Criminal Justice*, 23 (1): 4.

Laub, J. and Sampson, R. (2001) *Understanding Desistance from Crime.* Chicago: University of Chicago Press.

Laub, J. and Sampson, R. (2003) *Shared Beginnings, Divergent Lives: Delinquent Boys to age 70.* Cambridge, MA: Harvard University Press.

Lewis, L., Vennard, J., Maguire, M., Rayner, P., Vanstone, M., Raybold, S. and Rix, A. (2003) *The Resettlement of Short term Prisoners: An Evaluation of Seven Pathfinders*, RDS Occasional Paper No. 83. London: Home Office.

Lofland, J. (1969) *Deviance and Identity.* Englewood Cliffs, NJ: Prentice Hall.

Loucks, N. (2004) 'Women in prison', in G. McIvor (ed.), *Women Who Offend.* London: Jessica Kingsley.

Loucks, N., Malloch, M., McIvor, G. and Gelsthorpe, L. (2006) *Evaluation of the 218 Centre.* Edinburgh: Scottish Executive Justice Department.

McIvor, G. (ed.) (2004) *Women Who Offend.* London: Jessica Kingsley Publishers.

McMahon, G. and Seemungal, F. (2003) *The Employment and Educational Needs of Women Prisoners*, Occasional Paper. Oxford: University of Oxford, Centre for Criminological Research and Probation Studies Unit.

McNeill, F. (2003) 'Desistance-focused probation practice', in W. Chui and M. Nellis (eds), *Moving Probation Forward: Evidence, Arguments and Practice.* Harlow: Pearson Educational.

MacRae, R., McIvor, G., Malloch, M., Barry, M. and Murray, L. (2006) *Evaluation of the Scottish Prison Service Transitional Care Initiative.* Edinburgh: Scottish Executive Social Research. (See: www.scotland.gov. uk/Publications/2006/02/08110928/0.)

Maguire, M., Raynor, P., Vanstone, M. and Kynch, J. (1998) Voluntary After-care, Research Findings No. 73. London: Home Office.

Maguire, M., Raynor, P., Vanstone, M. and Kynch, J. (2000) 'Voluntary after-care and the Probation Service: a case of diminished responsibility', *Howard Journal*, 39: 234–48.

Malin, S. (2004) *Supporting People: Good News for Women Ex-Prisoners?*, Research Paper 2004/1. London: Griffins Society.

Maruna, S. (1999) *Desistance and Development*, British Society of Criminology Conference Proceedings Vol. 2. London: British Society of Criminology.

Maruna, S. (2001) *Making Good: How Ex-convicts Reform and Build their Lives.* Washington, DC: American Psychological Association.

Morris, A., Wilkinson, C., Tisi, A., Woodrow, J. and Rockley, A. (1995) *Managing the Needs of Female Prisoners.* London: Home Office.

National Offender Management Service and National Probation Service (NOMS/NPS) (2006) *Delivering Effective Services for Women Offenders in the Community: A Good Practice Guide.* London: Home Office.

Raynor, P. (2004) 'Opportunity, motivation and change: some findings from research on resettlement', in R. Burnett, and C. Roberts (eds), *What Works in Probation and Youth Justice.* Cullompton: Willan.

Roberts, C. (2000) *A Study of the Hereford and Worcester Probation Service's Women's Programme.* Oxford: Probation Studies Unit, University of Oxford.

Roberts, J. (2002) 'Women-centred: the West Mercia community-based programme for women offenders', in P. Carlen (ed.), *Women and Punishment: The Struggle for Justice*. Cullompton: Willan.

Rumgay, J. (2004a) *When Victims Become Offenders: In Search of Coherence in Policy and Practice*, Occasional Paper. London: Fawcett Society.

Rumgay (2004b) *The Asha Centre: Report of an Evaluation*. Worcester: Asha Centre.

Rumgay, J. (2004c) 'Scripts for safer survival: pathways out of female crime', *Howard Journal of Criminal Justice*, 43: 405–19.

Sampson, R.J. and Laub, J.H. (1993) *Crime in the Making: Pathways and Turning Points Through Life*. London: Harvard University Press.

Social Exclusion Unit (2002) *Reducing Re-offending by Ex-prisoners*. London: Office of the Deputy Prime Minister.

Todd, M. (1996) *Opening Doors: An Evaluation of the Cultural Sensitivity of Offender Provision in Greater Manchester*. Manchester: Greater Manchester Probation Service.

Trotter, C., Sheehan, R. and McIvor, G. (2006) 'Women After Prison'. Unpublished report funded by the Catholic Social Services Management Committee and the Australian Research Council. (Available from Monash University Social Work Department: chris.trotter@med.monash.edu.au.)

Uggen, C. and Kruttschnitt, C. (1998) 'Crime in the breaking: gender differences in desistance', *Law and Society Review*, 32 (2): 339–66.

Vaughn, P. and Badger, D. (1995) *Working with the Mentally Disordered Offender in the Community*. London: Chapman & Hall.

Wedderburn, D. (2000) *Justice for Women: The Need for Reform*, Report of the Committee on Women's Imprisonment. London: Prison Reform Trust.

Wilkinson, C. (2004) 'Women's release from prison: the case for change', in G. McIvor (ed.), *Women Who Offend*. London: Jessica Kingsley.

Wincup, E. (1996) 'Mixed hostels: staff and resident perspectives', *Probation Journal*, 43 (3): 147–51.

Women in Prison (2006) *Finding Somewhere to Live: The Resettlement Needs of Young Women in Prison*. London: Women in Prison. (See: www.womeninprison.org.uk to download this report.)

Worrall, A. (2002) 'Rendering them punishable', in P. Carlen (ed.), *Women and Punishment: The Struggle for Justice*. Cullompton: Willan.

Yorkshire and Humberside National Offender Management Service (2006) Second Newsletter, September.

Youth Justice Board (2006) *Annual Statistics*. London: Youth Justice Board.

Zaplin, R. (1998) *Female Offenders. Critical Perspectives and Effective Interventions*. Gaithersberg, MD: Aspen.

Chapter 10

The resettlement of black and minority ethnic offenders

Kate Williams, Susie Atherton and Douglas Sharp

Introduction

The resettlement needs of black and minority ethnic (BME) offenders have been largely ignored by research, meaning that very little is known about them. Indeed, it can be questioned whether research is required, as BME offenders comprise only a minority of those facing resettlement. However, it is important to acknowledge that BME groups comprise a significant minority of the prison population, due to the fact that they are a growing and already over-represented group within our prison system and the criminal justice process as a whole. The risk factors associated with reoffending have been widely documented, and include a lack of basic educational skills and unemployment (Niven and Olagundoye 2002), problems with securing good quality and stable accommodation (May 1999), problematic drug and alcohol use which is particularly associated with prolific offending (Hough 1996), difficulties in accessing treatment for mental health problems after imprisonment (Social Exclusion Unit 2002) and a lack of social support (Niven and Stewart 2003). Yet, there is very little known about the specific resettlement needs of BME ex-offenders, based on their cultural and religious backgrounds, and also their potentially different socio-economic circumstances.

This chapter draws upon current literature and a study conducted in the West Midlands by the authors,[1] in order to present the key issues surrounding the resettlement needs of BME offenders and the services available to them. We aim to subject these findings to critical questioning and analysis in order to move forward our current understanding.

'BME': what's in a name?

First, it is important to highlight that for this chapter, the currently fashionable term 'black and minority ethnic' is used with some caution and hesitation, due to our recognition of its invariable 'lumping together' of such a wide range of different groups with potentially vastly differing experiences and needs. The fact that this term is currently so widely used and accepted is in itself an interesting indicator of a lack of official understanding or appreciation of these possible differences, in the sense that this group is currently deemed by the label 'BME' to be 'everything other than white'. Notwithstanding this, the term does not recognise the ever changing and potentially increasing nature of those who fall within it – for example, with the rise in the number of Eastern Europeans in the UK, certain white groups may also be regarded as ethnic minorities.

Furthermore, the use of the term 'BME' also tends to discount gender differences, which are highlighted in another chapter in this book (see Chapter 9), or any other factors including age, religion or sexuality. Where possible throughout this chapter we attempt to draw out the resettlement differences within the groups that comprise 'BME' offenders, and also gender differences, although at times data are extremely limited due to the lack of information regarding these specific groups of prisoners.

The experiences of BME groups in the criminal justice process

BME minority communities are more likely than white groups to experience discrimination and marginalisation beyond the criminal justice process, such as accessing good quality housing, education and training opportunities, proper healthcare and employment prospects (Commission for Racial Equality (CRE) 2004; Social Exclusion Unit 2000). However, levels of social exclusion and over-representation experienced in relation to criminal justice processes are also a cause for concern. There is now a significant and increasing amount of literature addressing issues of racism within criminal justice processes, which have found discrimination against BME groups at all stages, from police stop and search and arrest decisions, to prosecution, court proceedings and sentencing practices (see, for example, Calverley *et al.* 2004; Commission for Racial Equality 2004; Edgar and Martin 2004; Ellis *et al.* 2004; Fletcher *et al.* 2002; Macphérson Report 1999; Smith 1997; Social Exclusion Unit 2002). In particular, there has been a strong focus on the interactions between the police and BME groups, specifically young people (Bland *et al.* 2000; Foster *et al.* 2005; Norris *et al.* 1992; Phillips and Bowling 2003; Stone and Tuffin 2000).

In this context, it is important to highlight some key reports, which have demonstrated the existence and impact of racism within the criminal justice process. One of the first, the Scarman Report (1981), stemmed from concerns regarding the treatment of BME groups by the police, specifically in their response to the Brixton riots in 1981. After the racist murder of Stephen Lawrence in south London in 1993, the Macpherson Report (1999) identified additional and ongoing problems within the Metropolitan Police. This report identified 'institutional racism' as a major factor contributing to the failures of the police to charge and convict the main suspects. The report also presented recommendations for the police to implement policy and practices to improve relations with BME communities, such as more accurate recording and monitoring of the use of stop and search.

In an assessment of the impact of the Macpherson Report on British policing as a whole, Foster *et al.* (2005) found that many improvements had been made, specifically with regard to the use of stop and search powers and consultation with local communities. However, the findings also suggested there were still many inconsistencies in implementing the Macpherson recommendations. There was a tendency among police forces to address immediately 'identifiable and achievable' targets, and this, coupled with the lack of understanding of the term 'institutional racism', has meant that 'despite the intentions of police forces and their staff, certain groups still receive an inappropriate or inadequate service because of their ethnic culture or ethnic origin' (Foster *et al.* 2005: 97).

Despite the recommendations from both the Scarman and Macpherson reports, both of which focused on the use of stop and search powers and relations with BME communities, there are still concerns regarding the treatment of people from BME groups by the police and criminal justice process as a whole. The latest Home Office statistics on the experiences of BME groups within the criminal justice system as suspects, defendants, offenders and prisoners show that BME groups are over-represented at all stages of the criminal justice process (Home Office 2006a). While there may be some legitimate explanations for this, including socio-demographic factors and methodological issues, the fact remains that they are treated differently to their white counterparts. Black people are six times more likely to be stopped and searched by the police than white people and Asians twice as likely to be stopped and searched compared with white people (Home Office 2006b). Black people are less likely to be cautioned than white people and more likely to be tried at the Crown Court which may be explained partly by the increased likelihood that defendants from BME groups plead not guilty and elect jury trail due to a lack of confidence in the court system (Ashworth and Redmayne 2005; Brown and Hullin 1993; Hood 1992; Jefferson and Walker 1992). BME offenders are more likely to be acquitted at Crown Court than white defendants (Home Office 2006a). In June 2005, among British nationals, there were five times more black people in prison than white people (relative to the population), and twice as many people from mixed ethnic backgrounds (Home Office 2006a).

Discrimination against BME groups within the Probation Service is less well researched. However, Knight and Bailey (2003: 2) quote the National Probation Directorate, who expressed concern that, 'the proportions of minority ethnic prisoners suggest that all agencies, including the National Probation Service for England and Wales, may not be serving them as well as their white counterparts'. An example of this can be seen in research conducted by Hassan and Thiara (2001) for the Association of Black Probation Officers, which found disparities in access to rehabilitative groups and less choice of groups for black offenders. The most comprehensive research so far was conducted by Calverley et al. (2004) who studied the experiences of minority ethnic groups on probation. They found that the criminogenic needs of BME and white offenders were similar although white offenders had higher levels of need. They suggested that this may result from differential sentencing practices. Generally, BME offenders had favourable experiences of probation and had experienced similar levels of social exclusion and disadvantage as the white offenders in the study. Where BME and white offenders' experiences diverged, however, was in relation to their explanations of their social exclusion which related to racial prejudice, hostility and discrimination. They were particularly critical of other areas of the criminal justice system, especially the police.

BME groups in prison

Currently, 8 per cent of the national population identify themselves as BME.[2] However, BME groups comprise 25 per cent of the male prison population and 28 per cent of the female prison population (Home Office 2005a: 86). Clearly, these figures demonstrate that the BME prison population is three times the size that it should be if it were to be representative of the national population. A more detailed analysis of these figures, looking at the rates of imprisonment for individual ethnic groups per 1,000 of the general population, shows that it is primarily black British nationals[3] who are over-represented (Home Office 2005b: 86). This group accounts for 7 per 1,000 compared with 1.4 per 1000 for white people. Those from mixed ethnic backgrounds are also over-represented (3 per 1,000), but not to the same extent as black British nationals. Asian groups have a similar imprisonment rate to white people (1.5 per 1,000). These trends remain regardless of gender or age (Audit Commission 2004). The differences in imprisonment rates between the BME and white populations are increasing. The number of prisoners from BME groups rose by 124 per cent between 1992 and 2002 compared with an overall increase in the prison population of 55 per cent (Smart Justice 2004). BME prisoners are also more likely to be serving longer sentences. Forty-seven per cent of white adult offenders were serving sentences of four years or more compared with 63 per cent of black and 58 per cent of Asian adult offenders (Social Exclusion Unit 2002). Some of these differences are explained by disparities in types of offences. BME groups in prison – particularly black females - are more likely to have committed drug-related offences compared to white offenders (Home Office 2004: 90). The longer sentences of BME offenders may partly explain why these groups are more likely to be held in closed prisons.

There is also evidence that BME prisoners are discriminated against in prison. Studies have found evidence of racist behaviour by prison staff and other prisoners including physical assaults, racial stereotyping by prison staff and in prison records and discrimination in relation to work allocation, accommodation and disciplinary matters (CRE 2003; Edgar and Martin 2004; Genders and Player 1989; Gordon 1983). These issues were brought into stark relief by the racist murder of Zahid Mubarek in Feltham Youth Offenders Institution in 2000. Zahid Mubarek was an Asian prisoner who was kept in a cell with Robert Stewart who had a previous history of violent behaviour, had expressed racist views and had mental health problems. After Zahid was fatally attacked in his cell by Robert Stewart, questions were asked about why prison officers, who knew about Stewart's history, felt it appropriate and safe to place him in a cell with a prisoner from a minority ethnic group.

The Council for Racial Equality held an inquiry into the murder. Their investigation found the Prison Service guilty of racial discrimination (CRE 2003). They found 'unlawful discrimination' and 'persistent failures' to tackle racism in the three prisons they studied. The report highlighted problems with the general culture in prisons, including the treatment of staff and prisoners from BME groups and inadequate procedures for dealing with reports of racism. Issues were also raised about a general lack of understanding of such prisoners' needs. For example, dietary requirements were often ignored, the faith needs of non-Christian religions were not met and BME prisoners were over-represented in the disciplinary processes and at the basic level of the Incentives and Earned Privileges scheme (IEP). Accessing work, both inside and outside the prison was also found to be affected by ethnicity in that BME prisoners were under-represented among working prisoners. The incidences of racist abuse, intimidation and taunting of both BME staff and prisoners reported to the CRE were often not treated seriously when staff or prisoners did complain, and in some cases resulted in further victimisation. Discretion among prison staff in their day-to-day decision-making was found to be a key factor in further discrimination against BME prisoners, for example, being locked in their cells, subjected to drug tests and banned from leisure activities. Prisoners also reported a failure of prison staff in dealing with racist incidents and protecting those who made complaints (CRE 2003).

Eventually, the family of Zahid Mubarek won their fight for a public inquiry into the murder. The subsequent report (House of Commons 2006) was a damning indictment of the Prison Service. The report suggested that the Prison Service was suffering from 'institutional religious intolerance' and found evidence of institutional and overt racism. It named 19 culpable individuals and 186 failings which contributed to the 'preventable' murder. In particular, it highlighted missed opportunities to identify Stewart as a risk because prison officers failed to recognise the importance of particular incidents or evidence or did not take them seriously. The inquiry was also critical of the wider Prison Service, particularly in relation to the practice of cell sharing as a result of overcrowding. While recognising that the Prison Service was working with the CRE to tackle racism, the inquiry made 88 recommendations which included improving officers' awareness of the needs and experiences of prisoners from BME groups through training, and also helping them to better understand the role of race relations officers and how complaints of racism should be investigated (House of Commons 2006).

Within the prison system, racism, whether in the form of insensitive remarks or discriminatory practices, has been explained in part by difficulties with the implementation of anti-racist policy and the lack of understanding of the impact of this among staff (HMIP 2005). Another report by the Commission for Racial Equality (2003) emphasised the complexities involved in understanding and responding to racism within prisons, where the environment was highly pressurised and sometimes dangerous and the primary aim is to maintain security and control. This is especially problematic within a prison system running at full capacity and in some institutions overcrowding. This inevitably impacts upon prison staff's attempts to ensure the welfare of offenders and to develop strategies to aid their resettlement (Tkachuk and Walmsley 2001).

The resettlement needs of BME groups

A stated aim of resettlement is the 'effective re-integration of imprisoned offenders back into the community' (Gelsthorpe 2004). Reintegration embraces reconciliation, reinclusion, removal of shame and forgiveness, or 'reintegration into the moral/social community as well as physical community' (Maruna 2004). In the 'Reducing Re-offending National Action Plan', addressing diversity is seen as an 'essential component' (Home Office 2004). There is clear evidence, as aforementioned, regarding the multiple needs ex-offenders present, which in turn requires a multi-agency approach to intervene and prevent reoffending (McGuire 2002).

The resettlement needs of BME groups may be further complicated by several factors. Not only are they over-represented in prison (thereby directly impacting upon resettlement services), but they also serve longer sentences (therefore potentially requiring greater assistance with resettlement), face racism within the criminal justice process, and experience higher levels of social exclusion and marginalisation (prior to and as a result of imprisonment). The key questions posed by such findings include the need to investigate the connections between the over-representation and length of sentences that BME prisoners serve with racist policies and practices within the criminal justice process and society overall, how this may impact upon their resettlement, why current resettlement strategies appear to be less than effective and how they can be improved by better addressing the needs of this group.

We conducted a small-scale qualitative research study in the West Midlands in 2005 to specifically consider the resettlement needs of BME offenders (Sharp et al. 2006). The West Midlands was an ideal site to conduct research into this area for several reasons. It is an ethnically and socio-economically diverse region, particularly when compared to the rest of England and Wales. Its population includes a wide range of BME groups, and it also comprises rural communities, prosperous inner-city and suburban areas and areas of deprivation (Centre for Urban and Regional Studies 2004). In 2004/5, a total of 6,825 offenders were received into prisons in the West Midlands Region. Of these 972 were classed as black or black British, 955 as Asian or Asian British, 31 as Chinese or 'other' and 194 as being from mixed ethnic backgrounds (Home Office 2005b: 87). Clearly, in accordance with the trends previously described, these figures illustrate an over-representation of BME groups in prisons in the West Midlands.

Semi-structured interviews were conducted with 72 BME prisoners and ex-offenders (36 black offenders, 20 Asian, 12 mixed race and 4 'other'), as well as prison staff and resettlement service providers in the community (including statutory, voluntary and faith-based groups). These interviews asked about a range of resettlement issues, including plans for accommodation; employment, training or education; financial support; and opinions of the resettlement services. We strived where possible to keep our sample of prisoners representative of the BME prison population in terms of age, gender, ethnicity and length of sentence in order to put into context the potentially differing needs faced by the target samples. However, due to availability of prisoners on our visits and the relatively short time period in which the research was conducted, younger prisoners and ex-offenders (between the ages of 21 and 30)[4] on short-term sentences were over-represented in our sample.

Lack of awareness, lack of confidence?

A key finding from Sharp et al.'s (2006) study was a distinct lack of awareness of any type of resettlement strategy within the prisons and the community. Indeed, many interviewees had not heard of, let alone received, been contacted by or used any type of resettlement service. This lack of knowledge regarding resettlement services among BME prisoners unsurprisingly led to a perception of a dearth of help and support being available to them. Although some prisoners reported that they were aware that community and voluntary services existed, they had no further knowledge of what they were or the services that were offered. Within the prisons, most prisoners stated that they had not seen any information or been presented with any by prison staff or other agencies. This also concurs with previous research, including Knight and Bailey (2003) who found that knowledge about the role of the Probation Service was limited among minority ethnic prisoners.

Additionally, we found that a general perception of a lack of available practical support overall was exacerbated by barriers which existed to accessing services. These included the need for referrals from statutory agencies, which acted as a barrier to many who would have preferred a walk-in service. This also applied to completing forms and attending interviews, which many prisoners felt ill-equipped to do. One female prisoner explained:

> ... it's so stupid ... they say they want to rehabilitate you back into the community ... well what structure is there? There's nothing in place. So they say one thing ... with their actions, it's totally different ... it's a farce.

Several interviewees emphasised that gaining resettlement support was primarily connected to personal motivation and initiative – without this, services would generally not be accessed. However, it was also clear that many prisoners and ex-offenders would not be in the position to take a proactive stance, considering the myriad of other significant difficulties they may be facing. As one male prisoner explained:

> ... people who ain't got no initiative are going to struggle ... you've got to want to help yourself to get by ... you've got to motivate yourself, but like 70 per cent of the prisoners are not really motivated, are they ... so that's where they probably just get caught in the loop ... like a trap, and start reoffending.

Indeed, this concern about the lack of support resulted in some prisoners feeling so fearful about their release that they felt 'safer' and 'more in control' in prison.

However, given what is known in terms of institutional racism within the criminal justice process, and within prisons in particular (CRE 2005; House of Commons 2006), it must be questioned to what extent this lack of awareness and use of resettlement services is directly affected by an overall lack of confidence and suspicion of statutory agencies. A study of the views from minority ethnic groups based on data from the British Crime Survey (Home Office 2000) suggested the lack of confidence in the criminal justice system resulted from a lack of respect for the rights of suspects and victims from BME groups. This was particularly apparent when respondents recounted their experiences with the police and prison services (Mirrlees-Black 2001: 3).

The study by Sharp *et al.* (2006) underlines this lack of trust and confidence. Indeed, one prisoner from the research described:

> The way society has moulded these people, they way prison moulds these people, the things they have to put up with in prison, they go out there, they don't want to work, they don't want no help off nobody. Do you know what I'm saying? They just want to do their own thing, which leads to obviously committing more offences ... it's because they've been victimised more because of their race ... they've never been given no help ... quite the opposite ... they go out there, they don't want to know ... they resent everyone.

Clearly, at least for some BME offenders, these negative experiences of both society in general and the criminal justice process and prisons more specifically (Edgar and Martin 2004) serve only to perpetuate a lack of confidence in the entire criminal justice process, which is likely to include resettlement services. In common with previous research another interviewee from the study by Sharp *et al.* (2006) felt that offenders from BME groups not only received harsher sentences and were treated more severely in prison (Commission for Racial Equality 2005), but also were given less help with resettlement from the Probation Service:

> I'd say they'd probably help, but not to the standard ... I was given a probation order ... and there was a few other people in the group, white people ... certain things like help for example, wasn't offered to me, but was offered to them, but on a private one-to-one basis ... I know it doesn't sound nice to think that ... but that's reality.

Conversely, one could argue that offenders from BME groups might well need greater help with resettlement due to the likelihood that they have served a longer prison sentence. Therefore, in this sense, the potentially disadvantaged nature of BME offenders' experiences of the criminal justice process appears to become increasingly focused and concentrated as it progresses through to resettlement. In turn, this of course may leave ex-offenders in a state of greater risk of reoffending and thus starting the cycle of arrest, sentencing and imprisonment once again.

The same needs?

Akin to BME experiences of prison and probation, there is also very little published research relating specifically to the resettlement needs of this group. One of the few studies which looks specifically at the resettlement of BME offenders (Calverley *et al.* 2004) found that – perhaps surprisingly – the majority of respondents' needs were in line with those of white offenders in terms of the types of services they expected and their evaluations of the programmes attended. Calverley *et al.* (2004) also found that although one-third indicated that they would like their probation officer to be someone from their ethnic group, over half reported that this did not concern them. Furthermore, there was very limited support for having groupwork programmes consisting only of BME offenders. Nonetheless, there is some evidence to point towards different needs among BME prisoners. For example, Knight and Bailey (2003) found that 63 per cent of their female interviewees felt that they had different needs in prison compared to other prisoners. They state, 'their responses highlighted that this was for predominantly multiple needs such as religious, cultural, personal and domestic needs. In particular significant responses were highlighted as dietary needs and hair and skin care needs' (2003: 22).

Sharp *et al.* (2006) support the overall assertion that the resettlement needs of BME groups are fundamentally very similar to those of all prisoners and ex-offenders. Clearly, without further in-depth research, it cannot be ascertained whether this is accurate or due to other factors including the small-scale nature of our study, or respondents' unwillingness and possible lack of motivation or trust to discuss a sensitive and complicated matter. Indeed, given our main findings in terms of lack of awareness, confidence, and suspicion of the criminal justice process, discussing this issue with a researcher might appear to be a somewhat pointless task. Nonetheless, the attitude of the majority of our interviewees was explained by one male prisoner:

> ... it doesn't matter what colour you are, what race you are, if you've been in jail, you're an ex-offender, everything is going to be difficult, full stop.

Indeed, like all offenders, the importance of fundamental resettlement requirements is paramount and has been well documented (see Calverley *et al.* 2004; Carter 2003; Farrall and Maruna 2004; Gill 1997; Harper and Chitty 2005; Home Office 2004; Lewis *et al.* 2005; Maxwell and Mallon 1997; McGuire 2002; NACRO 2001; Senior 2003; Social Exclusion Unit 2002). For example, the lack of suitable accommodation can be extremely problematic. Research by Grimshaw *et al.* (2002: 13) has demonstrated that this applies to 40 per cent of ex-offenders, with those from the black community being more likely to be in temporary housing. This supports suggestions that while the needs of BME groups may be similar to white prisoners, the nature and extent of the problems differ and consequently may be more difficult to resolve. Differences in the depth, severity and immediacy of needs between offenders may not be picked up adequately by assessment tools or research instruments, leaving the true extent of BME offenders' needs under-explored.

Sharp *et al.* (2006) also found that, invariably, the problem of homelessness led in many cases to reoffending, especially for ex-offenders staying with those that they had previously associated with during or prior to their offending. Without somewhere to live, other resettlement issues such as finding employment or keeping appointments with outside agencies can fall by the wayside. Although prison services had often attempted to secure housing for prisoners in time for their release, usually this did not materialise. For example, one female prisoner recounted that in her experience of 24 prison sentences, only once was she found accommodation for her release. This is despite performance targets set by the Home Office to secure housing for ex-prisoners on release (Home Office 2006b).

A high proportion of the prisoners and ex-offenders interviewed for our study – and particularly women – were also problematic drug users. The need to provide treatment and support for those prisoners and ex-offenders identified as problem drug users is clear, and it was suggested that there was a need for a more structured approach to rehabilitation in the community in order to reflect treatment services within the prison regime, for example CARATS (Counselling, Assessment, Referral, Advice and Through-care Services). However, problems arose if these services were not replicated in the community, in that prison was described as being 'wrapped up in cotton wool and separated from the real world' (Sharp *et al.* 2006: 14). Therefore the work done in prisons could be quickly undone on release without the necessary support (Sharp *et al.* 2006).

Resettlement services available to BME groups

Some distinct differences can be seen between statutory and non-statutory organisations in relation to the resettlement of BME groups. The role of the voluntary sector has been recognised as not only being more responsive to local needs, but has also been perceived by ex-offenders as having a less judgemental and authoritative approach in their services (Bhui 2006). This was demonstrated further in the study by Sharp *et al.* (2006) in which some voluntary services reported that BME ex-offenders felt excluded from statutory services, namely probation. Explanations for this included language and cultural differences, and in particular a mistrust of 'authoritarian organisations' as a result of their experiences of the criminal justice process as a whole. Indeed, it has also been found that a Probation Service initiative created to address the gaps in statutory provisions for BME groups 'lacked substance', and was not perceived by clients to address all their needs (Hucklesby and Wincup 2005).

In addition, in contrast to the Prison and Probation Services, whose attitude was fundamentally that resettlement was not specifically a 'BME issue', staff interviewed in voluntary and faith-based organisations in the West Midlands were inclined to believe that BME ex-offenders may have certain specific needs stemming from the different experiences in society. In turn, this was viewed as potentially impacting upon the type of offending they engage in and their motivations to reoffend, which may be due not only to continuing deprivation, but was also linked, in some cases, to the existence of gang culture in the more deprived areas included in the study (Sharp *et al.* 2006).

To counteract these issues, it was also found that organisations based in the West Midlands typically provided a crucial alternative to statutory services, such as probation or employment agency provisions. These included providing information and training literature in various languages and also the utilisation of outreach teams. There was a greater sense of the importance of looking beyond the practical measures and support required by ex-offenders, and to offer services to meet spiritual, social and emotional needs. One service provider based in the West Midlands emphasised the vital nature of counselling and mentoring for BME ex-prisoners, and peer-group mentoring was cited as being especially useful in relation to gang culture and violent offending among young BME males. Mentoring services were also reported to be of value, specifically to BME ex-offenders who had little or no family contact (Sharp *et al.* 2006). Previous findings have alluded to the role of mentoring in supporting BME ex-offenders but further exploration is required, perhaps to better determine its effectiveness in reducing reoffending (Stephens *et al.* 2004) and also to examine who is best placed to provide such a service. Overall, many community organisations felt that the Prison Service needs to think differently and more creatively about resettlement in relation to race and religion, including how it can link with community and faith-based organisations (Sharp *et al.* 2006). Nonetheless, among the prisons visited as part of our study, there was recognition of the need to replicate the cultural need of BME groups as far as possible given security and resource considerations, including dietary needs and religious ceremonies, for example. It was also found that BME prisoners tended to use the multi-faith chaplaincy to a greater extent than other inmates, viewing it as a supportive environment.

A further finding of the study by Sharp *et al.* (2006) was the issue of funding for some community-based organisations. This can be particularly problematic and frustrating for those initiatives which are effective and successful, yet were implemented on a short-term and small-scale basis due to funding not being available to sustain them over longer periods or on a wider scale. This may be potentially exacerbated due to the need to compete with statutory organisations in the provision of resettlement services with the advent of the NOMS, where there may be a lack of expertise in putting together business plans or demonstrating cost-effectiveness and efficiency (Allen 2004; see also Hucklesby and Worrall, this volume).

Conclusion

Significant difficulties and barriers to the effective resettlement of BME offenders have been shown to be the result of poor communication among different criminal justice agencies, specifically the Prison and Probation Services (Knight 2004; Knight and Bailey 2003; Sharp *et al.* 2006). There appears to be a continuing need for prison staff to establish and most importantly publicise links with community, voluntary and faith-based services due to a lack of knowledge exhibited by BME prisoners and ex-offenders regarding the facilities available to them. Where logistically possible, this may be aided by having a clearly designated, accessible space with facilities for prisoners to use in preparing for resettlement. For example, in one prison in the West Midlands, staff had developed a 'resettlement zone', which was a section of the prison containing separate offices for staff to help prisoners with housing, employment and financial support, and was regarded as very useful among the prisoners interviewed (Sharp *et al*. 2006). In addition, the lack of awareness of services and support extends beyond statutory services to voluntary and faith-based organisations based in the community. There is a clear need for such organisations to promote their services more widely to statutory providers, ex-offenders and the community as a whole, together with generally taking a more proactive stance, including continuing to make contact with prisoners prior to their release. Faith-based services in particular can also utilise the important role of religion for many BME groups and overcome any language barriers to reach those ex-offenders who feel unable to access other sources of support (Sharp *et al*. 2006).

However, this key message from Sharp *et al*. (2006) of a lack of awareness of the availability of resettlement services may also be fuelled by a mistrust of the criminal justice process and statutory agencies in particular. We suggest, therefore, that while recognising that many of the resettlement needs of BME offenders are similar to the rest of the prison population, the context of their needs differs in terms of their over-representation in the prison population and the discrimination in prisons and wider society. The inquiries into the deaths of Stephen Lawrence and Zahid Mubarek have highlighted ongoing problems with race relations in the police and Prison Service, which are further emphasised in statistics illustrating over-representation of BME groups at each stage of the criminal justice system (see Home Office 2006a; Smith 1997). To what extent this situation of over-representation of BME groups within the criminal justice process is directly attributable to the lack of effective resettlement services and/or their utilisation, or institutionalised racism within the criminal justice process and society as a whole, is unknown.

This is surely a cause for concern, which requires further investigation and more in-depth research to explore the needs of BME groups in resettlement and their overall attitudes towards the criminal justice process generally in much greater detail. In addition, such research needs to focus on the different groups within the 'BME' label in order to better understand the particular reasons why, and how we can prevent, the disproportionate imprisonment of BME groups, and the difficulties they face in resettling and reintegrating after imprisonment.

Notes

1 Our research in the West Midlands was funded by Government Office West Midlands (GOWM) and is published as a report: Sharp *et al.* (2006). Our thanks to GOWM for their kind permission to publish this research.
2 According to the Census (ONS 2001).
3 Foreign nationals are not included in our chapter, but it should be noted that they comprise 12 per cent of the male prison population and 19 per cent of the female prison population, and present their own set of resettlement needs (Bhui 2004).
4 BME offenders under the age of 18 were not within the scope of our study.

References

Allen, R. (2004) 'Fund communities, not prisons', *Safer Society*, Autumn. London: Nacro.

Ashworth, A. and Redmayne, M. (2005) *The Criminal Process*. Oxford: Oxford University Press.

Audit Commission (2004) *A Review of the Reformed Youth Justice System, Criminal Justice Briefing*. London: Audit Commission.

Bhui, H.S. (2004) *Going the Distance: Developing Effective Policy and Practice with Foreign National Prisoners*. London: Prison Reform Trust.

Bhui, H.S. (2006) 'Anti-racist practice in NOMS: reconciling managerialist and professional realities', *Howard Journal of Criminal Justice*, 45 (2): 171–90.

Bland, N., Miller, J. and Quinton, P. (2000) *Upping the PACE? An Evaluation of the Recommendations of the Stephen Lawrence Enquiry on Stops and Searches*, Police Research Series Paper 128. London: Home Office.

Brown, I. and Hullin, R. (1993) 'A study of sentencing in the Leeds magistrates' courts', *British Journal of Criminology*, 32 (1): 41–53.

Calverley, A., Cole, B., Kaur, G., Lewis, S., Raynor, P., Sadeghi, S., Smith, D., Vanstone, M. and Wardak, A. (2004) *Black and Asian Offenders on Probation*, Home Office Research Study No. 277. London: Home Office.

Carter, P. (2003) *Managing Offenders, Reducing Crime*. London: Home Office.

Centre for Urban and Regional Studies (2004) *West Midlands Prisoner Resettlement Strategy Framework*. Birmingham: University of Birmingham.

Clements, J. (2002) 'Diversity and equality: moulding a new future around racial equality', *Prison Service News*, July/August.

Commission for Racial Equality (2003) *Towards Racial Equality: An Evaluation of the Public Duty to Promote Race Equality and Good Race Relations in England and Wales*. London: CRE.

Commission for Racial Equality (2004) *Implementing Race Equality in Prisons*. London: CRE.

Commission for Racial Equality (2005) *Race Equality in Prisons: A Formal Investigation by the Commission for Racial Equality into HM Prison Service of England and Wales (Part 2)*. London: CRE.

Edgar, K. and Martin, C. (2004) *Perceptions of Race and Conflict: Perspectives of Minority Ethnic Prisoners and of Prison Officers*, Home Office Online Report 11/04. London: Home Office.

Ellis, T., Tedstone, C. and Curry, D. (2004) *Improving Race Relations in Prisons: What Works?*, Home Office Online Report 15/04. London: Home Office.

Farrall, S. and Maruna, S. (2004) 'Desistance-focused criminal justice policy research: introduction to a special issue on desistance from crime and public policy', *Howard Journal of Criminal Justice*, 43 (4): 358–67.

Fletcher, H. Providence, B., Mulixidwa, J. and Asafo-Agyei, H. (2002) *Race, Discrimination and the Criminal Justice System*. Available from: www.blink.org.uk/abpoa.htm.

Foster, J., Newburn, T. and Souhami, A. (2005) *Assessing the Impact of the Stephen Lawrence Enquiry*, Home Office Research Study No. 294. London: Home Office.

Gelsthorpe, L. (2004) 'Making it on the out: the resettlement needs of women offenders', *Criminal Justice Matters*, 56. London: Centre for Crime and Justice Studies.

Genders, E. and Player, E. (1989) *Race Relations in Prison*. Oxford: Clarendon Press.

Gill, M. (1997) 'Employing ex-offenders: a risk or an opportunity?' *Howard Journal of Criminal Justice*, 36 (4): 337–51.

Gordon, P. (1983) *White Law: Racism in the Police, Courts and Prisons*. London: Pluto.

Grimshaw, R. (2002/3) 'A place to call your own: does housing need to make a difference to crime?', *Criminal Justice Matters*, 50. London: Centre for Crime and Justice Studies.

Grimshaw, R., assisted by Pegg, G. and King, J. (forthcoming) *Accommodation and Offending – What Works? An International Literature Review*, Centre for Crime and Justice Studies, School of Law, King's College.

Harper, G. and Chitty, C. (eds) (2005) *The Impact of Correction on Re-Offending: A Review of 'What Works'*, 2nd edn. London: Home Office Research, Development and Statistics Directorate.

Hassan, E. and Thiara, R. (2001) 'Black prisoners' experiences of rehabilitative programmes, Centre for Research in Ethnic Relations, University of Warwick: Association of Black Probation Officers', *Probation Journal*, 48 (3): 219–21.

Her Majesty's Inspectorate of Prisons (HMIP) (2005) *Parallel Worlds: A Thematic Review of Race Relations in Prisons*. London: HMSO.

Her Majesty's Inspectorate of Prisons and Probation (2001) *Through the Prison Gate: A Joint Thematic Review*. London: HMSO

Home Office (2000) *The 2000 British Crime Survey England and Wales*, Home Office Statistical Bulletin 18/00. London: Home Office.

Home Office (2004) *Reducing Re-offending National Action Plan*. London: Home Office.

Home Office (2005a) *Criminal Justice Act 1991: Race and the Criminal Justice System: An Overview to the Complete Statistics 2003–4*. London: Home Office.

Home Office (2005b) *Statistics on Race and the Criminal Justice System*. London: Home Office.

Home Office (2006a) *Criminal Justice Act 1991, Section 95 Statistics 2004/5 on Race and the Criminal Justice System*. London: Home Office.

Home Office (2006b) *Performance Report on Offender Management Targets (PROMT) – April 2006 – September 2006*. London: Home Office.

Hood, R. (1992) *Race and Sentencing*. Oxford: Oxford University Press.

Hough, M. (1996) *Drugs Misuse and the Criminal Justice System: A Review of the Literature*. London: Home Office.

House of Commons (2006) *The Zahid Muburek Inquiry: Report*. London: HMSO.

Hucklesby, A. and Wincup, E. (2005) 'Evaluation of the Connect Project: Final Report'. Unpublished report to West Mercia Probation Board.

Jefferson, T. and Walker, M.A. (1992) 'Ethnic minorities in the criminal justice system', *Criminal Law Review*, 81: 83–95.

Knight, V. (2004) 'An investigation into minority ethnic prisoners' knowledge and perceptions of the Probation and Prison Service in the East of England', *Community Safety Journal*, 3 (2): 28–31.

Knight, V. and Bailey, R. (2003) 'An Investigation into Minority Ethnic Prisoners' Perceptions and Knowledge of the Probation and Prison Service in the East of England'. Unpublished report for the National Probation Service (East of England).

Lewis, S., Raynor, P., Smith, D. and Wardak, A. (2005) *Race and Probation*. Cullompton: Willan.

McGuire, J. (2002) *Offender Rehabilitation and Treatment: Effective Programmes and Policies to Reduce Re-Offending*. Chichester: John Wiley & Sons.

Macpherson, W. (1999) *The Stephen Lawrence Inquiry: Report of an Inquiry by Sir William Macpherson of Cluny. Advised by Tom Cook, The Right Reverend Dr John Sentamu and Dr Richard Stone*, Cmnd 4262-1. London: Home Office.

Maruna, S. (2004) 'What's love got to do with it?', *Safer Society*, 22: 12–14.

Maxwell, P. and Mallon, D. (1997) 'Discrimination against ex-offenders', *Howard Journal of Criminal Justice*, 36 (4): 352–66.

May, C. (1999) *Explaining Reconviction Following a Community Sentence: The Role of Social Factors*, Home Office Research Study No. 192. London: Home Office.

Mirrlees-Black, C. (2001) *Confidence in the Criminal Justice System: Findings from the 2000 British Crime Survey*, Research Findings No. 137. London: Home Office.

NACRO (2001) *Women Behind Bars: A Positive Agenda for Women Prisoners Resettlement*. London: NACRO.

NACRO (2003) *Recruiting Ex-offenders: The Employers' Perspective*. London: NACRO.

Niven, S. and Olagundoye, J. (2002) *Jobs and Homes: A Survey of Prisoners Nearing Release*, Home Office Research Findings No. 173. London: Home Office.

Niven, S. and Stewart, D. (2003) *Resettlement Outcomes on Release from Prison in 2003*, Research Findings No. 248. London: Home Office.

Norris, C., Fielding, N., Kemp, C. and Fielding, J. (1992) 'Black and blue: An analysis of the influence of race on being stopped by the police', *British Journal of Sociology*, 43 (2): 207–24.

Office for National Statistics (ONS) (2001) National Census. See: www.statistics.gov.uk/census2001.

Phillips, C. (2005) 'Facing inwards and outwards? Institutional racism, race equality and the role of black and Asian professional associations', *Criminal Justice*, 5 (4): 357–77.

Phillips, C. and Bowling, B. (2003) 'Racism, ethnicity and criminology: developing minority perspectives', *British Journal of Criminology*, 43 (2): 269–90.

Scarman, Lord (1981) *The Scarman Report: The Brixton Disorders*, Cmnd 8427. London: HMSO.

Senior, P. (2003) *Pathways to Resettlement*. Sheffield: Sheffield Hallam University Press.

Sharp, D., Atherton, S. and Williams, K. (2006) *Everyone's Business: Investigating the Resettlement Needs of Black and Minority Ethnic Groups in the West Midlands*. Birmingham: Government Office West Midlands (GOWM).

Smart Justice (2004) *The Racial Justice Gap Race and the Prison Population Briefing*. Available from: www.smartjustice.org.

Smith, D. (1997) 'Ethnic origins, crime and criminal justice', in R. Maguire, R. Morgan and R. Reiner (eds), *The Oxford Handbook of Criminology*, 2nd edn. Oxford: Oxford University Press.

Social Exclusion Unit (2000) *Minority Ethnic Issues in Social Exclusion and Neighbourhood Renewal: A Guide to the Work of the Social Exclusion Unit and the Policy Action Teams So Far*. London: Social Exclusion Unit.

Social Exclusion Unit (2002) *Reducing Re-offending by Ex-prisoners*. London: Office of the Deputy Prime Minister.

Stephens, K., Coombs, J. and Debidin, M. (2004) *Black and Asian Offenders Pathfinder: Implementation Report*, Home Office Development and Practice Report No. 24. London: Home Office.

Stone, V. and Tuffin, R. (2000) *Attitudes of People from Minority Ethnic Communities towards a Career in the Police Service*, Police Research Series Paper No. 136. London: Home Office.

Tkachuk, B. and Walmsley, R. (2001) *World Prison Population: Facts, Trends and Solutions*, HEUNI Papers No. 15. Finland: HEUNI.

Chapter 11

The resettlement of prolific offenders: policy and practice

Julie Vennard

Introduction

The focus of this chapter is on the resettlement of prisoners whose high rates of offending bring them within the ambit of the national Prolific and Other Priority Offenders (PPO) Strategy. Launched by the Government in 2004, the strategy falls squarely within its crime and disorder reduction programme. The aim is to reduce reoffending by those targeted and to achieve an impact on levels of crime overall. A spur to the decision to focus upon a small group of highly active offenders was the realisation that a relatively small proportion of the active offender population accounts for a high proportion of recorded crime. Home Office statistics estimated that some 100,000 offenders (10 per cent of the active offender population) were responsible for half of all crime in England and Wales (Home Office 2001).[1] Those targeted by the strategy are predominantly acquisitive offenders, a high proportion of whom are drug-dependent. Two years after the launch of the PPO programme, the Government claimed that it is '… not only making a substantial contribution to crime reduction, but … is also demonstrating how joined-up multi-agency, offender-focused partnership work can contribute to the Government's vision of safer and stronger communities'.[2] The chapter begins with a brief discussion of recent insights into the process of desistance from drug use and offending that appear relevant to the rehabilitative and resettlement aims of the PPO strategy. It then summarises the origins and main elements of the PPO strategy and considers what lessons might be drawn from early evaluations of local schemes.

Supporting and sustaining desistance from offending and drug misuse: insights from research

In a discussion of recent developments in mainstream resettlement policy, Maguire and Raynor (2006) noted that theories on why and how offenders might be encouraged to desist from crime have been largely absent from the Government's plans for change in practice, notably the Reducing Re-offending National Action Plan (Home Office 2004e). The same may be said of the PPO strategy. However, an understanding of how people become locked into chronic drug use and offending, and of what may trigger the process of desistance, clearly *ought* to inform resettlement policy and practice (McNeill 2006).

A number of studies have drawn attention to the significant scale of drug abuse among offenders and to the association between chaotic drug use and prolific offending (Bennett 2000; Liriano and Ramsay 2003; McSweeney and Hough 2006). There is also evidence that chronic drug use and offending coexist with other complex personal and practical problems, including poor mental health, homelessness and long-term unemployment (May, 1999; Niven and Stewart 2005; Social Exclusion Unit 2002). Sources of friendship and support also tend to be within the same social networks that encourage continued crime and drug abuse. Withdrawing from such an environment and gaining access to new social worlds can only take place over an extended period.

Of particular relevance to those involved in working with prolific offenders is the notion of desistance as a complex *process* rather than an event. This process may be triggered by a combination of 'objective' changes in offenders' lives and 'subjective' assessments of their significance (Farrall 2002). The process may be lengthy and, in the case of drug users, interrupted by relapses (Burnett 2004; Farrall 2002; McSweeney and Hough 2006; Worrall and Mawby 2004). The concept of a 'cycle of change', developed by Prochaska and DiClemente (1992), identifies a number of stages through which someone can be expected to pass on the way to recovery. Relapse and reversion to an earlier stage of the cycle are regarded as integral to the process of change. According to this model, drug-free and offence-free periods may be achieved, but sustained desistance over an extended period involves an underlying change in the way in which offenders perceive themselves (Farrall 2002; Maruna 2001).

How can criminal justice practitioners and drug workers prompt and sustain this process? The difficulty in generating motivation to seek an alternative lifestyle tends to be underestimated in many rehabilitative programmes (Rumgay 2004). Studies of criminal careers among drug dependent offenders report that this group are the least likely to access formal support services or to succeed in treatment (Rumgay 2004: 252). However, a consistent message from the literature is that motivation to sustain treatment is open to external influence. Timely access to clinical assistance and a speedy response to requests for help are vital (Fox *et al.* 2005). Factors that influence perseverance in treatment include a supportive environment, the availability of social support and therapists who encourage feelings of self-efficacy (Eley *et al.* 2005; Fox *et al.* 2005; Rumgay 2004). Research into styles of offender supervision also suggest that offenders are likely to be more responsive when encouraged to become active participants rather than treated as passive recipients of services and opportunities (Chapman and Hough, 1998; Partridge 2004; Robinson 2005; Robinson and Dignan 2004).

These findings echo a key theme of the desistance literature, which is that a sustained commitment to lifestyle change is achieved primarily through decisions made by offenders themselves (Maguire 2004; Maruna *et al.* 2004). In the case of substance abusing offenders there is evidence that entry into treatment can be prompted by external factors, but that successful completion of programmes and longer-term desistance requires personal commitment to change (Harman and Paylor 2005; Rumgay 2004). As demonstrated by Hough *et al.* (2003) in a pilot study of Drug Treatment and Training Orders (DTTOs), coerced treatment can be effective, at least in the short term, in reducing both drug use and offending among those who comply and complete their orders. However, strict enforcement tends to result in high rates of revocation and reconviction among non-completers. Mirroring the wider desistance literature, it has been argued that a balance needs to be struck between coercion and strict enforcement on the one hand, and responsiveness to individual needs and circumstances on the other (Hedderman and Hough 2004; Rumgay 2004).

A related insight is that practitioners can support desistance by helping offenders to acquire a stake in conformity (typically a job or family ties) that they value more highly than gains derived from a criminal lifestyle (e.g. Burnett and Maruna 2004). It is claimed that motivation is enhanced if interventions pay attention not only to offenders' *capacity* to lead crime-free lives (for example by addressing poor cognitive skills) but also their self-esteem and access to *opportunities* ('social capital') (Farrall 2002; Rex, 1999). In similar vein, Burnett and Maruna (2004) have argued that 'strengths-based' resettlement, in which offenders are given opportunities to make amends and make positive contributions to their communities, promotes and sustains the desistance process (see Hucklesby and Wincup, this volume).

These broad messages from the desistance literature accord with findings from studies of the way in which resettlement and aftercare services can support offenders' efforts to reintegrate. A key theme of such studies is that continuity of interventions and supportive relationships across the custody/community boundary can have a major impact on subsequent drug use and offending (Hough *et al.* 2003; Robinson and Dignan 2004; Turnbull *et al.* 2000). An evaluation of resettlement 'Pathfinders' that were targeted on prisoners serving short sentences (a high proportion of whom were persistent drug users) confirmed the importance of continuity of contact 'through the gate' with a member of the resettlement team (Clancy *et al.* 2006; Lewis *et al.* 2003; Lewis *et al.* 2007). This evaluation also indicated that offenders are better equipped to overcome the obstacles they encounter if, prior to release, they are well motivated, set clear goals and have realistic plans to achieve them (Maguire and Raynor 2006).

Evolution of prolific offender schemes

In England and Wales the earliest intensive interventions designed to curb the behaviour of persistent/prolific offenders were developed in the 1970s. Between 1972 and 1974 four Probation Services participated in what was known as the Intensive Matched Probation and After-Care Treatment (IMPACT) experiment (Folkard *et al.* 1976). As described by Mair *et al.* (1994), this experiment was the first systematic attempt to reduce offending through a combination of smaller caseloads and correspondingly higher levels of contact (Folkard *et al.* 1976). Mair *et al.* (2004: 3) concluded that in these early schemes the term 'intensive' simply meant 'more social work, more counselling, more guidance'. The traditional treatment model of probation employed by IMPACT staff made few demands upon the offenders targeted. Moreover, there was little evidence that supervisors collaborated with other agencies in addressing problems associated with high rates of offending (Worrall and Mawby 2004).

During the early 1980s the Probation Service found itself under pressure to adopt a more rigorous approach towards recidivist

247

offenders. This was partly a response to a rising prison population. At the same time, the government was heavily influenced by the well documented 'nothing works' movement, associated with Martinson's (1974) claim that 'treatment' (including intensive supervision) was ineffective in reducing reoffending. In an effort to persuade sentencers that community penalties offered a credible alternative to custody, new forms of intensive supervision were introduced that began to make more demands on offenders and imposed greater restrictions on their liberty (Home Office 1988). This new generation of programmes was principally designed to satisfy the demand for punishment and increased surveillance, largely through increased contact with supervisors and electronic monitoring. As Gendreau *et al.* (2001) observed in respect of similar intensive schemes implemented in North America during this period, besides serving a retributive purpose, the expectation was that these tough programmes would achieve conformity and crime reduction through the threat of punishment. This was despite the growing body of North American literature indicating the ineffectiveness of intensive programmes in which there is little or no attempt to engage in any form of rehabilitative work (see, for example, Andrews 1995; Gendreau *et al.* 2001). However, there was some evidence of a reduction in recidivism in the few programmes in which supervisors continued to provide assistance with offending-related problems and sought to motivate participants to change their lifestyle (Gendreau *et al.* 2001; Petersilia and Turner 1993).

The Government's current emphasis on the apprehension and rehabilitation of recidivist offenders can be traced back to the 2001 election manifesto pledge to narrow the gap between the number of crimes recorded and those that result in the perpetrator being brought to justice. In *Narrowing the Justice Gap* attention was drawn to the fact that in 80 per cent of all crimes recorded by the police offenders remain unpunished (Home Office 2002). Greater effectiveness in catching and punishing persistent offenders was seen as a means of reducing the 'gap' and also raising the level of public confidence in the criminal justice system. Studies of criminal careers lend support to this argument. The most recent findings of the Cambridge Study in Delinquent Development indicate that some 7 per cent of males accounted for approximately half of officially recorded offences (Farrington *et al.* 2006).

The rationale for focusing on a relatively small group of offenders has been challenged by those who have pointed out that offences resulting in conviction make up a very small proportion of all offences committed (e.g. Garside 2004). Garside has contended that the PPO strategy will be used to justify heavy-handed treatment of the 'usual suspects' while distracting attention from offenders who cause greater harm to society. It is undoubtedly true that criminal activity is more widespread than the official statistics suggest: the Cambridge Study shows for example that nearly half of all offences are committed by *unconvicted* males (Farrington *et al.* 2006). However, critics of the Government's policy concede that the activities of those targeted, such as prolific burglars, can have considerable impact on the neighbourhoods in which they operate. There is also evidence that the impact of crime is often felt most keenly by victims who are socially and economically disadvantaged, and by the most deprived and vulnerable communities (Social Exclusion Unit 2002). Furthermore, the financial costs associated with the prevalence of dependent drug use within the offending population are high. It was estimated that in 2000, costs to the criminal justice system and wider 'social costs' of drug-related offending – including those incurred by victims – were in the range of £17 billion (Godfrey *et al.* 2002).

The Persistent Offender Scheme was implemented in 2002 as part of the *Narrowing the Justice Gap* strategy. The scheme was aimed at adult offenders 'who have been convicted of six or more recordable offences in the last year and other offenders identified as persistent on the basis of local intelligence' (Home Office 2002: 13). Although the prime objective was to contribute to the Government's crime reduction targets, it was acknowledged that there was a greater chance of achieving this if, once caught and punished, participants received help in tackling the problems related to their offending. In the following year the Carter Review of Correctional Services similarly argued that a punitive response to persistent offending was needed, but that such an approach should be combined with efforts to rehabilitate and prioritise offenders for services (Carter 2003).

A Joint Inspection of the Persistent Offender Scheme (Home Office 2004a) found widespread support for a model of intensive intervention that pursued the twin aims of rehabilitation and crime reduction. However, the definition of a 'persistent offender' that was employed had drawn in an unmanageable number of offenders, many of whom had been convicted of relatively minor offences – principally shoplifting – which were not those causing the greatest harm to their local community. Moreover, the scheme did not impose any requirement upon the Police and Probation Services to implement the strategy, nor provide guidance on how it was to operate. Following the recommendations of the inspection team, the Government introduced the National Prolific and Other Priority

Offender (PPO) programme in 2004. Local schemes were to focus their efforts on a more limited number of offenders who commit a high volume of acquisitive crime, but were free to determine their own definitions of 'prolific' and 'other priority' offenders.

The current PPO strategy

The current PPO strategy comprises as an integrated initiative made up of three complementary strands. The first, 'prevent and deter', targets young people who are at risk of becoming involved in crime and those who are already committing offences but who are not yet highly active. The second and third strands – 'catch and convict' and 'rehabilitate and resettle' – are intended to work together. The 'rehabilitate and resettle' element aims to offer support to those brought within the ambit of the scheme and afford them priority access to services, both in custody and in the community. At the same time offenders are to be closely monitored in order to ensure a swift response to any breach of licence conditions (Home Office 2004b). In the language of the 2006 Green Paper *Rebalancing the Criminal Justice System in Favour of the Law-Abiding Majority*, those targeted by local schemes are offered a 'hard choice' between accepting help to change their lives and being fast-tracked through the courts if they fail to comply with the terms of community orders or licences (Home Office 2006a: 28).

Statistics gathered for performance management purposes indicate that in the period July to September 2006 local schemes were targeting around 11,000 adult recidivist offenders and 4,000 young offenders deemed to be at risk of becoming the next generation of prolific offenders (Home Office 2006c). Of the 11,000, around 40 per cent are in prison at some point during their involvement in the programme. It is noteworthy that only 18 per cent of those within the scheme were serving sentences of more than 12 months and were thereby subject to statutory post-release supervision. A further 38 per cent were serving sentences of 12 months or less and would not therefore have benefited from the intensive support offered to targeted offenders who were released on licence. This has important implications for the rehabilitative and resettlement strands of the strategy. Although voluntary aftercare is offered to short sentence prisoners, take-up is low with the most recent monitoring statistics indicating that only 2 per cent of targeted offenders were at liberty and subject to 'voluntary rehabilitative intervention' (Home Office 2006c).

The strategy is led at the local level by existing Crime and Disorder Reduction Partnerships (CDRPs) in which the Police and Probation Services are already key players.[3] Schemes are expected to forge links with Youth Offending Teams, who are required to pursue the same broad resettlement policies and practices in the case of persistent young offenders passing through young offender institutions (Youth Justice Board 2005). Unlike the earlier Persistent Offender Scheme, the current PPO strategy is explicit in its emphasis on the central role that prisons are to play in the case of targeted offenders who receive custodial sentences. Anticipating the implementation of the National Offender Management Service (NOMS), the 'rehabilitate and resettle' component of the strategy is expected to provide 'end-to-end offender management' through all stages of sentences (NOMS 2005). Prisons are to play a key role in providing pre-release support to those targeted and to work closely with the Probation Service through offender managers. Furthermore, prisons holding offenders designated 'prolific' are required to prioritise them for services in custody and ensure successful completion of sentence plans (Home Office 2004c).

From the start of the PPO initiative, the Government has sought to ensure close partnership with the Drug Interventions Programme (DIP) with the aim of working more effectively with highly prolific offenders whose criminality is drug-related. In high crime areas central government funding has been provided to enable Drug Action Teams to respond more effectively to drug-users who commit high levels of acquisitive crime. They are expected to work in partnership with the Probation Service and with prison healthcare and drug treatment services (Home Office 2004d). DIP is also expected to address the broader range of offenders' needs and to broker access to services such as housing, employment and education.

Whereas engagement with the Drug Interventions Programme had been voluntary, from 2004 coercive elements were introduced into the DIP/PPO partnership. These included restriction on bail, which requires defendants who test positive for Class A drugs at the police station to undergo assessment and appropriate treatment as a condition of bail with the threat of custodial remand if they refuse (Hucklesby et al. 2007). In a relaunch of the PPO programme in autumn 2006, the Government has placed greater emphasis upon strict enforcement and sanctions in the event of non-compliance. Those who test positive for Class A drugs will be required to undergo mandatory drug testing, drug treatment and follow-up assessment. Refusal may result in 'tough new sanctions' in the form of a fine or imprisonment (Home

Office 2006a: 28). For some offenders the 'choice' may be between accepting treatment and intensive supervision, or the new 'extended sentences' proposed in the case of the most prolific offenders.[4]

The 'rehabilitate and resettle' strand of the PPO strategy is conceived as a multi-agency approach in which CDRPs work with a range of other partners at local authority and regional level in supporting the needs of PPOs. This is to be achieved by following the 'Pathways' set out in the Government's Reducing Re-offending National Action Plan (Home Office 2004d), which in turn reflects the recommendations of the Social Exclusion Unit report (SEU 2002). In addition to drug and alcohol services, schemes are expected to address resettlement problems in relation to accommodation, unemployment, mental and physical health, finances and relationships with family (see Hedderman, this volume). Also implicit in the PPO strategy is a recognition that schemes need to address attitudes and motives underpinning a lifestyle of drug use and criminality.

Effective offender management, modelled on NOMS (Home Office 2004c), is seen as the way to overcome the poor coordination of services highlighted in the research literature. Offender managers are also expected to provide 'intensive supervision' and close monitoring of offenders post-release, although the guidance accompanying the launch of the strategy did not specify the frequency of contact with supervisors and partner agencies.[5] Experience in working with persistent offenders in schemes that predated the PPO strategy suggested a need for at least four (breachable) contacts with offenders per week in the first three months of supervision. Thereafter the preference was flexibility in levels of contact in order to cater for variations in needs and risk of reoffending (Homes *et al.* 2005). This model has been widely adopted as best practice, although for reasons outlined below it is not always achievable.

Probation Services are expected to take the lead in prioritising targeted offenders for the provision of *all* interventions for which they have been assessed as suitable.[6] However, the PPO programme was introduced without additional central government funding. Local schemes and partner agencies are expected to utilise existing resources, including funding allocated to support other programmes such as DIP. The rationale for relying on existing funding was that reductions in offending would generate savings across these funding streams. As will be argued later in the chapter, reliance on short-term funding has compromised the quality of prison-based and post-release resettlement provision. The policy also raises an issue of principle concerning the prioritisation of prolific offenders for services over others (non-offenders in some instances) who may be regarded as more deserving.

Lessons from early evaluative studies

The NOMS Offender Management Model has only recently begun to be implemented in respect of offenders in custody. It was not until September 2006 that prisons were required to play their part in the sentence management of offenders within the PPO programme (National Probation Directorate 2006). That said, certain lessons may be drawn from the experience of local schemes in supporting participants while they are in custody and in preparing them for release. One such scheme, which operated in Avon and Somerset from 2003, sought to provide the 'through the gate' service envisaged in the NOMS resettlement model. This scheme was regarded by the architects of the national PPO strategy as a model of good practice, not least because the Prison, Probation and Police Services were formal partners in the enterprise.

The Bristol component of the Avon and Somerset scheme was evaluated by the author of this chapter with a colleague from Bristol University (Vennard and Pearce 2004). The evaluation focused on the scheme's operation in Bristol between 2002 and 2004. We drew on the experiences of managers and staff from the Police, Prison and Probation Services. In addition, we sought the views of 17 participants when they first joined the scheme and a year later. Consistent with the scheme's selection criteria, all 17 offenders had histories of acquisitive crime and drug addiction and all were at high risk of reoffending.[7] The majority had spent a large proportion of their adult lives in prison and had multiple problems associated with their drug misuse and offending.

Rehabilitative and resettlement provision in custody

The probation team seconded to the Bristol Prolific Offender Unit regarded their small caseloads as critical to their ability to fulfil their role effectively while participants were in custody. Visits to prison enabled them to build relationships, motivate participants to take advantage of enhanced opportunities to participate in drug treatment and other programmes, and contribute to sentence management and resettlement planning. In the early days of the scheme probation staff were expected to maintain frequent contact with participants throughout their sentence and to review progress on a regular basis. As reported by probation staff involved in the earlier persistent offender schemes, staff were able to maintain contact with participants serving custodial sentences to an extent that was unrealistic in mainstream probation (Homes *et al.* 2005).

Participants who were targeted by the Avon and Somerset scheme while in custody welcomed the promise of continuity of support throughout their sentence. This support, coupled with prioritisation for drug services, was perceived as more likely to provide the motivation they needed to desist from further offending than the coercive elements of the scheme. Well aware of the risks of relapse into drug abuse and offending on their release, many of these offenders described themselves as having reached a point at which they felt motivated to make fundamental changes in their way of life. As expressed by 'Mike', this was something most had never previously been offered:

> I've never had any help – I've been in prison all my life – all my life in and out – but no one's actually sat down and talked to me. I've had people in prison saying they want me to do this scheme and that – you do that because you're bored in prison – it's something to do. You go along, answer their questions – sometimes you might even enjoy it – but it does nothing for you whatsoever once you leave the prison. But this [the Bristol scheme] is actually outside and they're going to stick with you. They're not going to give up on you – like everyone else has.

However, it proved impossible to maintain this ideal, even with caseloads that were far smaller than in mainstream probation, as the Bristol scheme expanded throughout Avon and Somerset, and as participants began to be transferred to prisons at a greater distance from Bristol. Visits began to be restricted to the initial remand period and to the last few weeks of the sentence. Members of the probation team were critical of this managerial decision, fearing that motivation would be lost if personal contact was not sustained. Participants whom we interviewed a second time while they were in custody commented adversely on the decline in the number of visits they received from their supervisors. 'Robin', who had breached the terms of his licence, expressed his disappointment at the lack of continuity:

> I was given a chance and I blew it. But it's not like I just wandered off and didn't tell them where I was. I made proper

arrangements. I told them where I'd be ... I've failed so many times in my life. That's what I thought this was about – because I can't do it and because it's not going to be easy. I thought they were going to be ready for this. If you've been trying so long, what makes them think you're going to do it first time? It's not going to happen, it's going to take a while. It's not going to be easy ... It seems like you just get one chance and if you fail it, that's it. For seven months I've seen none of them.

Had these disgruntled participants returned to Bristol prison for the last few weeks of their sentences their supervisors would have been able to renew contact prior to their release. In practice, despite their pressing resettlement needs, this was seldom achieved. The probation team was thus unable to play as full a part in preparing participants for their release as had been envisaged at the outset. This undermined supervisors' ability to maintain motivation to engage with the scheme and avoid further offending in the critical post-release period (see also Clancy *et al.* 2006; Lewis *et al.* 2003).

The presence of dedicated prison staff in HMP Bristol, and of liaison officers in other prisons throughout the South West, partially offset these limitations in pre-release contact with probation staff. This enabled the field probation team to secure priority access for participants to certain services within the prison, such as the 'drug-free' wing that offered a short treatment programme. The dedicated team within Bristol prison was also able to arrange transfers to prisons in the South West that were willing to prioritise participants for certain programmes. Some participants who completed programmes or courses at training prisons progressed to Category D establishments with open conditions. The Bristol prison team was enthusiastic about the scope for progression that some offenders were able to exploit. One team member reported:

A lot of these lads year in year out spend their time in Cat. B or at best Cat. C training establishments. Now they are actually progressing through their sentence. You can't make anyone change, but if someone is ready we can actually give them the tools to make that transition.

Unlike the arrangement in Bristol prison, liaison officers located in other prisons were not formally seconded to the scheme. Nonetheless, these officers contributed to prisoners' sentence plans, helped facilitate access to programmes and kept the probation team informed of transfers. Probation staff compared this arrangement favourably with their experience in mainstream probation, where communication between prison and probation was generally considered to be poor.

Despite the benefits derived from these informal liaison arrangements, the partnership forged by the Bristol scheme with prison authorities was not sufficiently robust to counter the demands of population management within the prison system. When pressure from overcrowding became acute in Bristol prison, as occurred in the course of the evaluation, requests to delay transfer were often overridden, with the result that many participants left before there had been a full assessment of their needs. These same institutional pressures also prevented schemes from returning participants to Bristol prison six to eight weeks prior to release to take advantage of the Resettlement Unit's intensive programme. As the Avon and Somerset scheme expanded, some prison governors began to express unease at the presence in their establishment of an increasing number of priority 'prolific' offenders. From their perspective these offenders were but one category of prisoner who might benefit from treatment and training facilities. After all, prisoners are overwhelmingly young, male, repeat offenders who tend to be characterised by high levels of unemployment, homelessness, relationship difficulties and, increasingly, drug misuse (Lewis et al. 2003; Social Exclusion Unit 2002). Resource constraints within prisons are such that only a small minority of prisoners can gain access to rehabilitative and resettlement facilities.

Tension between the Avon and Somerset scheme and prison authorities in respect of the dispersal of participants around the prison system highlighted differences in organisational values and priorities. Other important areas of disagreement were in relation to the programmes participants should attend, and whether or not they should be released on Home Detention Curfew. Notwithstanding the organisational merger of the Prison and Probation services, it seems likely that these differences, coupled with prison overcrowding, will limit the extent to which schemes are able to achieve the pre-release resettlement goals to which the PPO strategy aspires.

Intensive post-release supervision and monitoring

Probation staff involved in prolific offender schemes placed a high premium on frequent contact following the release of offenders from custody – even more frequently than the customary four contacts per week when participants' needs are greatest. This was seen as crucial if staff were to respond promptly to unacceptable behaviour, sustain motivation and help participants deal with problems that placed them at risk of drug relapse or reoffending. Both in the Avon and Somerset and the Stoke-on-Trent prolific offender schemes, participants whose offending was drug-related relied heavily on the probation team for intensive (sometimes daily) support. Worrall *et al.* (2003) concluded that, while the Stoke project was clearly supportive, mandatory appointments also brought structure to participants' lives. As in respect of pre-release contact, probation staff regarded small caseloads (in the region of 13 participants to one member of staff) as essential if they were to work effectively on the multiple personal and practical difficulties these offenders faced on release. Such small caseloads also enabled schemes to extend support to participants' partners and families in an effort to rebuild relationships.

Scheme participants generally perceived the intensive supervision they received as beneficial. Those involved in the Bristol scheme spoke of the structure this had brought to their lives, not only in terms of the one-to-one meetings with their supervisors but through the tasks set for them in connection with future employment, attendance at relevant courses and drug counselling (see also Worrall and Mawby 2004). Those who wanted help to overcome drug dependency valued the encouragement they had received in efforts to distance themselves from drug-using associates. Others said their supervisors had helped them gain a measure of self-reliance and had encouraged them to set their own targets for change in a way that was new to them. Such accounts lend support to a model of desistance that emphasises the importance of self-determination and identifies a role for probation staff in encouraging and facilitating this process (Maguire and Raynor 2006; McNeill 2006).

Consistent with the findings reported by Dawson and Cuppleditch (2006) on the impact of the PPO programme, offenders who participated in the Bristol scheme compared their experience favourably with previous experience of probation supervision. This tended to be portrayed as a combination of minimal and meaningless contact and an authoritarian approach. In contrast, supervisors working within the prolific offender scheme were seen as available in times of need, concerned about participants' problems and willing to exercise discretion. As the following extracts from interviews with scheme participants illustrate, considerable importance was attached to relationships developed with supervisors:

I thought – 'What's happening here – why are they taking so much interest?' It made me think what they were saying was what they were meaning. I feel all these people are genuine. I'll be gutted if they're not. I'll be devastated if it all comes to nothing.

They ring me up; they genuinely want me to stay clean. They are there for me; I'm not just any statistic.

Intensive surveillance and monitoring is a striking extension of the multi-agency management and monitoring arrangements that have, to date, been reserved for those assessed as posing a risk of serious harm to the public. Indeed, from the perspective of the Probation Service, such close collaboration with the police, coupled with an expectation that information about targeted offenders will be shared between the various agencies involved in local schemes, may sit uncomfortably with the Service's rehabilitative traditions. At the outset of the Bristol and Stoke schemes such concerns were expressed by some probation staff. However, with experience, the partnership came to be regarded as central to the Probation Service's ability to protect the public from the harm that is inflicted by prolific offenders. Worrall and Mawby (2004) similarly observed that, in the Stoke scheme, support and surveillance were seen as complementary. Co-location of police and probation staff were widely favoured (Dawson 2006; Homes et al. 2005; Worrall and Mawby 2004). The arrangement was thought to convey to offenders that police and probation staff shared the same goals; it also reinforced the programme's crime-reduction ethos.

It might be thought that the policy of strict and speedy enforcement in the event of non-compliance with demanding reporting requirements runs the risk of high levels of revocation and return to custody. Such a policy may also undermine efforts to tailor interventions to the circumstances of individual offenders. As noted earlier in this chapter, drug dependent offenders are likely to be slow to engage with such a demanding regime and a robust approach to enforcement runs the risk of high rates of failure. Furthermore, if offenders are brought within the ambit of the PPO programme when their offending, though persistent, is relatively minor, there is a risk of inappropriate resort to custodial sentences. Such concerns were not shared by staff involved in the Avon and Somerset scheme. Indeed, they regarded early detection and disruption of further offending as beneficial, both to society and to participants. One senior prison officer expressed this as follows:

Offenders are fast-tracked back in before they've done too much damage to themselves and the community. If someone relapsed and stays out for some time it can take 6–12 months to bring them back – they can be as bad if not worse than at first contact. With this scheme quite often they are a couple of steps on from where they started. So there is something to build on.

For this reason, staff seldom viewed the high breach rate (two-thirds of participants were breached at some stage) as necessarily indicating failure on the part of the scheme. A prompt response to drug relapse and/or reoffending enabled staff to stabilise participants' drug use and prevent a further spree of offending, with the associated risk of lengthy prison sentences. As in the case of the Stoke scheme, relapse and recall to prison were not viewed as an end point. If prolific offenders returned to the scheme staff were able to build on any progress made and continue supporting their efforts to abstain from further offending (Worrall and Mawby 2004).

Offenders whom we interviewed who had been breached appeared to accept that this action was in their interests. As noted by Dawson and Cuppleditch (2006), the 'carrot and stick' approach was fairly well understood by offenders and tended to be seen as an effective way of helping them keep out of trouble. Although a few offenders interviewed in the course of the Avon and Somerset evaluation were uncomfortable that the police knew so much about their movements and associations, most accepted the fact that close attention from probation and police officers curbed their offending.[8]

Accessing services in the community

Consistent with wider studies of prisoners' resettlement needs (see, for example, Lewis et al. 2003), it is clear that those targeted by the PPO scheme face a range of resettlement problems which, if not addressed, undermine their reintegration. Priority needs following release are almost invariably in relation to their drug addiction and housing (Homes et al. 2005; Tupman et al. 2001; Vennard and Pearce 2004). Drug treatment is regarded as an essential element of schemes and access to such treatment following release needs to be swift (Homes et al. 2005). Equally, as observed by Lewis et al. (2003), until ex-prisoners are satisfactorily housed, they are unlikely to achieve stability in other areas of their lives or to overcome drug and alcohol addiction. A high proportion of offenders targeted by schemes are homeless or are at risk of returning to unsuitable accommodation

(Dawson 2006). Difficulties in securing accommodation have been noted in several evaluations of local persistent and prolific offender schemes and are discussed in Maguire and Nolan (this volume). The Bristol prolific offender team identified a pressing need for a range of suitable housing, including hostels that do not tolerate drug use and independent housing of an acceptable standard. As noted by Homes *et al.* (2005), many local housing associations refuse to house anyone with rent arrears or a criminal conviction (see Maguire and Nolan, this volume).

In the case of offenders whose acquisitive offending is fuelled by drug use, the CARATS (Counselling, Assessment, Referral, Advice and Throughcare Service) initiative, operational in prisons throughout England and Wales, is the core treatment service for drug users in custody. The service also has a clear remit to provide throughcare support for this group in terms of preparation for release, referral to other agencies and post-release support where needed (HM Prison Service 2002). As noted by Harman and Paylor (2005), Prison Service guidance explicitly directs CARATS workers to take a holistic approach to offenders who misuse drugs, ensuring that they address other needs, including housing and employment (HM Prison Service 2002). In practice, however, high levels of demand for the CARAT service have restricted workers' ability to engage effectively in the resettlement process (Harman and Paylor 2005). Harman and Paylor note that the gap in provision is particularly wide in the case of drug-using offenders serving short sentences who are not subject to statutory aftercare, for whom CARATS is the main statutory coordinator of post-release support.

In the case of offenders who participated in the early persistent/ prolific offender schemes the CARATS initiative appears not to have played a significant role in providing continuity of treatment through the prison gate. Schemes experienced difficulties in fast-tracking participants into non-residential drug services and in ensuring that drug maintenance plans were closely monitored. In Bristol waiting lists for the main prescribing drug service were lengthy, so the scheme had begun to rely on local GPs to prescribe medication. One solution to this gap, adopted by the Stoke scheme, was to fund a GP to provide such a service. The GP became a full-time team member of the scheme, saw offenders in times of crisis and provided immediate medication where needed (Worrall *et al.* 2003). The Avon and Somerset scheme experienced the withdrawal of ring-fenced funding for residential treatment. This entailed joining waiting lists, competing for places with other priority drug users and, as one probation officer put it, 'becoming bogged down in bureaucracy'. The Government's plans to align the DIP more closely with the PPO programme may go some way towards dealing with these difficulties since, although the DIP client group is far larger than that of the PPO programme, both programmes aim to break the cycle of drug misuse, offending and return to custody.

Supporting and maintaining desistance

In accordance with the crime reduction aspirations of the Prolific Offender Strategy, it will be judged primarily in terms of levels of reconviction among targeted offenders and its impact upon local crime rates. Guidance issued by the Home Office to those responsible for managing local schemes has set a mandatory indicator of effectiveness: to reduce recorded reconviction rates among a cohort of PPOs tracked for a minimum of two years. On the basis of an interim evaluation of the PPO programme, areas are expected to reduce recorded convictions among those targeted by 15 per cent per annum (Home Office 2006b).[9]

There are indications of a reduction in offending among those who have been targeted by persistent and prolific offender schemes. For example, within the Avon and Somerset scheme, local crime statistics, coupled with information on the progress of participants, suggested that the combination of intensive support and a swift response to further offending had resulted in modest reductions in the level of drug use and offending. Other evaluations reported similar results while offenders are actively participating in schemes (Worrall *et al.* 2003; Worrall and Mawby 2004). However, these early studies were necessarily based on small numbers of participants and lacked well-matched comparison groups. A more recent examination of the conviction rates of a large cohort of offenders targeted by the PPO strategy indicated a sharp reduction in convictions following entry onto the programme. Comparing the sum of convictions in the 17 months prior to and following entry on the programme showed a 43 per cent reduction across the cohort (Dawson and Cuppleditch 2006). This reduction in convictions was not attributable to a sudden increase in custodial sentences among those targeted. At the individual level, the average rate of offending fell from 0.51 convictions per month in the 12 months prior to entry onto the scheme to 0.39 for the 12 months following entry, a reduction of 24 per cent. However, as the authors caution, it is not possible to ascertain how much of the decrease in levels of convictions is directly attributable to the PPO programme. Neither is it clear to what extent these positive findings can be attributed to rehabilitative and resettlement elements of the programme.

A consistent finding of the research is that participants in local schemes attribute a cessation or reduction in their offending while they are under supervision to a combination of three factors: drug treatment and other helpful interventions, the intensity and structure of PPO schemes and the deterrent effect of regular monitoring. As yet there is no firm evidence that such results are sustained when supervision and monitoring comes to an end. Indeed, analysis of conviction rates among offenders who participated in the Stoke-on-Trent scheme showed that the number of convictions actually increased in the post-project period (Worrall *et al*. 2003). One of the main lessons Worrall and Mawby (2004) drew from their evaluation was that although offenders may reduce their levels of criminal activity while they are actively engaged on a scheme, progress is not always maintained when support and close monitoring are withdrawn. The same pattern was evident in the Avon and Somerset scheme.

Such findings support the view that desistance from substance misuse and offending is a lengthy and complex process. This was reflected in the expectation of those involved in schemes that contact will continue beyond the statutory licence/community sentence if this is requested by offenders. In Bristol staff were reluctant to terminate contact until the risk of drug relapse and a return to offending were much reduced. Terms such as 'phased exit' and 'moving on' were used to convey a preference for a flexible approach in which staff assisted participants in their efforts to take responsibility for an increasing range of tasks. Guidance issued by the Home Office (2005) on the criteria for removing a prolific or other priority offender from a scheme supports this decision. In selecting new offenders, schemes are meant to ensure that the overall numbers do not jeopardise the ability of prison and probation services to work effectively with existing participants. If schemes reach their capacity a decision to remove an existing PPO should not disrupt a drug treatment plan or result in the withdrawal of other services (such as housing and debt counselling). Drug Action Teams are expected to continue to provide a service to such offenders within the context of the DIP/PPO partnership arrangements. The guidance appears uncontroversial, but with finite resources and a premium on small caseloads, the decision to terminate contact with targeted offenders is likely to be as critical as the initial selection.

Conclusions

The 'rehabilitate and resettle' strand of the PPO strategy is expected to play a key role in reducing offending by those brought within its ambit. Evaluations of local schemes underline the importance of close collaboration between the prison and probation services if these goals are to be met. Where this partnership worked well, as in HMP Bristol, participants benefited from the support of dedicated prison officers and a degree of prioritisation for drug treatment and other services. However, there are likely to remain substantial challenges to the seamless sentence ideal underlying the PPO strategy within a prison system that is running at maximum capacity. The creation of the roles of 'Offender Supervisors' and 'Offender Manager Units' within the National Offender Management Model has the potential to address some of these challenges. But if the number of offenders included in the national PPO scheme continues to rise, the prioritisation for pre-release resettlement services envisaged in the strategy may prove to be unattainable.

Restricted probation caseloads enabled schemes to deliver a level of post-release support that is not as readily achievable within mainstream probation. The benefits that participants derived from a high level of support indicate that probation supervisors can play a pivotal role in fostering the process of reintegration and desistance (see, for example, Rex 1999). This feature may also enable probation staff to help build the 'social capital' (opportunities) and human capital (motivation and capacity) that is necessary if the offenders targeted by the PPO programme are to achieve a different lifestyle (Farrall 2002; McNeill 2006). However, at a time of expanding probation caseloads, there is a risk that PPO schemes will be unable to sustain the intensive supervision and monitoring that may be key to their effectiveness.

It must be acknowledged that prolific offender schemes have significant resource implications for agencies expected to prioritise offenders for their services. The Government sees a clear case for 'resources following risk' (Home Office 2004c), but such a policy has to be considered in the context of competing demands for services – in prison but also of course among law-abiding citizens who may be regarded as more deserving. Moreover, compelling or persuading poorly motivated participants into drug treatment not only risks high levels of relapse, but may also be seen as squandering scarce resources (Rumgay 2004). Quite apart from the cost implications of such an approach, the prioritisation of drug-misusing recidivists for treatment and other services raises difficult issues of principle that need to be acknowledged and addressed.

Meanwhile there are early indications that, in the short term, the partnership between the police and probation services can curtail offending through a combination of close monitoring and a speedy response to breach of licence conditions. Achieving desistance over an extended period among a group of highly prolific offenders, many with intractable problems, calls for a sustained investment of resources such as to test the political will of any government. However, given the scale of their offending, if only a modest proportion of those targeted were to desist there would be compensatory savings as well as clear social benefits.

Notes

1 These estimates were based on an analysis of the available statistics on individuals convicted of standard list offences in England and Wales.

2 Extract from letter dated 21 March 2006 from the Director General, Home Office Crime Reduction and Community Safety Group, and from the Chief Executives of NOMS and the Office for Criminal Justice Reform.

3 The 1998 Crime and Disorder Act established partnerships between the police, local authorities, probation services, health authorities, the voluntary sector and local businesses. Co-located within the Government Offices for the 10 Regions of England and Wales, Crime and Disorder Reduction Partnerships were well placed to coordinate the various strands of the PPO strategy.

4 With a view to giving the courts more power to put tough conditions on a small number of the most prolific offenders, the Government has proposed the introduction of a period of post-release licence during which the offender would be prohibited from, for example, approaching areas in which they have previously been active burglars or from going out at night (Home Office 2006a).

5 Guidance accompanying the 'rehabilitate and resettle' strand merely stated that PPOs will be supervised in accordance with Home Office National Standards.

6 Prioritisation of prolific offenders for these services is intended to reduce the risk that they represent. However, the operational guidance accompanying the launch of the PPO strategy signalled that the concept of 'resources following risk' may need to be overridden if this would displace offenders who pose a greater risk of serious harm – namely violent and sex offenders (Home Office 2004c).

7 The offenders scored highly on the Offender Assessment System (OASys) which measures the risk of reoffending.

8   PPO monitoring statistics indicate that in September 2006 just 2 per cent of participants were subject to 'proactive targeting by the police'.

9   In their first six months on the scheme there was a 10 per cent reduction in recorded convictions for the first PPO cohort compared with the six months prior to their allocation (Dawson 2005). No attempt was made in this evaluation to disentangle the effects of the PPO programme from other relevant factors such as changes in overall levels of crime and convictions for targeted offences.

References

Andrews, D.A. (1995) 'The psychology of criminal conduct and effective treatment', in J. McGuire (ed.), *What Works: Reducing Re-offending – Guidelines from Research and Practice*. Chichester: Wiley.

Bennett, T. (2000) *Drugs and Crime: The Results of the Second Developmental Stage of the NEW-ADAM Programme*, Home Office Research Study No. 205. London: Home Office.

Burnett, R. (2004) 'To re-offend or not to re-offend: the ambivalence of convicted property offenders', in S. Maruna and R. Immarigeon (eds), *After Crime and Punishment: Pathways to Offender Reintegration*. Cullompton: Willan, pp. 152–80.

Burnett, R. and Maruna, S. (2004) 'So "prison works", does it? The criminal careers of 130 men released from prisons under Home Secretary Michael Howard', *Howard Journal*, 43 (4): 390–404.

Carter, P. (2003) *Managing Offenders, Reducing Crime: A New Approach*. London: Prime Minister's Strategy Unit.

Chapman, T. and Hough, M. (1998) *Evidence Based Practice: A Guide to Effective Practice*. London: Home Office.

Clancy, A., Hudson, K., Maguire, M., Peake, R., Raynor, R., Vanstone, M., and Kynch, J. (2006) *Getting Out and Staying Out: Results of the Prisoner Resettlement Pathfinder*. Bristol: Policy Press.

Dawson, P. (2005) *Early Findings from the Prolific and Other Priority Offenders Evaluation*. Development and Practice Report. London: Home Office.

Dawson, P. (2006) *The National PPO Evaluation – Research to Inform and Guide Practice*, RDS Online Report 09/07. London: Home Office.

Dawson, P. and Cuppleditch, L. (2006) *An Impact Assessment of the Prolific and Other Priority Offenders Programme*, RDS Online Report 08/07. London: Home Office.

Eley, S., Beaton, K. and McIvor, G. (2005) 'Co-operation in drug treatment services: views of offenders on court orders in Scotland', *Howard Journal of Criminal Justice*, 44 (4): 400–10.

Farrall, S. (2002) *Rethinking What Works with Offenders: Probation, Social Context and Desistance from Crime*. Cullompton: Willan.

Farrington, D., Coid, J., Harnett, L., Jolliffe, D., Soteriou, N., Turner, R. and West, D. (2006) *Criminal Careers and Life Success: New Findings from the Cambridge Study in Delinquent Development*, Home Office Findings No 281. London: Home Office.

Folkard, M.S., Smith, D.E. and Smith, D.D. (1976) *IMPACT Vol. 11: The Results of the Experiment*, Home Office Research Study No. 36. London: Home Office.

Fox, A., Khan, L., Briggs, D., Ress-Jones, N., Thompson, Z. and Owens, J. (2005) *Throughcare and Aftercare: Approaches and Promising Practice in Service Delivery for Clients Released from Prison or Leaving Residential Rehabilitation*, RDS Online Report 01/05. London: Home Office.

Garside, R. (2004) *Crime, Persistent Offenders and the Justice Gap*. London: Crime and Society Foundation.

Gendreau, P., Goggin, C. and Fulton, B. (2001) 'Intensive supervision in probation and parole settings', in C. Hollin (ed.), *Handbook of Offender Assessment and Treatment*. Chichester: Wiley.

Godfrey, C., Eaton, G., McDougall, C. and Culyer, A. (2002) *The Economic and Social Costs of Class A Drugs Use in England and Wales, 2000*, Home Office Research Study No. 249. London: Home Office.

Harman, K. and Paylor, I. (2005) 'An evaluation of the CARAT initiative', *Howard Journal of Criminal Justice*, 44 (4): 357–73.

Hedderman, C. and Hough, M. (2004) 'Getting tough or being effective: what matters?', in G. Mair (ed.), *What Matters in Probation*. Cullompton: Willan, pp. 146–69.

Her Majesty's Prison Service (2002) *Counselling, Assessment, Referral, Advice and Throughcare Services*, Prison Service Order 3630. London: HM Prison Service.

Home Office (1988) *Punishment, Custody and the Community*, Cmnd 424. London: HMSO.

Home Office (2001) *Criminal Justice: The Way Ahead*. London: HMSO.

Home Office (2002) *Narrowing the Justice Gap*. London: HMSO.

Home Office (2004a) *Joint Inspection Report into Persistent and Prolific Offenders*. London: Home Office.

Home Office (2004b) *Prolific and Other Priority Offenders Strategy. Initial Guidance, Catch and Convict Framework*. London: Home Office.

Home Office (2004c) *Prolific and Other Priority Offenders Strategy. Initial Guidance, Rehabilitate and Resettle Framework*. London: Home Office.

Home Office (2004d) *Criminal Justice Interventions Programme and Prolific and Other Priority Offenders Programme: Partnership Guidance for CJITs and PPO Schemes*. London: Home Office.

Home Office (2004e) *Reducing Re-offending National Action Plan*. London: Home Office.

Home Office (2005) *Criteria for Removing a Prolific and Other Priority Offender from a Scheme*. London: Home Office.

Home Office (2006a) *Rebalancing the Criminal Justice System in Favour of the Law-Abiding Majority*. London: Home Office.

Home Office (2006b) *Prolific and Other Priority Offenders: Guidance on Local Area Agreements (LAAs) for Government Offices*. London: Home Office.

Home Office (2006c) *Prolific and Other Priority Offenders Strategy Performance Management Headline Measures Report, September 2006*. London: Home Office. Available at: www.crimereduction.gov.uk/ppo/ppominisite07.htm.

Homes, A., Walmsley, R. and Debidin, M. (2005) *Intensive Supervision and Monitoring Schemes for Persistent Offenders: Staff and Offender Perceptions*, RDS Development and Practice Report. London: Home Office.

Hough, M., Clancy, A., McSweeney, T. and Turnbull, J. (2003) *The Impact of Drug Treatment and Testing Orders on Offending: Two-Year Reconviction Results*, Home Office Findings 184. London: Home Office.

Hucklesby, A., Eastwood, C., Seddon, T. and Spriggs, A. (2007) *The Evaluation of the Restriction on Bail: Final Report*, RDS Online Report 06/07. London: Home Office.

Lewis, S., Maguire, M., Raynor, P., Vanstone, M. and Vennard, J. (2007) 'What works in resettlement? Findings from seven Pathfinders for short-term prisoners in England and Wales', *Criminology and Criminal Justice*, 7 (1): 33–53.

Lewis, S., Vennard, J., Maguire, M., Raynor, P., Vanstone, M., Raybould, S. and Rix, A. (2003) *The Resettlement of Short-Term Prisoners: An Evaluation of the Seven Pathfinders*, RDS Occasional Paper No. 83. London: Home Office.

Liriano, S. and Ramsay, M. (2003) 'Prisoners' drug use before prison and the links with crime', in M. Ramsay (ed.), *Prisoners' Drug Use and Treatment: Seven Research Studies*, Home Office Research Study No. 267. London: Home Office, pp. 7–22.

McNeill, F. (2006) 'A desistance paradigm for offender management', *Criminology and Criminal Justice*, 6 (1): 39–62.

McSweeney, T. and Hough, M. (2006) 'Supporting offenders with multiple needs: lessons for the "mixed economy" model of service provision', *Criminology and Criminal Justice*, 6 (1): 107–25.

Maguire, M. (2004) 'Resettlement of short-term prisoners: some new approaches', *Criminal Justice Matters*, 56: 22–3.

Maguire, M. and Raynor P. (2006) 'How the resettlement of prisoners promotes desistance from crime: or does it?', *Criminology and Criminal Justice*, 6 (1): 19–38.

Mair, G., Lloyd, C., Nee, C. and Sibbit, R. (1994) *Intensive Probation in England and Wales: An Evaluation*, Home Office Research Study No. 133. London: Home Office.

Martinson, R. (1974) 'What works? Questions and answers about prison reform', *Public Interest*, 35: 22–54.

Maruna, S. (2001) *Making Good*. Washington, DC: American Psychological Association.

Maruna, S., Immarigeon, R. and LeBel, T. (2004) 'Ex-offender reintegration: theory and practice', in S. Maruna and R. Immarigeon (eds), *After Crime and Punishment: Pathways to Offender Reintegration*. Cullompton: Willan.

May, C. (1999) *Explaining Reconviction Following a Community Sentence: The Role of Social Factors*, Home Office Research Study No. 192. London: Home Office.

National Offender Management Service (NOMS) (2005) *The NOMS Offender Management Model*. London: National Offender Management Service. See: www.probation2000.com/documents/NOMS%20Offender%20Managemen t%20Model.pdf.

National Probation Directorate (2006) *Offender Management for Custodial Sentences*, Probation Circular 09/2006. London: Home Office.

Niven, S. and Stewart, D. (2005) *Resettlement Outcomes on Release from Prison in 2003*, Home Office Research Findings No. 248. London: Home Office.

Partridge, S. (2004) *Examining Case Management Models in the Community*, Home Office Online Report 17/04. London: Home Office.

Petersilia, J. and Turner, S. (1993) 'Intensive probation and parole', *Crime and Justice*, 17: 281–335.

Prochaska, J. and DiClemente, C. (1992) 'Stages of change in the modification of problem behaviour', in M. Hersen, R. Eisler and P. Miller (eds), *Progress in Behavior Modification*, Vol. 25. Illinois: Sycamore, pp. 154–216.

Rex, S. (1999) 'Desistance from offending: experiences of probation', *Howard Journal*, 38: 66–83.

Robinson, G. (2005) 'What works in offender management?', *Howard Journal of Criminal Justice*, 44 (3): 254–68.

Robinson, G. and Dignan, J. (2004) 'Sentence management', in A. Bottoms, S. Rex and G. Robinson (eds), *Alternatives to Prison*. Cullompton: Willan, pp. 313–40.

Ross, R.R. and Fabiano, E.A. (1985) *Time to Think: A Cognitive Model of Delinquency Prevention and Offender Rehabilitation*. Johnson City, TN: Institute of Social Sciences and Arts.

Rumgay, J. (2004) 'Dealing with substance-misusing offenders in the community', in A. Bottoms, S. Rex and G. Robinson (eds), *Alternatives to Prison*. Cullompton: Willan, pp. 248–67.

Social Exclusion Unit (2002) *Reducing Re-offending by Ex-prisoners*. London: Office of the Deputy Prime Minister.

Tupman, B., Hong Chui, W. and Farlow, C. (2001) 'Evaluating the Effectiveness of Project ARC'. Unpublished report, University of Exeter.

Turnbull, P., McSweeney, T., Webster, R., Edmunds, M. and Hough, M. (2000) *Drug Treatment and Testing Orders: Final Evaluation Report*, Home Office Research Study No. 212. London: Home Office.

Vennard, J. and Pearce, J. (2004) *The Bristol Prolific Offender Scheme: An Evaluation*. Safer Bristol website at: www.crimebristol.org.uk.

Worrall, A. and Mawby, R. (2004) 'Intensive projects for prolific/persistent offenders', in A. Bottoms, S. Rex and G. Robinson (eds), *Alternatives to Prison*. Cullompton: Willan, pp. 268–99.

Worrall, A., Mawby, R., Heath, G. and Hope, T. (2003) *Intensive Supervision and Monitoring Projects*, Home Office Online Report 42/03. London: Home Office.

Youth Justice Board (2005) *Youth Resettlement: A Framework for Action*. London: Youth Justice Board.

Chapter 12

Dangerous offenders: release and resettlement

Hazel Kemshall

Introduction

Recent high-profile murders by released prisoners (e.g. John Monckton by Damien Hanson and Naomi Bryant by Anthony Rice) have raised the issue of safe release and effective resettlement and risk management of 'dangerous' and sexual offenders in the community. The key issue raised by such cases is how 'dangerous offenders' are identified and risk assessed prior to release, and whether such offenders can be effectively resettled into the community.

'Dangerous' and sexual offenders present significant issues in terms of their resettlement, most notably due to the high levels of anxiety, public fear and stigmatisation that often accompanies them (Kitzinger 2004). As a consequence, sex offenders have been dubbed 'the ultimate neighbour from hell' (Kitzinger 1999). Public reactions to the release of Robert Oliver and Sydney Cooke (see Thomas 2005) and the calls for a 'Sarah's Law' following the murder of Sarah Payne in 2000 have all emphasised public intolerance of this particular offender group.

Reoffending by 'dangerous' and sexual offenders creates political as well as public disquiet. Following the Serious Further Offence Inquiries on Damien Hanson and Elliot White,[1] and Anthony Rice[2] (HMIP 2006a, 2006b) the incoming Home Secretary, John Reid, summed up the political and public mood by stating that: 'The public has the right to expect that everything possible will be done to minimise the risk from serious violent and dangerous offenders' (Home Secretary 2006: 1). This expectation has been quickly translated into a 'dramatic overhaul of public protection arrangements' and a rebalancing of justice between offenders and victims (Home Office 2006a, 2006b; Home Secretary 2006).

This chapter will explore the resettlement issues facing these offenders, and the challenges they present to practitioners and the key agencies tasked with their supervision and management in the community. It examines questions such as how can such offenders be successfully reintegrated and resettled while maintaining public safety and victim protection? What is the appropriate balance between public protection and rehabilitation? The role of Multi-Agency Public Protection Arrangements (MAPPA) in the assessment and management of high-risk offenders will also be explored, along with the lessons learnt from recent risk management failures and evaluations of MAPPA.

The current context

The safe release of prisoners into the community has been a perennial problem, reflected in the development of a parole predictor by Burgess in the late 1920s (1928, 1936). Who to keep in and who to let out has been a long-standing question, given added weight by the high cost of prison places and the increased use of custody over time (Flynn 1978). The Carlisle Report (1988) focused on risk and harm reduction and placed risk as the central concern of parole decision-making. Carlisle crystallised a bifurcated approach to parole, with an emphasis upon distinguishing between high-risk prisoners who must be kept in, and lower-risk prisoners who could be safely released. This twin-track approach is economically rational, but very difficult to operate in practice. Bifurcation presumes easily distinguishable thresholds between risk categories, accurate risk assessment within prisons and classification of prisoners and fail-safe parole decisions, and that risk remains static upon release. These are unsound assumptions (Kemshall 2003) and create systemic flaws in the operation of a bifurcated approach. Damien Hanson, for example, was classified as medium risk but this escalated substantially upon release (HMIP 2006a). The Hanson Serious Incident Inquiry Report (HMIP 2006a) noted that there was a lack of clarity about how the Parole Board should respond to significant changes in release plans and circumstances prior to prisoners' release date. In essence, Hanson's resettlement plan was compromised prior to release because of the changes in his circumstances and risk which had taken place.

Parallel to these concerns around parole and public protection has been a broader concern with reducing reoffending, expressed in the Reducing Re-offending National Action Plan (Home Office 2004b). The plan identifies seven pathways to resettlement and reduction in offending: accommodation; education, training and employment; mental and physical health; drugs and alcohol; finance, debt and benefit; children and families of offenders; attitudes, thinking and behaviour. From this national plan both regional and local objectives are stated. For example, the national objective on 'attitudes, thinking and behaviour' translates into the following local requirement: 'to ensure that high-risk/sexual offenders have completed relevant interventions and a risk management plan is in place' (Home Office 2004b: 42). This requires that risk management plans are adequate, robust and properly delivered, and that pre-release arrangements with local MAPPA are sound (Kemshall et al. 2005). This chapter will explore some of the pathways and how challenging they can be for dangerous and sexual offenders to traverse.

Resettlement of high-risk offenders

Stigmatisation, public anxiety, and the resulting social exclusion can make the resettlement and reintegration of high-risk offenders particularly challenging. Many will have offended against vulnerable groups (particularly children, including in many cases their own), and in some smaller, tight-knit communities both they and their victims may be well known. This literally makes re-entering the community a tricky and risky business, open to a multitude of risks ranging from reoffending and harm to the public, vigilante action and public disorder, and attacks on offenders. The period following the murder of Sarah Payne saw numerous vigilante actions (Nash 2006; Petrunik 2003), and while less reported currently, they still present a major concern to police and local MAPPA (Wood and Kemshall 2007). This makes the first resettlement pathway of accommodation especially problematic. Sex offenders in particular can be notoriously difficult to rehouse. For example, risk management dictates that sex offenders should not be housed near to schools, parks or leisure areas that attract children. In some instances local authority housing departments may refuse to rehouse sex offenders, or their location in small, tight-knit communities can result in their 'outing'. Sex offenders are often excluded by parole conditions from residing or approaching particular areas or addresses (i.e. locations where previous victims reside), and can find themselves released from custody into restrictive conditions within a hostel setting. Approved premises are seen as a key resource in managing risk in the community (NOMS 2007). Their use is often appropriate for the level of risk posed and provides intensive levels of supervision and surveillance post-custody. However, approved premises are often used primarily as a way of monitoring risk rather than as a tool to aid resettlement and reintegration. Consequently, they may increase barriers to resettlement particularly as resettlement activities may be restricted by the location of many hostels, offenders' separation from the community and 'normal' life and the fact that offenders do not choose to go there.

Employment is another area where resettlement ambitions can be restricted. While employment involving direct contact with children is prohibited for sex offenders, some employment is 'borderline', such as taxi driving which may involve drivers undertaking the school run. The re-entry of young sex offenders to college and training can also be problematic. To facilitate employment and training where possible (commensurate with the risk presented), some areas are now pursuing formal contracts with offenders and third parties (e.g. employers and colleges) to control the risks and facilitate safe reintegration (Wood and Kemshall 2007). This may include controlled disclosure.[3] This involves limited disclosure to a named person (such as a class teacher or tutor) to facilitate their involvement in risk management including notifying any signs of relapse to supervisors (Wood and Kemshall 2007). This reflects increasing attempts to balance protection with rehabilitation on the basis that it facilitates longer-term self-risk management and that reintegration itself can contribute to community safety (for a full review of this approach see Wood and Kemshall 2007).

Traditionally, much more emphasis has been placed upon the monitoring and surveillance of high-risk offenders than on their resettlement and reintegration. This has included the introduction of registration requirements for sex offenders and latterly violent offenders. Sex offenders are subject to registration requirements under the Sex Offender Act 1997 (amended by the Sex Offences Act 2003), and must notify their address and any subsequent changes to the police. It is routine for police officers to use address notification requirements as a mechanism for making home visits to check up on sex offenders (Kemshall *et al.* 2005), and even sex offenders who are not subject to parole licence conditions can find themselves being monitored by the police in this manner. While often presented in terms of help and support, visits are also an essential ingredient of the community surveillance provided by MAPPA (Kemshall *et al.* 2005; Wood and Kemshall 2007). However, the UK sex offender register has high levels of compliance (currently 97 per cent) in marked contrast to its US counterpart where compliance is between 10 and 40 per cent lower (Nash 2006: 138).

Another tool often used in an attempt to reduce the chances of reoffending are conditions including tagging, surveillance, exclusion and curfews. However, more recent public protection work is attempting to balance monitoring and surveillance with attention to thinking patterns, attitudes and behaviours via intensive treatment programmes as well as dealing with employment, accommodation and welfare needs. Intensive community-based sex offender programmes are supported by relapse prevention programmes, one-to-one support from case officers (e.g. the Northumbria sex offender programme), supported accommodation and return to work or training wherever possible. While these measures are often accompanied by monitoring and surveillance and adherence to registration requirements, this presents a more holistic and multi-modal approach to risk management, which incorporates many of the key facets of the resettlement plan for reducing reoffending (Kemshall *et al.* 2005).

Involving offenders in release planning also appears to be successful. Recently interviewed offenders who had been informed of their release conditions and who had been involved in their risk management planning were able to explain what was required of them and why (Wood and Kemshall 2007). They also accepted the plans as 'realistic', 'common sense' and in their interests (Wood and Kemshall 2007). Both staff and offenders interviewed for the study advocated a more balanced approach to public protection and rehabilitation, believing that one assisted the other (Wood and Kemshall 2007). In essence, resettlement could be achieved with low risk in most cases if the appropriate steps were taken and resettlement was seen to contribute to self-risk management, stability and commitment to change. Offenders interviewed who were experiencing these regimes appeared to be informed and confident about what was happening to them and why and more actively engaged in their own supervision. They were more likely to comply, and to experience higher levels of 'well-being' and linkage to their communities in contrast to offenders who were fearful of vigilante action and 'outing', and who resented the imposition of conditions and the surveillance of MAPPA (Wood and Kemshall 2007).

Not all high-risk offenders are sex offenders. The Hanson case illustrates the difficulties of resettling and successfully managing the risks posed by violent offenders in the community. In this case, risk had been under-assessed, principally because of a failure to take sufficient account of dynamic risk factors and failing to recognise his violent offending as 'instrumental' rather than emotional (HMIP 2006a). Again Approved Premises are often a critical factor in successfully resettling violent offenders safely, particularly where exclusion from previous victims must be monitored. Intensive intervention programmes are also seen as crucial, but as the recent MAPPA evaluation showed areas are struggling to develop them and the national provision of intensive treatment programmes is patchy (Wood and Kemshall 2007). However, similar case management principles apply to violent offenders, along with prompt response to escalating risk and deteriorating behaviour (see Kemshall *et al.* 2006).

The evaluation indicated that good practice with high-risk offenders largely comprised effective co-working across relevant agencies, including close work between police and probation, and the use of other staff and voluntary agencies for the 'needs'-based work (Wood and Kemshall 2007; for previous research see Kemshall *et al.* 2005). This prevented supervising officers losing the public protection focus but ensured that such issues were not neglected or allowed to stymie risk management plans. Tight liaison between staff running treatment groups and case officers facilitated prompt follow-up and implementation of programme material. Attention to relapse prevention was seen by offenders as particularly beneficial. However, what may be termed a 'protectively rehabilitative' approach to the resettlement of high-risk offenders requires a careful assessment not only of risk, but of motivation and compliance levels. This also necessitates a risk management plan which can appropriately balance offenders' capacity for internal controls with the number and type of external controls imposed. This requires careful assessment by practitioners of the risk factors present, how imminently harmful activity might take place if the external controls are lessened, what protective factors are present and how they might be strengthened, and offenders' capacity for self-risk management (see Kemshall *et al.* 2006, for training material on this). The next section will consider some of these issues.

Managing risk in the community

As the recent cases involving serious further offences have reminded us, effectively managing the risk posed by offenders upon release is crucial to their effective resettlement. This requires a careful balance between external and internal controls. The most frequently used external controls are: licence conditions (e.g. curfews, exclusion zones, accommodation restrictions); behavioural restrictions (for example, restricting leisure activities to limit grooming behaviours); and restrictions to limit contact with past or potential victims (Kemshall et al. 2005; Wood and Kemshall 2007). Internal controls are those used by offenders to limit their own offending behaviours and tend to focus on the recognition and avoidance of key triggers, the avoidance of risky situations and relapse prevention techniques. Sex offender programmes, supported by focused one-to-one work are one way of promoting internal controls, although access to such programmes can be variable with long waiting times (Wood and Kemshall 2007).

- Electronic tagging
- Supervised accommodation
- Restricting access to school locations
- Identification and intensive one-to-one work on key triggers, e.g. mood change, attitudes to offending, sexualisation of children
- Use of local police surveillance and police intelligence
- Victim empathy work

(*Source*: Kemshall *et al.* 2005: 18.)

Figure 12.1 A typical risk management package for known sex offenders

A typical risk management package for sex offenders as shown in Figure 12.1 may be supported by a resettlement focus on accommodation, employment, help and support (as outlined above) to provide a more holistic approach to risk management. The following have a proven track record for effective risk management in the community (adapted from Kemshall *et al.* 2005; Kemshall *et al.* 2006):

- *Proactive planning before release from prison* – enables appropriate licence/parole conditions to be imposed, accommodation to be secured, victim protection and support work to take place, and surveillance and reporting requirements to be set up.

- *Police intelligence* – helps to monitor grooming and targeting activities, and to identify offenders' networks.

- *Boundaries and swift enforcement* – written contracts with offenders can reinforce such conditions and hold offenders to account for programme attendance and compliance with conditions.[4]

- *Targeted surveillance* – establishes key contacts and offenders' movements and provides evidence of further offending and to justify rapid recall.

- *Supervised accommodation* – can be crucial for effective risk management. It provides stability, and can be combined with curfews, intensive treatment-based work, CCTV surveillance, electronic monitoring and high levels of staff contact.

- *Accredited programmes* – can be used with positive effect with some offenders (see Kemshall 2001). However programme selection and work must be done with care and as part of a wider risk management strategy. Offenders may present false compliance and on occasion a false reassurance to workers that risk is falling. In some cases offenders will have experienced similar programmes in prison or under earlier supervision and have 'learnt the responses'.

- *Victim protection* – can include providing information, personal alarms, rapid response police numbers, restraining orders, conditions on licences or supervision orders.

- *Addressing criminogenic and welfare needs* – failing to meet basic needs of offenders (e.g. benefit claims or accommodation) can undermine the risk management plan. However, these should not be the sole focus of the risk management plan. In some probation areas the welfare tasks are devolved to probation service officers (PSOs), leaving probation officers to concentrate on the risk management plan. There is some limited evidence that this approach is effective (Kemshall *et al.* 2005; Wood and Kemshall 2006).

In a more recent evaluation of MAPPA, Wood and Kemshall (2007) found a number of factors were critical to the effective supervision of high-risk offenders. Some were procedural, such as pre-release MAPPA assessments and regular attendance of prison personnel at panel meetings, which enables specific risk management plans with the appropriate conditions and restrictions to be put into place prior to release. The attendance of victim liaison workers to present victim issues is also helpful as it enables a focus on victim protection strategies such as rapid response phone contact, alarms and so on. Early risk assessment can also facilitate appropriate referral to community-based treatment/group work programmes supported by tightly focused one-to-one work. Effective case management is also crucial, comprising offence-focused work, teaching relapse prevention techniques, rapid and consistent enforcement of conditions/restrictions, and the use of home visits to be 'lifestyle vigilant' – in some MAPPA areas these visits are made jointly by police and probation.

The recent joint thematic inspection (HMIP/HMIC/HMIP 2006a: 22–44) noted a number of strengths in joint work with high-risk offenders, but also a number of areas for improvement in risk management planning and in the delivery of effective supervision. In brief, these were a lack of information exchange especially pre-release, a lack of attention given to OASys, a lack of integration of victims' perspectives; and a requirement for a more rapid response to changes in risk level. During the MAPPA evaluation staff also noted significant barriers to the effective management of high-risk offenders; most notably these were: the absence of relevant treatment programmes (especially for sex offenders) and long waiting times, a lack of hostel provision or supervised housing and an absence of specialist groupwork programmes for some offenders, especially those with low functioning and/or learning difficulties. Rolling programmes with swift access for offenders appear to reduce attrition but not all probation areas are able to provide these (Wood and Kemshall 2007).

Recent work has also identified a pro-social approach with offenders, (including high-risk ones) as helpful in reducing reoffending (e.g. Trotter 2000). While most often associated with the supervision of 'young, high-risk, violent and drug-using offenders' (McNeill and Batchelor 2002: 38), there is growing evidence of the effectiveness with adult high-risk offenders (Wood and Kemshall 2007). Pro-social modelling is underpinned by an assumption that in most cases offenders, if given the opportunities to engage effectively, can and will change behaviours. Trotter (1993, 1999, 2000) suggests that the characteristics of both supervisors and supervision practices can promote change. In order to do this a number of conditions must be met. Firstly, the supervisory role must be clear, including the purpose and expectations of supervision, the appropriate use of authority and the role of enforcement. Secondly, clear distinctions need to be made between acceptable and unacceptable values and behaviours in order to discourage pro-criminal attitudes and values. This should be undertaken using rewards to reinforce acceptable behaviour and challenging undesirable behaviours. Thirdly, problem-solving should be negotiated with clear objective-setting and monitoring and accountability of offenders' progress. Finally, honest, empathic relationships between supervisors and offenders are required with an emphasis upon persistence and belief in offenders' capacity to change (adapted from McNeill and Batchelor 2002: 38; Trotter 1999, 2000).

Rex (1999; see also Rex and Matravers 1998) has also indicated that a number of factors play a significant role in the supervisory relationship and in subsequent desistance from offending. The most notable are negotiated engagement with offenders and a partnership in problem-solving, with support provided through home visits. Also important is intensive work to improve the offenders' decision-making either during group programmes or in individual work, with a particular focus on pro-social decisions and relapse prevention techniques. Commitment, professionalism, genuine interest and attention to the personal and social problems of offenders are also significant along with the feelings of commitment and loyalty probation officers can inspire in offenders.

Compliance and enforcement have also been seen as crucial to effective risk management (HMIP 2006a, 2006b), with particular emphasis upon enforcement of licence conditions. Since 2000 the number of recalls to custody has increased by 350 per cent (Harding 2006; HMI Prisons 2005), with the recall population making up 11 per cent of the custodial population in 2005 (Harding 2006). In part this reflects the climate of increased accountability and enforcement within probation. It is also a sign of the growing preoccupation with public protection and risk avoidance as evidenced by recent attempts to rebalance the criminal justice process towards the 'law-abiding majority' (Home Office 2006a, 2006b). However, many practitioners believe that a balance between rehabilitation and public protection is important to effective risk management and resettlement (Wood and Kemshall 2007). The issue of offenders' rights versus victim and public protection has attracted much recent comment, not least from the Chief Inspector of Probation (HMIP 2006a, 2006b) and Home Secretary (Home Secretary 2006). This 'rebalancing' is continuing and is subject to both debate and test cases (see Padfield 2006).

MAPPA

An increasing proportion of high-risk cases in the community now come under the auspices of MAPPA, which provides a multi-agency framework for risk assessment and risk management (Home Office 2004a). This section will consider the role of MAPPA in the risk management and resettlement of high-risk offenders.

Multi-Agency Public Protection Arrangements (MAPPA) were formally created by sections 67 and 68 of the Criminal Justice and Court Services Act 2000, although they had evolved from multi-agency arrangements in the late 1990s for the assessment and management of sex offenders subject to the sex offender register. These arrangements were consolidated by the Criminal Justice Act 2003 (CJA), which made Police, Probation and Prisons 'responsible authorities' and gave other agencies a 'duty to cooperate'. These arrangements place a statutory responsibility on the three main agencies to assess and manage high-risk offenders. MAPPA are concerned with three categories of offenders (Home Office 2004a):

- *Category one* – registered sex offenders who have been convicted or cautioned since September 1997 of certain sexual offences (s. 327(2), CJA 2003), and are required to register personal and other relevant details with the police in order to be effectively monitored. The police have primary responsibility for identifying category one offenders.

- *Category two* – violent and other sexual offenders receiving a custodial sentence of 12 months or more since April 2001, a hospital or guardianship order, or subject to disqualification from working with children (s. 327(3–5), CJA 2003). All these offenders are subject to statutory supervision by the National Probation Service and consequently probation is responsible for the identification of category two offenders.

- *Category three* – other offenders considered by the Responsible Authority to pose a 'risk of serious harm to the public' (s. 325(2), CJA 2003). Identification is largely determined by the judgement of the Responsible Authority based upon two main considerations: firstly, offenders must have a conviction that indicates that they are capable of causing serious harm to the public; and secondly, the Responsible Authority must reasonably consider that offenders may cause harm to the public. The responsibility of identification lies with the agency that deals initially with offenders.

MAPPA also has a three-tier pyramid structure, aimed at targeting resources at the highest level of risk or 'critical few' (Home Office 2004a: paras. 111–116):

- *Level one* (ordinary risk management) – where the agency responsible for offenders can manage the risk without the significant involvement of other agencies. This is only appropriate for category one and category two offenders who are assessed as presenting a low or medium risk.

- *Level two* (local inter-agency risk management) – where there is 'active involvement' of more than one agency in risk management plans, either because of a higher level of risk or because of the complexity of managing offenders. Responsible Authorities should decide the frequency of panel meetings and also the representation and quality assurance of risk management.

- *Level three* (MAPPA) – includes offenders defined as the 'critical few' who pose a high or very high risk in addition to having a media profile and/or management plan drawing together key active partners who will take joint responsibility for the community management of offenders. Level three cases can be 'referred down' to level two when risk of harm deflates.

Connelly and Williamson (2000) have described such formal and statutory procedures for the management of offenders' risk as a 'community protection model'. Such an approach emphasises restrictive conditions, surveillance, monitoring and control, compulsory treatment and intensive interventions. These 'special measures' are delivered almost exclusively by statutory agencies, usually in partnership through the MAPPA (Kemshall *et al.* 2005).

While MAPPA itself does not supervise or assume the case management of offenders, it has a statutory responsibility to ensure effective risk assessment and management of those offenders who fall within its remit. In practice, this may involve case conference-style panel discussions to assess risk, formulating risk management plans that involve more that one agency, and authorising decisions to permit controlled disclosure to third parties. The value-added by MAPPA is that it facilitates the pooling and exchange of information, the formulation of risk management plans which go beyond the capacity of a single agency to deliver and the provision of additional resources for community management, sometimes quickly when unexpected release decisions are made or in the case of escalating risk and deteriorating behaviour.

MAPPA contributes to the holistic and in-depth risk assessment of offenders, and at its best provides a multi-disciplinary perspective on high-risk behaviours (although the contribution of mental health services remains problematic in some areas – see Kemshall *et al.* 2005). For those prisoners approaching release, best practice dictates that they are referred to MAPPA if their risk level meets the MAPPA criteria (Home Office 2004a), and early assessment and risk management planning for their effective management in the community takes place. As stated by the Chief Inspector of Probation, it is the quality of the risk management plan that enables high-risk prisoners to be released safely into the community, including level three offenders (HMIP 2006b: para. 6.9.9: 20).

Effective and robust risk management planning is dependent upon the quality of the interface between the prison, parole and MAPPA system, and the quality of the inter-agency working between police, probation and prisons. However, there is a discontinuity of public protection work. Most notably, the Prison Service was not initially a statutory partner and therefore did not establish the processes, systems or key networks to link with MAPPA (Kemshall *et al.* 2005; Mate 2006). The inclusion via the Criminal Justice Act 2003 was an attempt to deal with the problems arising from this initial omission.[5] A further remaining flaw in procedures identified by the Anthony Rice SFO report (HMIP 2006b) is that there are no direct links between the Parole Board and MAPPA. The public protection system requires excellent communication between MAPPA and the Parole Board. Nevertheless, the Parole Board does not attend MAPPA panels and is dependent upon the information provided by MAPPA (usually through probation officers) and the risk management plans made by MAPPA. The failings of this interrelationship were highlighted in the probation inspectorate reports (HMIP 2006a, 2006b; see also Kemshall 2007, for a full review). Importantly the Inspectorate reminds us that Parole Boards do not directly control the risk management packages delivered by either MAPPA or single agencies (such as probation). The consequence of this is to divide responsibility for release decisions from that of risk management. This has already led to blurred responsibility for recall and enforcement decisions between MAPPA and the Parole Board (e.g. the Anthony Rice case – see HMIP 2006b).

Measures of effectiveness for MAPPA remain underdeveloped (Kemshall *et al.* 2005; Wood and Kemshall 2007). The police, for example, have no key performance indicator for this area of work, hence resources remain low and it is under-prioritised. There is a similar picture for the Prison Service and to a lesser extent for the National Probation Service. Nevertheless, in recent research Wood and Kemshall (2007) found that MAPPA personnel defined effectiveness largely as lack of reconvictions (especially for the 'critical few'), lack of serious further offences and 'holding difficult people in the community for long periods of time'. Prompt recall in the face of escalating risk, deteriorating behaviour or breach of restrictive conditions was also presented as an effectiveness measure – in effect preventing further serious harm before it could occur. Nationally 2005/6 saw a reduction in the number of serious further offences in the MAPPA caseload from 79 (0.6 per cent) to 61 (0.44 per cent) (Home Office 2006c) with the biggest impact at level three.[6] The same Home Office study noted that the:

> ... data relating to breach of licence and court orders is positive as this reflects an increase in action taken in level two and three cases prior to them having opportunity to commit serious further harm, i.e. to recall offenders to prison. A similarly encouraging picture emerges from a reading of the data on various sex offender provisions ... Action taken to enforce the sex offender registration requirements through caution and conviction increased by 30 per cent from last year and affected 1,295 offenders, 4.3 per cent of the total registered in the community. There was also considerable use made of the range of new civil orders available under the Sex Offences Act 2003 (sexual offences prevention orders, notification orders, foreign travel orders). In total 973 orders have been granted this year, an increase of 446. (Home Office 2006c: 7)

The joint thematic review also highlighted the difficulties in measuring performance and noted the contribution that standards and guidance had made to improving practice (HMIP/HMIC/HMIP 2006b). They stated that 'planned interventions were generally effective in containing offending behaviour' but that 'planned objectives were only achieved in under half the cases examined' (HMIP/HMIC/HMIP 2006b: 5). However, evidence from both research and inspections would support the view that generally resources are well managed and that MAPPA is effective in managing high-risk offenders (HMIP/HMIC/HMIP 2006a; Kemshall *et al.* 2005; Wood and Kemshall 2007).

Conclusion: blending protection and rehabilitation

The community protection model which emphasises restrictive conditions, surveillance and control (Connelly and Williamson 2000) has been critiqued for adopting an almost exclusively controlling, restrictive and exclusionary approach to the community management of high-risk offenders, and in particular sex offenders (Kemshall and Wood 2007; Nash 2006). In essence the emphasis upon control and enforcement is seen to compromise treatment, reintegration and rehabilitation. This can be understood as a clash between the often short-term goals of immediate victim safety and community protection and the longer-term goals of behaviour change and desistance. An overemphasis upon external controls for offenders without attention to the development of internal controls and relapse prevention techniques in effect means that offenders fail to develop self-risk management techniques. Offenders without such techniques are unlikely to be able to maintain offending-free lifestyles once the external controls are removed.

However, protection and rehabilitation are not mutually exclusive, and indeed they are often effectively combined in practice (a point Connelly and Williamson themselves identified in some jurisdictions within Western Europe and in New Zealand). Wood and Kemshall (2007) in their recent review of supervision strategies with high-risk MAPPA offenders identified practice which effectively blended protection and rehabilitation and which provided high degrees of resettlement (in accommodation, employment and with welfare needs met) without compromising public safety. These techniques (discussed in detail earlier) could be labelled 'protective resettlement' and offer a balanced approach to the community management of high-risk offenders that is achieving the desired outcome of reducing serious further offences of the critical few, holding difficult people in the community safely for long periods and protecting the public. They also have the added benefit of sustaining offenders in longer-term intensive treatment, teaching relapse prevention techniques and facilitating longer-term self-risk management.

High-risk offenders, especially sex offenders, present key challenges to effective resettlement and community risk management. Their resettlement is taking place against a general climate of public intolerance, fear and anxiety, and in a political climate that is risk averse. The Government's designated seven pathways to resettlement are not impossible to achieve with this group, but they are difficult. As the Serious Further Offence Reviews indicate it only takes one case to critically challenge the integrity and credibility of the systems and personnel involved. Failures attract a lot of attention but the daily routine of good practice attracts rather less. Accommodation, employment and training, and safe social integration are perhaps the most challenging. However, recently developing supervisory techniques under MAPPA, predominantly a blended approach of surveillance with support accompanied by careful controlled disclosure and attention to intensive interventions alongside a reduction of presenting needs is achieving positive outcomes without 'outing' offenders or alienating them from the supervisory process. The approach is underpinned by concern for the offenders' reintegration and a commitment to pro-social modelling and constructive challenge around problematic behaviours. Wherever possible, offenders are positively engaged in their own resettlement and risk management plan, and where this had been achieved offenders exhibited both understanding and compliance with what had been asked of them.

Positive resettlement and successful risk management are also dependent upon early pre-release planning and effective information exchange across the whole system, including the parole board and MAPPA. Recent Serious Further Offence Reviews have highlighted some difficulties here, and while corrective action is underway, increasing attention to the system requirements of effective resettlement is required. 'Protective resettlement' requires not only good practice but the appropriate systems to support it.

Acknowledgement

Thanks are extended to my colleague Jason Wood for all his generous support on a number of joint projects cited here and joint publications referred to in this chapter.

Notes

1 Damien Hanson and Elliott White were convicted of the murder of John Monkton and attempting to murder his wife, Homeyra, while on licence.
2 Anthony Rice was convicted of murdering Naomi Bryant in 2005 while on life licence.
3 See MAPPA Guidance (Home Office 2004a: paras 93–95) for full explanation of controlled disclosure.
4 While not legally binding, such contracts may engender a stronger commitment by the offender and can be used in conjunction with a clear warning system and swift enforcement, including rapid parole recall.
5 The Criminal Justice Act 2003 had an implementation date of April 2004 for the Prison Service to become a Responsible Authority. Until this

change the Prison Service had a 'duty to cooperate' under the Criminal Justice and Court Services Act 2000.

6 The Home Office study urges caution in interpreting these figures as they are based on a two-year database and the low figures concerned can have a potentially distorting effect.

References

Burgess, E.W. (1928) 'Factors making for success or failure on parole', *Journal of Criminal Law and Criminology*, 19 (2): 239–306.

Burgess, E. W. (1936) 'Protecting the public by parole and parole prediction', *Journal of Criminal Law and Criminology*, 27: 491–502. As reprinted in L.S. Cottrell Jr, A. Junter and J.F. Short Jr (eds) (1973) *Ernest W. Burgess on Community, Family and Delinquency*. Chicago: University of Chicago Press.

Carlisle, Rt Hon Lord of Bucklow (1988) *The Parole System in England and Wales. Report of the Review Committee*. London: HMSO.

Connelly, C. and Williamson, S. (2000) *Review of the Research Literature on Serious Violent and Sexual Offenders*, Crime and Criminal Justice Research Findings No. 46. Edinburgh: Scottish Executive Central Research Unit.

Flynn, E. (1978) 'Classifications for risk and supervision', in J. Freeman (ed.), *Prisons Past and Future*. Cambridge: Cambridge Studies in Criminology.

Harding, J. (2006) 'Some reflections on risk assessment, parole and recall', *Probation Journal*, 53 (4): 389–96.

Her Majesty's Inspectorate of Probation (HMIP) (1998) *A Guide to Effective Practice*. London: HMIP.

Her Majesty's Inspectorate of Probation (HMIP) (2006a) *An Independent Review of a Serious Further Offence Case: Damien Hanson and Elliot White*. London: Her Majesty's Inspectorate of Probation.

Her Majesty's Inspectorate of Probation (HMIP) (2006b) *An Independent Review of a Serious Further Offence Case: Anthony Rice*. London: Her Majesty's Inspectorate of Probation.

Her Majesty's Inspectorate of Probation, Her Majesty's Inspectorate of Constabulary and Her Majesty's Inspectorate of Prisons (HMIP/HMIC/HMIP) (2006a) *Putting Risk of Harm into Context: An Inspection Promoting Public Protection: A Joint Thematic Inspection*. London: Home Office.

Her Majesty's Inspectorate of Probation, Her Majesty's Inspectorate of Constabulary and Her Majesty's Inspectorate of Prisons (HMIP/HMIC/HMIP) (2006b) *Putting Risk of Harm into Context: An Inspection Promoting Public Protection: A Joint Thematic Inspection*, Inspection Findings 3/06. London: Home Office.

Her Majesty's Inspectorate of Prisons (2005) *Recalled Prisoners: A Short Review of Recalled Adult Male Determinate-sentenced Prisoners*. London: Her Majesty's Inspectorate of Prisons.

Home Office (2004a) *MAPPA Guidance (Version 2)*. London: Home Office.

Home Office (2004b) *Reducing Re-offending National Action Plan*. London: Home Office.

Home Office (2006a) *Rebalancing the Criminal Justice System in Favour of the Law-Abiding Majority: Cutting Crime, Reducing Reoffending and Protecting the Public*. London: Home Office.

Home Office (2006b) *The Home Secretary's Five Year Strategy for Protecting the Public and Reducing Reoffending*. London: Home Office.

Home Office (2006c) *MAPPA – The First Five Years: A National Overview of the Multi-Agency Public Protection Arrangements 2001–2006*. London: Home Office.

Home Secretary (2006) *Annual Speech to the Parole Board, May 2006*. London: Home Office website: www.press.homeoffice.gov.uk, accessed 8 August 2006.

Kemshall, H. (2001) *Management of Known Sexual and Violent Offenders: A Review of Current Issues*, Police Research Unit Paper 140. London: Home Office. Available at: www.homeoffice.gov.uk/rds/prgpdfs/prs140.pdf.

Kemshall, H. (2003) *Understanding Risk in Criminal Justice*. London: Open University Press.

Kemshall, H. (2007) 'MAPPA, parole and the management of high-risk offenders in the community', in N. Padfield (ed.), *Who Gets Out? Parole and Criminal Justice*. Cullumpton: Willan.

Kemshall, H. and Wood, J. (2007 forthcoming) 'Beyond public protection: an examination of the community protection and public health approaches to public protection', *Criminology and Criminal Justice*.

Kemshall, H., Mackenzie, G., Miller, J. and Wilkinson, B. (2006) *Risk of Harm Guidance and Training Resource*, CD-ROM. Leicester: DeMontfort University and the National Offender Management Service.

Kemshall, H., Mackenzie, G., Wood, J., Bailey, R. and Yates, J. (2005) *Strengthening the Multi-Agency Public Protection Arrangements*, Development and Practice Report No. 45. London: Home Office.

Kitzinger, J. (1999) 'The ultimate neighbour from hell: media framing of paedophiles', in B. Franklin (ed.), *Social Policy, Media and Misrepresentation*. London: Routledge.

Kitzinger, J. (2004) *Framing Abuse: Media Influence and Public Understanding of Sexual Violence Against Children*. London: Pluto Press.

McNeill, F. and Batchelor, S. (2002) 'Chaos, containment and change: responding to persistent offending by young people', *Youth Justice*, 2 (1): 27–43.

Mate, P. (2006) 'The development of the Prison Service as a "Responsible Authority" within Multi Agency Public Protection Arrangements in England and Wales (2004–2005)', *Prison Service Journal*, 163: 50–4.

Nash, M. (2006) *Public Protection and the Criminal Justice Process*. Oxford: Oxford University Press.

National Offender Management Service (NOMS) (2007) Available at: www.noms.homeoffice.gov.uk/protecting-the-public-/managing-risk-in-cusdody/ (accessed 15 February 2007).

Padfield, N. (2006) 'The Parole Board in transition', *Criminal Law Review*, 3–22.

Petrunik, M. (2003) 'The hare and the tortoise: dangerous and sex offender policy in the United States and Canada', *Canadian Journal of Criminology and Criminal Justice*, 45 (1): 43–72.

Rex, S. (1999) 'Desistance from offending: experiences of probation', *Howard Journal of Criminal Justice*, 38 (4): 366–83.

Rex, S. and Matravers, A. (1998) *Pro-social Modelling and Legitimacy*. Cambridge: Cambridge Institute of Criminology.

Thomas, T. (2005) *Sex Crime: Sex Offending and Society*. Cullompton: Willan.

Trotter, C. (1993) *The Supervision of Offenders – What Works? A Study Undertaken in Community Based Corrections*. Victoria: Social Work Department, Monash University and the Victoria Department of Justice, Melbourne.

Trotter, C. (1999) *Working with Involuntary Clients: A Guide to Practice*. London: Sage Publications.

Trotter, C. (2000) 'Social work education, pro-social modelling and effective probation practice', *Probation Journal*, 47: 256–61.

Wood, J. and Kemshall, H. with Maguire, M., Hudson, K. and Mackenzie, G. (2007) *The Operation and Experience of Multi-Agency Public Protection Arrangements*. London: Home Office.

Chapter 13

Conclusion: opportunities, barriers and threats

Anthea Hucklesby and Lystra Hagley-Dickinson

There are many reasons to be optimistic about the future of resettlement policy and practice. Resettlement is high on the policy agenda. The new Offender Management Model promises to provide 'end-to-end' management of offenders and there are many smaller local initiatives operating currently. However, the work undertaken as part of these initiatives could easily stall. One of the greatest threats to effective resettlement work is the ever-increasing prison population. At the time of writing the prison population has risen to over 80,000 and is predicted to continue to rise (HM Prison Service 2007; Home Office 2006b). Statutory services and resettlement initiatives are already being overwhelmed by the number of prisoners who require help and this pressure will increase as the available population rises. Initiatives are also being hampered by the constant movement of prisoners between prison establishments to cope with overcrowding which results in resettlement planning being disrupted or discontinued altogether (Hudson, this volume; Lewis *et al.* 2003; Vennard, this volume). Overcrowding in the prison estate inevitably means that an increasing number of prisoners are held considerable distances from their homes making resettlement planning and continuity of provision much more difficult.

A further threat to resettlement work is financial resources. Currently, a substantial amount of resettlement work is undertaken on 'soft' money available only in the short term. This results in initiatives constantly having concerns about where the next funding will come from and whether they can continue to operate and employ workers. Furthermore, as discussed in Chapter 6, often the funding source sets boundaries for the work which can be undertaken and limits the adaptability and innovation of projects. The statutory funding pledged under contestability has the potential to put funding on firmer foundations but problems are likely to remain. Under the new regime, short-term contracts are set to continue and projects will be required to demonstrate their effectiveness. The uncertainties surrounding the timetable for the introduction of contestability and exactly what it will mean in practice have also caused problems. Statutory funding is not a panacea. With it will come requirements to demonstrate effectiveness in terms of reoffending and strict contracts about the work to be undertaken with attached targets. This presents particular challenges for the voluntary and community sector (VCS) (see Chapter 8). Variety, innovation and small locally based projects are likely to be the losers as demonstrated by the development of drug services in prisons (Sampson 2002) and discussed in Chapter 8.

Narrowing the focus of resettlement work in the statutory sector is already underway. As one of us was recently told by a Prison Service manager, 'we don't talk about resettlement any more, it's all about preventing reoffending.' The ultimate aim of any resettlement policy must be to stop prisoners from offending but resettlement has broader aims and for many prisoners desistance is an unrealistic goal in the short term. Interim measures related to offending including reductions in frequency and severity of offending are one of the alternatives. However, prisoners have multiple and entrenched needs (SEU 2002) and there is normally no quick-fix solution to their problems or their offending. Focusing on reoffending whether in terms of total desistance or distance travelled and measuring success only in these terms is risky, especially when the evidence base for what brings about offenders' desistance is limited. The evaluation of the resettlement pathfinders suggested that increasing prisoners' motivation and attitudes and thinking skills in addition to dealing with practical issues such as housing and benefits and equipping prisoners with job and life skills (i.e. human capital) are important elements of effective resettlement work (Clancy et al. 2006; Lewis et al. 2003). In other words, resettlement projects need to ensure that offenders take responsibility for their own resettlement and take an active role in preparations for release. Doing things for offenders simply cultivates dependence and has minimal long-term benefits.

Current resettlement policy takes the form of the seven pathways set out in the National Reoffending Action Plan (Home Office 2004). Inevitability, the seven pathways prioritise some areas over others and it has already been suggested that several pathways, most notably drugs and alcohol and education, training and employment, should be split making a total of nine pathways. It is difficult to see how the number of pathways will not proliferate further when other issues are identified and gain priority. Some pathways are more developed than others and these tend to be those which relate either to urgent and immediate needs like housing and/or to key performance targets (KPTs). In an environment dictated by limitations on resources the potential exists for these pathways to be allocated the lion's share of resources and time and effort of workers, leaving the less developed but no less important pathways to fall further behind. The creation of pathways also creates artificial boundaries, which compartmentalises resettlement practice. This may produce barriers to the provision of holistic resettlement services, which are required to deal effectively with prisoners' diverse and multiple needs.

Resettlement policy takes no account of diversity within the prison population and the potentially different resettlement needs. The pathways are assumed to apply to all prisoners in the same way and to a similar extent. Additionally, different groups are assumed to relate to services in similar ways. Several chapters in this volume suggest a more complicated picture. In Chapter 6 on PS Plus it was argued that women seek and respond to generic resettlement services, which are able to deal with a wide range of resettlement needs. By contrast, men are more likely to seek help for single issues. If further evidence confirms this, it indicates that the pathways approach adopted by NOMS is more suited to male than female prisoners. The evidence on whether different groups of prisoners have different needs is limited and mixed (see Chapters 9 and 10). However, what is made clear by Williams et al. in Chapter 10 is that the context in which prisoners from minority ethnic groups access services may differ as their confidence in statutory services is generally limited as a result of past encounters. The resettlement of sex offenders is particularly difficult and is dictated largely by external issues relating to risk rather than the needs of offenders. As Kemshall points out in Chapter 12 the measures put in place to manage risk often militate against the reintegration of these offenders and present particular challenges to resettlement policies and practices.

Effective resettlement practice may be undermined by efforts to measure effectiveness. Setting key performance targets (KPTs) around resettlement practice has the advantage of signalling its priority but only in those areas which relate to the KPTs. KPTs may be inappropriate and counterproductive as evidenced by the Prison Service's accommodation KPT. The original KPT related to accommodation being arranged for prisoners on release and required that prisoners had somewhere to sleep when they left prison. It took no account of the quality, suitability or sustainability of the accommodation. In practice, this meant that some prisoners had one night's accommodation found in a local hostel or bed and breakfast while others were encouraged to return to unsuitable accommodation linked to their offending or substance use. Additionally, it resulted in resettlement workers and the Prison Service concentrating on meeting accommodation targets at the expense of sourcing more sustainable accommodation and working on other resettlement needs. This reinforced the tendency for resettlement work to be concentrated on immediate practical requirements which are more easily resolved rather than focusing on more entrenched needs or issues which may result in more sustainable longer-term outcomes.

Resettlement work currently involves partnerships between Prison and Probation Services and the voluntary and community sector (VCS). These are crucial particularly to ensure continuity of services through the prison gate. While relationships between these organisations have improved recently and examples of exemplary practice exist, a key task of NOMS is to bring about much closer working relationships. Some of the challenges involved in instigating this were explored by Hucklesby and Worrall in Chapter 8 and relate to both cultural and practical issues. Partnerships are based on mutual respect and trust (Crawford 1998) and historically these have been lacking between the three major players involved in prisoners' resettlement. The expectation that the VCS involvement in resettlement and other areas of criminal justice will increase upon the introduction of contestability makes dealing with these issues more urgent. Precursors to greater cooperation and integration involve the VCS demonstrating their creditability, professionalism and high standards of working and the Prison Service trusting other organisations to manage issues of security. Even greater issues are raised by the potential for the private sector to become involved in the provision of resettlement services.

One of the biggest challenges for resettlement practice is providing continuity of provision 'through the prison gate'. The evidence is that this is crucial to effective resettlement and that it is more effective when services are provided by the same individuals (Lewis *et al.* 2003; Clancy *et al.* 2006). Nonetheless, so far this has been an elusive aim. The practical difficulties and the resources required to follow prisoners out into the community are enormous, particularly if the prisons in which they were held are some distance from their resettlement areas (see Chapters 3 and 11). The problems encountered have resulted in many initiatives concentrating on providing services either in prison or in the community, or handing over cases to different teams when prisoners are released (see Chapter 6 for an example). All these models have limitations (see Chapter 3). The Offender Management Model attempts to deal with these issues as one person will be providing 'end-to-end' management of cases. However, problems are likely to remain or be exacerbated, particularly as 'ownership' issues will arise because offenders held in any one prison will continue to return to many different geographic regions and offenders from regions are likely to be housed in several different prisons. Maintaining continuity of provision raises particular issues for women and longer-term offenders who are often held long distances from their resettlement area.

Resettlement is under-theorised and sparsely evidenced. While we know something about pathways into offending much less is known about pathways out. The seven pathways set out in the National Reoffending Action Plan (Home Office 2004) are based on those identified by the Social Exclusion Unit (SEU 2002). Nonetheless, only limited evidence is presented in the SEU report to support its conclusions and recommendations. Additionally, government policy assumes that the same factors are involved in desistance as offending. Even if the ingredients which lead to offending and desistance are similar the relative importance of factors may vary. Available evidence suggests, also, that the issues represented in the pathways may be necessary for effective resettlement to take place but may not instigate it. Consequently, more exploration of the links between the pathways and desistance needs to be undertaken to clarify the relationship between them.

Many contributors to this volume have suggested that desistance research is the most promising avenue to explore in terms of providing a theoretical basis for resettlement. We know that many offenders grow out of crime as part of a process of 'maturation' (Bottoms et al. 2004; Maruna 2001; Rutherford 1986). This has been linked to a number of factors, namely finding employment, settling down with a partner and having children amongst others (Farrall 2002; Farrall and Calverley 2006; Laub and Sampson 2003; Maruna 2001). Bottoms et al. (2004: 384) suggest that desistance is linked to '[a] safe job as an employee of a stable company, enough money, some consumer luxuries, a steady girlfriend and (possibly) kids'. Evidence is mounting about the links between these factors and desistance and how these relate to resettlement practice is certainly worth investigating. However, so far desistance research has not explored in any depth questions about why and how these factors are linked to desistance, which is crucial to informing resettlement policy and practice.

The most important contribution that desistance research has made to resettlement so far is that it has highlighted that desistance is a process, not a single event, and that setbacks can and do occur (Farrall 2002; Maruna 2001). It is important for policymakers and resettlement workers to take this into consideration, as it is easy to dismiss projects as failures and/or workers to become demoralised because prisoners return to prison after work has been done and reoffending targets are missed. Conceptualising desistance as a process or journey enables offenders who return to prison to be perceived positively as experiencing short-term setbacks which provide an opportunity for further work to be undertaken which will reinforce earlier interventions. In practice, however, the scope for this is limited as prisoners often return to different prisons where another resettlement project is operating and the process of assessment and referral begins again. This highlights the need not only for continuity of provision between prisons and the community but also between different prisons. While NOMS may provide this to a degree, its regional structure militates against consistent service provisions across regional boundaries.

A further potentially useful insight from desistance research is Maruna and LeBel's (2002, 2003) concept of strength-based resettlement. As discussed by Hucklesby and Wincup in Chapter 3 this approach focuses on the positive contribution which prisoners can make to society. By contrast, most resettlement work undertaken currently conforms to the deficit model, which assumes that offenders lack something, whether practical needs such as housing or money, or motivation or thinking skills. While there are issues about how the strength-based approach could be operationalised, its importance lies in the recognition that resettlement work should play to prisoners' strengths, working to empower prisoners to contribute positively to society and not concentrating exclusively on what they lack or are not doing.

Similarly, several contributors to this volume have drawn attention to the importance of the distinction between human and social capital (Farrall 2002; Farrall and Calverley 2006; McNeill 2006). It has been noted elsewhere that a large proportion of work with offenders on probation concentrates on improving offenders' human capital such as employment skills while little attention is paid to social capital, i.e. prisoners' social networks (Farrall 2004; McNeill 2003, 2006). A similar point could be made about the majority of resettlement work currently. While it is acknowledged that social capital can be linked to offending (Crawford 2006; Hucklesby, forthcoming), it may also play a significant role in desistance (Farrall 2004; McNeill 2006). As Hudson notes in relation to families in Chapter 5 this role is largely unrecognised and certainly underdeveloped in current resettlement practice. Families are not normally involved or encouraged to take part in the process of resettlement. The inclusion of families as one of the seven pathways to resettlement may change this but the practical and logistical difficulties of engaging families may militate against any improvement in the levels of their involvement. Awareness of the importance of social capital also opens up exploration of the role of the communities to which prisoners are returning (Farrall and Sparks 2006). As Maguire and Nolan note in Chapter 7 returning prisoners back to where they came from, while expedient in terms of accommodation provision, often sends them back to criminogenic environments, although communities may also support and enhance offenders' attempts to desist (Farrall and Sparks 2006).

Emphasising the role of pro-social capital in resettlement demonstrates the importance of the involvement of non-criminal justice agencies. Some of these agencies, most notably local authority housing departments (see Maguire and Nolan, Chapter 7), are reluctant to be involved with offenders and have erected significant barriers. If effective resettlement is to be achieved these obstacles need to be removed while recognising the issues raised by prisoners receiving priority access to limited services (see Vennard, Chapter 11). In reality, developmental work with housing and employment providers is often the first task to fall victim to workload pressures. Nevertheless, there is little point working with prisoners on employability and tenancy skills if there is no prospect of putting either into practice. A useful framework for these discussions is provided by the concept of state-obligated rehabilitation (Carlen 1989; Cullen and Gilbert 1982; Hudson 1987, 1993), which is discussed by Raynor in Chapter 2. In essence, state-obligated resettlement refers to a situation in which offenders are expected to comply with requirements imposed upon them which will assist in their resettlement, and in return the state is required to provide the services and support it promises. In other words, the state and offenders have a contract to work towards resettlement and desistance and both parties have rights, expectations and responsibilities. The state's role is crucial because all too often promises to provide services do not materialise and consequently, offenders do not receive the assistance they expected. In these circumstances, it is not surprising that offenders break their side of the contract. Indeed, broken promises and dashed expectations may have a more detrimental effect on offenders' future behaviour and cooperation than when no services are offered or expected.

While desistance theories and research may be useful to enhance our understanding of resettlement policy and practice it provides only a partial picture, particularly as resettlement has broader aims, especially in the short term. One significant short-term goal for resettlement, not often articulated in official discourse, is preventing offenders from being recalled to prison as a result of non-compliance with their Home Detention Curfew (HDC) or licence requirements. Both Hedderman and Kemshall draw attention to the high and increasing number of recalls to prisons which are explained largely by stricter enforcement policies (Harding 2006; HMIP 2005; Home Office 2006a; Padfield and Maruna 2006). Recalled prisoners comprise over a tenth of the prison population currently and increase the pressure on accommodation and services within the prison system (Harding 2006; Padfield and Maruna 2006). Compliance theories and research are also an under-researched area, but one which has the potential to provide insights of value to resettlement theory, policy and practice (see Bottoms 2001; Nellis 2006; Sherman *et al.* 2003; Tyler 1990, 1997, 1998; Zhang *et al.* 1999). Most notably, it highlights the importance of legitimacy and the ways in which offenders' perceptions of their treatment impacts upon compliance (Bottoms 2001; Nellis 2006; Sherman *et al.* 2003; Sparks *et al.* 1996; Tyler 1990, 1997, 1998; Zhang *et al.* 1999).

Resettlement tends to be conceptualised in terms of dealing with offenders' needs. Rarely is the role of enforcement and surveillance discussed in conjunction with it. Questions about how resettlement, enforcement and surveillance may be mutually supportive or work against each other remain largely unexplored. The aims of resettlement on the one hand and enforcement and surveillance on the other are often perceived to conflict and in practice sometimes do. Nevertheless, it is likely that they can support each other but evidence is sparse. Important questions to explore include whether electronic monitoring can support other interventions (see Hucklesby, forthcoming; Nellis 2004) or the extent to which the threat of recall promotes compliance and prevents offending for example.

This volume has brought together current theory and research on prisoner resettlement. What it has highlighted most starkly is how weak the evidence base is and how little we know about what works and why. As Wincup and Hucklesby point out in Chapter 4, the reasons for this are three-fold, namely a general lack of research, a concentration on evaluation and the failure to disseminate research findings. In order to build up an evidence base to inform policy developments systematic research is required which explores resettlement holistically and from a variety of perspectives, including offenders and practitioners. As discussed in Chapter 4, longitudinal research is the most effective way to achieve this despite its drawbacks in terms of resources and the time involved.

The outlook for resettlement looks promising and the climate appears to be right to foster and develop effective policy and practice. But resettlement is part of the government's broader crime reduction agenda and is, therefore, highly political. Not only does this mean that it is open to the vacillations of government policy but also that unplanned events can unravel developments very quickly. Policy changes have been rapid and what is required above all is a period of stability to enable policies and initiatives to consolidate and evidence about their effectiveness to be gathered.

References

Bottoms, A.E. (2001) 'Compliance and community penalties', in A. Bottoms, L. Gelsthorpe and S. Rex, *Community Penalties: Change or Challenges.* Cullompton: Willan.

Bottoms, A., Shapland, J., Costello, A., Holmes, D. and Muir, G. (2004) 'Towards desistance: theoretical underpinnings for an empirical study', *Howard Journal*, 43 (3): 368–89.

Carlen, P. (1989) 'Crime, inequality and sentencing', in P. Carlen and D. Cook (eds), *Paying for Crime.* Milton Keynes: Open University Press.

Clancy, A., Hudson, K., Maguire, M., Peake, R., Raynor, P., Vanstone, M. and Kynch, J. (2006) *Getting Out and Staying Out: Results of the Prisoner Resettlement Pathfinders.* Bristol: Polity Press.

Crawford, A. (1998) *Crime Prevention and Community Safety: Politics, Policies and Practices.* Harlow: Longman.

Crawford, A. (2006) 'Fixing broken promises?': neighbourhood wardens and social capital', *Urban Studies*, 43 (5/6): 957–76.

Cullen, F.T. and Gilbert, K.E. (1982) *Reaffirming Rehabilitation.* Cincinnati, OH: Anderson.

Farrall, S. (2002) *Rethinking What Works with Offenders.* Cullompton: Willian.

Farrall, S. (2004) 'Social capital and offender re-integration: making probation desistance focussed', in S. Maruna and R. Immarigeon (eds), *After Crime and Punishment: Ex-offender Reintegration and Desistance from Crime.* Cullompton: Willan.

Farrall, S. and Calverley, A. (2006) *Understanding Desistance from Crime*. Maidenhead: Open University Press.

Farrall, S. and Sparks, R. (2006) 'Introduction', *Criminology and Criminal Justice*, 6 (1): 7–17.

Harding, J. (2006) 'Some reflections on risk assessment, parole and recall', *Probation Journal*, 53 (4): 389–96.

Her Majesty's Inspectorate of Prisons (HMIP) (2005) *Recalled Prisoners: A Short Review of Recalled Adult Male Determinate-sentenced Prisoners*. London: Her Majesty's Inspectorate of Prisons.

Her Majesty's Prison Service (2007) *Prison Population and Accommodation Briefing*, 18 May. London: HM Prison Service.

Home Office (2004) *National Reoffending Action Plan*. London: Home Office.

Home Office (2006a) *Offender Management Caseload Statistics 2005, England and Wales*, Home Office Statistical Bulletin 18/06. London: Home Office.

Home Office (2006b) *Prison Population Projections 2006–2013 England and Wales*, Statistical Bulletin 11/06. London: Home Office.

Hucklesby, A. (forthcoming) 'Vehicles of desistance? the impact of electronically monitored curfew orders', *Criminology and Criminal Justice*.

Hudson, B. (1987) *Justice Through Punishment*. Basingstoke: Macmillan.

Hudson, B. (1993) *Penal Policy and Social Justice*. Basingstoke: Macmillan.

Laub, J.H. and Sampson, R.J. (2003) *Shared Beginnings, Divergent Lives*. Cambridge, MA: Harvard University Press.

Lewis, S., Vennard, J., Maguire, M., Raynor, P., Vanstone, M., Raybould, S. and Rix, A. (2003) *The Resettlement of Short-term Prisoners: An Evaluation of Seven Pathfinders*, RDS Occasional Paper No. 83. London: Home Office.

McNeill, F. (2003) 'Desistance-focused probation practice', in W.H. Chui and M. Nellis (eds), *Moving Probation Forward*. Harlow: Pearson Education.

McNeill, F. (2006) 'A desistance paradigm for offender management', *Criminology and Criminal Justice*, 6 (1): 39–62.

Makkai, T. and Braithwaite, J. (1994) 'Reintegrative shaming and compliance with regulatory standards', *Criminology*, 32: 361–85.

Maruna, S. (2001) *Making Good: How Ex-convicts Reform and Rebuild their Lives*. Washington, DC: American Psychological Association Books.

Maruna, S. and LeBel, T.P. (2002) 'Revisiting ex-prisoner re-entry: a buzzword in search of a narrative', in S. Rex and M. Tonry (eds), *Reform and Punishment: The Future of Sentencing*. Cullompton: Willan.

Maruna, S. and LeBel, T.P. (2003) 'Welcome home? Examining the "Re-entry Court" concept from a Strengths-based perspective', *Western Criminology Review*, 4 (2): 91–107.

Nellis, M. (2004) 'Electronic monitoring and the community supervision of offenders', in A. Bottoms, S. Rex and G. Robinson (eds), *Alternatives to Prison*, Cullompton: Willan.

Nellis, M. (2006) 'Surveillance, rehabilitation, and electronic monitoring: getting the issues clear', *Criminology and Public Policy*, 5 (1): 103–8.

Padfield, N. and Maruna, S. (2006) 'The revolving door at the prison gate: exploring the dramatic increase in recalls to prison', *Criminal Justice and Criminology*, 6 (3): 329–52.

Rutherford, A. (1986) *Growing Out of Crime*. Winchester: Waterside Press.

Sampson, A. (2002) 'Principles and pragmatism: surviving working with the Prison Service', in S. Bryans, C. Martin and R. Walker (eds), *Prisons and the Voluntary Sector*. Winchester: Waterside Press.

Sherman, L., Strang, H. and Woods, D. (2003) 'Captains of restorative justice: experience, legitimacy and recidivism by type of offence', in E. Weitekamp and H. Kerner (eds), *Restorative Justice in Context: International Practice and Directions*. Cullompton: Willan.

Social Exclusion Unit (2002) *Reducing Re-offending by Ex-prisoners*. London: Office of the Deputy Prime Minister.

Sparks, R., Bottoms, A.E. and Hay, W. (1996) *Prisons and the Problem of Order*. Oxford: Clarendon Press.

Tyler, T. (1990) *Why People Obey the Law*. New Haven, CT: Yale University Press.

Tyler, T. (1997) 'The psychology of legitimacy: a relational perspective on voluntary defence to authorities', *Personality and Social Psychology Review*: 323–4.

Tyler, T. (1998) 'Trust and democratic governance', in V. Braithwaite and M. Levi (eds), *Trust and Governance*. New York: Russell Sage Foundation.

Zhang, L., Messner, S. and Lu, Z. (1999) 'Public legal education and inmates' perceptions of the legitimacy of official punishment in China', *British Journal of Criminology*, 39 (3): 433–49.

Index

A–Z programme 127, 131
access to prisons 81–3
   and community-based initiatives 52
   and prison-based initiatives 47, 49–50
   and the voluntary and community sector
     (VCS) 58
accessing services 45, 57
   black and ethnic minority (BME) offenders
     232–3
   prolific offenders 259–61
accommodation 144–69, 292
   for black and minority ethnic (BME)
     offenders 162, 166, 235
   for high-risk and prolific offenders 162–3,
     167, 259–60
   improvements 163–7
     organisational and practical 164–7
     strategic developments 163–4
   options 147–59
     'crisis' facilities 157–9
     'floating support' 153, 155–6
     private rental 156–7
     returning to prior accommodation
      147–8, 164
     social housing see social housing
     supported accommodation see
      supported accommodation
     temporary accommodation with friends
      or family 148–9
   and relational continuity and motivational
     support 166
   for sex offenders 162, 272–3
   'throughflow', 'rescue' and 'move on' 156,
     165–6
   for women 159–60, 166, 206–7, 210–11
   for young prisoners 160–1, 166–7
accredited programmes 181, 219n
aftercare 29–30, 37

appropriation 48
Approved Premises 153, 162, 273, 275
Asha Women's Centre 205, 213–16
assessment
   and offender management 106–8
   techniques 45
   see also risk assessment
automatic conditional release (ACR) 31

Beneficiary Access Fund (BAF) 124–5
benefits, accessing 45
black and minority ethnic (BME) offenders
   224–39, 291
   accommodation 162, 166, 235
   available services 236–7
   awareness and use of services 231–3, 237–8
   and the criminal justice process 225–30
     trust and confidence in 233, 238
   in prison 227–30, 237
   resettlement needs 230–6
   see also ethnic minority women
bonding social capital 37–8
bridging social capital 37–8

CARATS (Counselling, Assessment, Referral,
   Advice and Throughcare Service) 45–6, 260
Care Services Improvement Partnership (CSIP)
   211–12
Carlisle Report (1988) 271
Carter Report (2003) 32–3, 249
Case Assessment and Tracking System (CATS)
   128
'case management' 44
CDRPs (Crime and Disorder Reduction
   Partnerships) 251, 252
Central After-Care Association 29, 30
Centre 218 209
'change, cycle of' 127, 245